# The Politics of Distribution

HARVARD POLITICAL STUDIES

Published Under the Direction of the
Department of Government in
Harvard University

# Harvard Political Studies

# The Politics of
# DISTRIBUTION

Joseph Cornwall Palamountain, Jr.

HARVARD UNIVERSITY PRESS

CAMBRIDGE · MASSACHUSETTS

1955

TO ANNE

## ACKNOWLEDGMENTS

I acknowledge most gratefully the debt I owe others for their wholehearted assistance and wise counsel in the preparation of this study. Only I can fully appreciate how much this debt is reflected throughout the book. For its errors and deficiencies alone can I claim exclusive ownership.

I am especially indebted to Professor Merle Fainsod for his initial suggestion of the general subject and for his careful scrutiny and criticism of the manuscript in all of its stages, to Professor V. O. Key for his careful reading and shrewd counsel, to Professor Charles Cherington, without whose encouragement and spirited injunctions to put pen to paper this work would still be in its research stages, to Dr. Robert Kuenne for tightening my grasp on several elusive economic tools, and to Professor Alan Campbell for his encouragement and criticism.

Mrs. Marjorie Thwing, Mrs. Jane Stonemetz, and Mrs. Ann Scanlin labored above and beyond the normal call of duty in reducing my scrawls to typescript and know how grateful I am.

I am also most grateful to the Harvard Department of Government, whose generous subsidy enables the publication of this work and thus illustrates how, in a political economy, governmental judgments may be substituted for the verdicts of a competitive market.

But the one to whom I am most indebted, and to whom I gratefully and lovingly dedicate this book, is my wife, who has, usually uncomplainingly, performed more services for the author and his manuscript than can be listed here.

Adams House
Harvard University
June 17, 1955

# CONTENTS

# The Politics of DISTRIBUTION

## Introduction: Economics and Politics

The politics of distribution are indissolubly wedded to its economics. Accordingly, this study of the political struggles that in the 1930's swirled up out of that galaxy of markets called distribution or marketing must deal with a complex inter-mixture of politics and economics. It focuses on that decade because it was then that the economic conflicts between large- and small-scale organization, between "mass distribution" and smaller, independent distributors, became most acute; consequently, it was also then that the political struggles precipitated out of these economic conflicts also reached their peak.

Although I shall try to breach the high wall that academic disciplines usually place between politics and economics, yet whatever novelty this study may have lies in the blending of the analytical tools of these two disciplines rather than in the development of new tools. For the problem of analysis is simply that the raw material to be analyzed is both political and economic. Both competition and power, political and economic, play roles in distributive processes, and similarly political processes are characterized by both political and economic factors. A mixture of competition and power occurs in both processes.

My primary concern will be a description and analysis of the policy-making process, but political processes cannot fully be understood in isolation; they are part of a seamless web of the political and the economic. Ours is a political economy in the sense that economic processes are often channeled and influenced by acts of government and in the sense that power often is an important part of economic relationships; and ours is an economic polity in the sense that the economy, in turn, importantly affects political and governmental processes and in the sense that economic power is often translated into political power. Both power and competition play their roles in distributive markets; neither alone is sufficient to explain market processes. The economic conflicts that characterized distribution during the 1930's became political conflicts and were fought out in legislative chambers. But these conflicts were often greatly altered by their transfer to political arenas, and the political settlement of them was importantly influenced and limited by economic factors.

Accordingly, this study will attempt to analyze the economic conflicts of distribution in the decade of the Great Depression — conflicts between large and small organization, conflicts centered on the issue of economic power and on the interaction of power and competition. It will attempt to trace the ways in which these conflicts were translated into political struggles, the ways in which this translation altered the original conflicts, and, most briefly, the extent to which the outcome of these political struggles altered or settled the original economic conflicts. In so doing, I shall use group analysis as a starting hypothesis. That politics has its economic bases has been long and widely recognized, and the usual approach has been an analysis that described public policy as the end result of a process of struggle and compromise among groups whose interests in the matter are for the most part economically determined.[1] Dissatisfied groups try to better their economic lot by invoking governmental aid, while other groups respond with attempts to

[1] E.g., a leading textbook states that "Three interests — business, labor, and agriculture — seek to determine . . . public economic policy. . . Each has its own primary objectives. . . Each, in turn, is a mosaic of many particular interests, not necessarily harmonious and frequently expressing their aspirations through independent political activity. The pattern of evolving public policy reflects the interplay of these interests, their strength and their weakness, their skill in accommodation, and their ability to capitalize such resources as they have at their disposal." Merle Fainsod and Lincoln Gordon, *Government and the American Economy* (New York: Norton; 1948), p. 21.

block or modify the initial proposals. Arthur Bentley, who first developed this method of analysis, at times virtually equates public policy with the mathematical result of the relative strengths and drives of interested groups.

The great task in the study of any form of social life is the analysis of . . . groups. . . When the groups are adequately stated, every-thing is stated. When I say everything, I mean everything.[2]

The configuration of their [groups'] interrelationships marks out the pattern and objectives of regulation. Government . . . can do little more than register the shifting balance of forces in the struggle for power. The interest or group of interests which captures control of them impresses its policy upon them. With realignment of power, a new conception of public policy is spelled out in terms of the claims of the new dominant combination. . . . At any given moment, public policy is the resultant of a parallelogram of operative forces; the substance of public policy is redefined as the balance of power shifts. Government institutions thus tend to be transformed into mere pawns in a struggle for supremacy. Deprived of independent creative force, the purposes which they serve simply mirror the changing fortunes of battle. . . . The idea of public interest becomes a fiction used to describe an amalgam which is shaped and reshaped in the furnace of . . . [group] conflicts.[3]

Yet group analysis cannot be applied in too crude a manner. A pseudomathematical approach that describes public policy as "the resultant of a parallelogram of operative (group) forces," while appealing because of its stark simplicity, cannot

[2] Arthur Bentley, *The Process of Government* (Bloomington, Indiana: Principia Press; 1935 reissue of 1908 ed.), pp. 208–209. "When we talk about government we put emphasis on the influence, the pressure, that is being exerted by group upon group. . . The balance of group pressure is the existing state of society. . . Law is activity, just as government is. . . It is a group process, just as government is. It is a forming, a systematization, a struggle, an adaption, of group interests. . ." *Ibid.*, pp. 258–259, 272. For the best and most comprehensive contemporary statement of the group hypothesis and for a description of the political role of groups, see David B. Truman, *The Governmental Process* (New York: Knopf; 1951).

[3] Merle Fainsod, "Some Reflections on the Nature of the Regulatory Process," in C. J. Friedrich and E. S. Mason (eds.), *Public Policy*, vol. I (Cambridge, Mass.: Harvard University Press; 1940), pp. 297–298. Fainsod here states the Bentley hypothesis in order to explain some of its limitations.

adequately register the complexities and subtleties of policy formation.[4] So simple an analysis so distorts the policy-making process as to give a quite false picture of the real process. Accordingly, this study will seek to work within the framework of group analysis in order to demonstrate some of its complexities, to show some of the reasons for the differing political effectiveness of economic groups, and to illuminate the process which lies between an economic grievance and governmental efforts to alleviate that grievance. In brief, I shall try to show that the economic environment enables, but does not guarantee, the creation of political groups, and that economic groups which seek to operate politically thereby enter a realm which exercises its own conditioning effects and which does far more than simply reflect the strengths and drives of economic groups.

[4] Even Truman, who pushes the group hypothesis fairly far, says that "it is only as the effects of overlapping memberships and the functions of unorganized interests and potential groups are included in the equation that it is accurate to speak of governmental activity as the product or resultant of interest group activity." Truman, p. 515.

# I

## Distribution: Economic Bases of Conflict

### A. RETAIL DISTRIBUTION

The group conflicts and political battles that characterized distribution during the 1930's reflected for the most part the impact of a surge of new methods of organizing the distributive function. This chapter will describe the participants in these struggles; [1] a more careful analysis of the economic conflicts is postponed until the second chapter.

Roughly synonomous with marketing, distribution consists of those economic activities which surround a product after its manufacture and before its final sale.[2] It is supremely the field of the "middleman" — he who stands between producer and consumer. By any measurement it is a large segment of the economy. About two million firms, or almost half of the nation's operating businesses, are in retail or wholesale trade, mustering

[1] Since our primary concern is with political conflicts of the 1930's, most of my statistics are drawn from the 1939 Census. Except for a few significant changes such as the growth of the supermarket, 1948 figures, although swollen by inflation, describe the same general picture of distribution as do the 1939 statistics.

[2] "It embraces the entire group of services and functions performed in the distribution of merchandise from producer to consumer, excluding only operations relating to changes in the form of goods normally regarded as processing or manufacturing operations." H. H. Maynard and T. N. Beckman, *Principles of Marketing*, 4th ed. (New York: Ronald Press Co.; 1946), p. 3. Or, it is "the addition of time and place utilities" (to goods). The Twentieth Century Fund, *Does Distribution Cost Too Much?* (New York: 1939), p. 6.

almost one fifth of the total labor force and generating about one fifth of the national income.

As these figures indicate, the field is still predominantly one of small firms, one in which large-scale organization has been relatively slow to develop. The average retail firm in 1939 made annual sales of less than $25,000 and hired less than three employees. But large-scale organization has appeared, winning a share of the market by dispossessing older, smaller retailers, and great differences in size of units now prevail. Of the five major innovations in retail distribution since the Civil War, four — the department store, the mail-order house, the chain store, and the supermarket — are successful attempts to increase substantially the size of retail units.[3] Even the fifth innovation — the voluntary chain — is an attempt to secure the advantages of large-scale organization while retaining small-scale ownership and management. While department stores and mail-order houses achieve great size as a consequence of their function — to offer a wide variety of many different lines of merchandise under one roof or between two covers — both originated in the nineteenth century and their greatest competitive impact had subsided by the 1920's.[4] The supermarket, which first appeared in the early 1930's, is by definition large, usually being defined as a self-service food store with annual sales of over $250,000. During the period under study, however, it was still in its comparative infancy, although its growth was rapid.[5]

[3] For descriptions of the origin and growth of these five forms of organization, see Maynard and Beckman, chs. 9–11. A sixth innovation, the discount house, has become of major importance only since World War II.

[4] Because most early department stores developed gradually from stores with a more limited line of merchandise, it is difficult to set a precise date of origin. Most authorities place its birth in Eastern cities in the decade following the Civil War. See, e.g., Maynard and Beckman, pp. 146–147. The mail-order house originated in the last quarter of the nineteenth century.

[5] In 1939 grocery stores with annual sales of $300,000 or more made 9.2 per cent of all food sales and 1.7 per cent of all retail sales. In 1948 they made 37.2 per cent of all grocery sales and 7.1 per cent of all retail sales. U.S. Dept. of Commerce, Bureau of the Census, Sixteenth Census of the United States,

It was the corporate chain store which has had by far the greatest success — and the greatest competitive impact on older distributive media. In 1949 department stores made 7.5 per cent of all retail sales, supermarkets about 7 per cent, mail-order houses (catalog sales) 0.9 per cent, while chain stores made 20.3 per cent.[6] Thus, of all the newer methods of distribution to arise in the past century, the chain store has had the greatest competitive impact. Moreover, its impact was intensified by the rapidity of its growth. It wrested most of its share of the market from competing retailing media in less than a decade, increasing its proportion of total retail sales from 9 per cent in 1926 to 25 per cent in 1933.[7] It truly revolutionized many trades during the late 1920's and early 1930's and was, naturally enough, the target of most political retaliations or redresses advocated by groups of older means of distribution.

Chains, too, represent a substantial increase in scale. In 1939 the average chain *unit*, making sales of about $75,000, was almost four times as large as its independent competitor, and the average *chain*, containing 19 units and making sales of almost one and a half million dollars, was over 70 times as large.[8] Furthermore, averages obscure the size of the large

Census of Business, vol. I, *Retail Trade: 1939*, part 1, p. 817 (hereafter cited as *1939 Census of Business*) and Census of Business, *1948*, vol. I, part 1, pp. 2.02–3 (hereafter cited as *1948 Census of Business*). However, these statistics reflect inflation as well as physical growth, since the food component of the BLS Consumer Price Index rose from 95.2 (1935–39 = 100) in 1939 to 210.2 in 1948.

[6] The supermarket percentage is an estimate. The others are computed from data in *Survey of Current Business*, October 1949, and July 1950, pp. S–8, S–9.

[7] As late as 1919 chain sales were but 4 per cent of total retail sales. In 1926 chain volume approximated 9 per cent; in 1928, 12 per cent; in 1929, 20 per cent; and in 1933, 25 per cent. T. N. Beckman and H. C. Nolen, *The Chain Store Problem* (New York: McGraw-Hill; 1938), pp. 24–25. These figures, as are those of the Census Bureau, are based on chains of four or more stores each.

[8] *1939 Census of Business*, vol. I, part 1, pp. 112, 120, 179. This difference in size of unit held true for most trades. Only among department stores, themselves a relatively new method of distribution, were chain units smaller than their independent counterparts, although differences in average size of chain and independent units in the liquor and the lumber and building materials trades were not large enough to be significant.

chain. Fifty-five per cent of all chain sales were made by chains with more than 100 units.[9] Thus the chances were good that an independent merchant competed with a chain unit which was part of a large organization, perhaps even a giant such as A & P.

Yet side by side with these giants exists a multitude of almost minute retail establishments. A conflict between newer and older methods of distribution is also a conflict between large- and small-scale organization, and most independents are very small indeed. As Table I shows, distribution is marked by great differences in the size of establishment. Now, of the six major size groups, all but the lowest make substantial percentages of total retail sales, and no one size group predominates. And this is what we might expect. The grand total of retail firms includes the few giant stores serving metropolitan centers, the more numerous moderately large units in large suburbs or small cities, still more firms of a moderate size serving towns and suburbs, and, finally, the thousands of small stores in residential and rural areas. In addition, typical size will vary with the trade. But this general picture of retailing hardly pre-pares one to expect so many extremely small units, which ac-count for but a small percentage of total sales. Certainly the most striking feature of Table I is the fact that over one half of all retail units make less than one tenth of all sales. This was also true in 1948, although then the lot of the bottom half was somewhat easier.[10] Thus there lies at the bottom of the distributive pyramid a broad, marginal, and depressed base.

Most of these nearly one million stores with an annual vol-ume of less than $10,000 were independents. While only 12.5 per cent of chain units had this low a volume, 943,533 inde-

---

[9] *Ibid.*, vol. I, part 1, pp. 179–182. Such chains contained 46 per cent of all chain units.

[10] 45.8 per cent of the total number made only 8.9 per cent of total retail sales. But they included merchants with volumes of up to $30,000. *1948 Census of Business*, vol. I, part 1, pp. 2.02–203. This increase in sales reflects moderate real growth, as well as much inflation.

TABLE I <sup>a</sup>

RETAIL TRADE ANALYSIS BY SIZE GROUPS, 1939

| Size Group | Stores | | | Sales | | |
|---|---|---|---|---|---|---|
| Annual sales | Number | Per cent | Cumulative per cent | Amount (add 000) | Per cent | Cumulative per cent |
| $300,000 and over: | 12,630 | 0.7 | 0.7 | $9,855,631 | 23.4 | 23.4 |
| $100,000 to $299,999: | 50,097 | 2.8 | 3.5 | 7,955,285 | 18.9 | 42.3 |
| $50,000 to $99,999: | 93,318 | 5.3 | 8.8 | 6,394,703 | 15.2 | 57.5 |
| $30,000 to $49,999: | 133,221 | 7.5 | 16.3 | 5,077,007 | 12.1 | 69.6 |
| $10,000 to $29,999: | 522,117 | 29.5 | 45.8 | 8,938,632 | 21.3 | 90.9 |
| Less than $10,000: | 958,972 | 54.2 | 100.0 | 3,820,532 | 9.1 | 100.0 |

<sup>a</sup> Abstracted from data in *1939 Census of Business*, vol. I, part 1, p. 48.

pendents — 57.3 per cent of all independent stores — made annual sales of under $10,000.[11] Even in 1948, after retail prices had more than doubled, almost 300,000 retailers enjoyed a volume of less than $10,000, and almost 600,000 a volume of less than $20,000.

Even in the absence of chain competition, the ownership of a small store offers no easy path to riches. How over one half of the nation's retail units could exist on a volume of less than $10,000 is not readily apparent. Even a volume of $12,000, for example, yields, after the payment of $9,000 for the merchandise sold, a gross margin of only $3,000 to cover all expenses.[12] Two fifths of this margin, or about $1,250, must be spent for rent, insurance, taxes, repair and upkeep of premises, light, heat, power, telephone, advertising (if any), and other un-

[11] *1939 Census of Business*, vol. I, part 1, pp. 671, 679.
[12] This analysis of a $12,000 volume store is based on U.S. Dept. of Commerce, Bureau of the Census, *1929 Census of Business*, vol. I, part 1, p. 15. (Hereafter cited as *1929 Census of Business*.)

avoidable operating expenses.[13] Thus the proprietor is left with $1,750 for his payroll and profit. A store of this size requires at least two salespeople. If the proprietor and his family man the store,[14] then they share an income of $1,750, hardly a munificent payment for the full-time labor of two or more people. If the proprietor is not aided by family members, then he must hire an employee (in fact, usually one full-time and one part-time employee) and realizes only the difference between the $1,750 and his payroll. This is the full reward for his labor and his entrepreneurial functions, and the profit on his working capital.

Yet such a merchant was doing better than were well over one half of his fellow retailers. For, to repeat, over one half of all independent retail stores sold less than $10,000 worth of merchandise. And many of these 950,000 merchants were extremely small businessmen. Almost two thirds of them, or over one third of all independent stores, had sales of less than $5,000! However, the proportion of very small retailers varies markedly from trade to trade. In 1939 three fourths of all independent groceries (without fresh meats) had sales of less than $10,000. The corresponding percentage for combination groceries (with fresh meats) was 39.5 per cent, drug stores 29.3 per cent, and new car dealers 6.5 per cent.[15]

The lot of these small retailers is not an easy one. Well over one half of our independent merchants realized for all of their retail services less than a thousand dollars each in 1939. Furthermore, if we assume a net profit of 2 per cent on sales — the national retail average — then we find that the market assays the risk-taking and entrepreneurial functions of each as worth less than sixty cents a day. Even if we take into account the

[13] It makes little difference, of course, whether the proprietor actually pays rent or whether, as owner of his premises, he has to meet the equivalent of rent in the form of fixed charges, depreciation, and interest.

[14] In 1939 over 900,000 members of proprietors' families, about 35 per cent of all workers in retail stores, worked in retail establishments. *1939 Census of Business*, vol. I, part 1, p. 85.

[15] *Ibid.*, vol. I, part 1, pp. 116–117.

fact that some stores are merely secondary or part-time activities of their proprietors [16] and that some proprietors sell services as well as merchandise,[17] it appears that there are probably well over half a million firms which command the bulk of their proprietors' economic activities but which yield them inadequate incomes.

The economic existence of these small merchants, if not solitary, certainly tends to be "poor, nasty, brutish, and short." They all too often enter retailing with scanty capital and insufficient experience. A small retailer at the best enjoys an inadequate income, one which makes it most difficult to build up capital and increase the scale of operations. The prices he can charge are usually limited by competition, "but there is nothing except his own ingenuity and sound credit rating to hold down the cost of the goods which he must purchase, and nothing but his own ability to hold down operating expenses." [18] He must maintain himself with the often thin margin between the ceiling of the prices which competition will allow him to charge and the floor of the costs which he must pay, and these costs are often maximized by the minuteness of his scale of operations. Consequently, retail mortality rates are high.[19] Only in-

[16] These stores include establishments selling products of the proprietor's industrial shop, stores that occupy only the spare time of the proprietor and/or family, and stores that are established in part to obtain wholesale prices on supplies (usually food and clothing) used by the proprietor and his family. No reliable estimates of the size of this group exist.

[17] E.g., caterers, repair shops, plumbing, electrical, and interior decorators' shops. While the often haphazard and casual nature of sales of service probably causes incomplete reporting, the 1939 Census classified only 1.6 per cent of total retail sales as payments for service, and such payments never exceeded 8 per cent in any trade. Vol. I, part 1, p. 145. In addition, some retailers receive a return for their services in the form of higher retail margins. E.g., an electrical appliance dealer may receive a margin of about 40 per cent as compared with 20 to 25 per cent for a grocer.

[18] *1929 Census of Business*, vol. I, part 1, p. 16.

[19] The term "mortality rate," although standard terminology, is perhaps unduly morbid, for far from all retail "deaths" are bankruptcies or failures. Many discontinuances occur upon the retirement of the owner or the sale of the business at no loss or no great loss. In the case of one-man enterprises, which constitute a majority of discontinuances, the liquidation of the firm often re-

complete data are available, but the general picture is clear. Only 42.3 per cent of the independent stores counted by the 1939 Census were more than ten years old.[20] And if we compare 1929 and 1939 Census statistics, we find that 49.2 per cent of the independent stores counted in the former year were not in existence in the latter.[21] But this percentage greatly understates actual mortality rates because it omits all stores opened after 1929 but closed before 1939 and because it measures the economic existence of the *store* rather than of the proprietor.[22] For recent years we have estimates of retail discontinuances, which show that the retail mortality rate was 6.7 per cent in 1940, 7.3 per cent in 1941, 6.1 per cent in 1947, and 8.4 per cent in 1948.[23] Thus an average annual mortality rate of at least 7 per cent seems to be indicated. Mortality is, of course, highest among small retailers.[24]

There also exist a number of more accurate and detailed local studies which, although they probably understate actual mortality,[25] indicate that average mortality rates in the 1920's

sults from the proprietor's securing employment elsewhere. Such a "death" really is a shift in employment rather than an outright failure. See A. D. H. Kaplan, *Small Business: Its Place and Its Problems*, Committee for Economic Development Research Study (New York: McGraw-Hill; 1948), pp. 55–56.

[20] *1939 Census of Business*, vol. I, part 1, pp. 170–174. These figures, of course, reflect technological and other changes as well as mortality rates. E.g., that more than 80 per cent of used car dealerships were less than ten years old reflects the newness of the trade, and that none of 1939's liquor dealers admitted operating in 1929 is understandable but signifies nothing about mortality rates.

[21] *Loc. cit.*, and *1929 Census of Business*, vol. I, part 1, pp. 47, 69, 71.

[22] The 1939 Census questionnaire asked for the "date (year) of original establishment of this business in this city." *1939 Census of Business*, vol. I, part 1, pp. 874–876.

[23] *Survey of Current Business*, July 1944, p. 13; 1949 Statistical Supplement, pp. 24–25. "Discontinuances" are so defined as to eliminate mere transfers, i.e., sales of operating businesses.

[24] In 1939 retail firms with more than three employees were 16.5 per cent of all stores but accounted for only 3.8 per cent of all discontinuances in the next year. *1939 Census of Business*, vol. I, part 1, pp. 87–89; *Survey of Current Business*, July 1944, p. 13.

[25] Because their basic sources make probable the omission of many short-lived enterprises and less well-organized types of establishment.

and 1930's ran somewhat higher, averaging about 10 per cent.[26] Some of these studies also show that mortality varies widely among different lines of trade. A grocery, for example, can anticipate an economic life only half as long as that of a drugstore.[27]

Yet these high mortality rates are usually matched by retail birth rates. There have always been "prospective, undiscerning proprietors . . . ready to step into the place of fallen comrades. Entry . . . is so easily accomplished and the competitive struggle so severe that a continuous seething occurs in the cauldron of trade." [28] The ranks remain full and the turnover high.

Why, if the competitive struggle is so rugged, the chances of survival so slim, and the economic rewards so scanty, are so many people willing and eager to enter such an uneven combat? In part, simply because they *can*. Since, with a few exceptions such as drugstores, retailing is easy to enter, it appeals to those who, perhaps enthused with optimistic hopes of emulating a Horatio Alger hero, prefer the risky possibility of entrepreneurial profits to the drab security of a salary or wages. In a society which lays great ideological stress on economic individualism but whose economic institutions have be-

[26] For a survey and recapitulation of these studies, see U.S. Temporary National Economic Committee (TNEC), Monograph No. 17, *Problems of Small Business*, by John H. Cover, Nathanael H. Engle, Earl D. Strong, Peter R. Nehenkis, William Saunders, Harold Vatter and Harold H. Weir (Washington: GPO; 1941), pp. 7–44. Also see R. G. Hutchinson, A. R. and Mabel Newcomer, "Study in Business Mortality," *American Economic Review*, vol. XXVIII, no. 3, September 1938, pp. 479–514; Paul D. Converse, *Business Mortality of Illinois Retail Stores from 1925 to 1930*, University of Illinois, Bureau of Business Research, Bull. No. 41; E. T. Halass, "Mortality of Retail Stores in Colorado," *University of Denver Reports*, Business Study no. 82, vol. XII, no. 3, June 1936; G. W. Starr and G. A. Steiner, "Births and Deaths of Retail Stores in Indiana, 1929–1937," *Dun's Review*, January 1940; E. A. Heilman, *Mortality of Business Firms in Minneapolis, St. Paul, and Duluth, 1926–30*, Employment Stabilization Institute, vol. II, no. 1 (Minneapolis: University of Minnesota Press; 1933); and A. E. Boer, "Mortality Costs in Retail Trades," *Journal of Marketing*, vol. II, no. 1, July 1937, pp. 52–60.
[27] Starr and Steiner, p. 27; Heilman, p. 13; Boer, p. 53.
[28] TNEC Monograph No. 17, p. 7.

come increasingly large-scale and bureaucratic, retail trade remains attractive to those who, unwilling or unable to subject themselves to the rigidities and disciplines of other economic occupations, want to be "their own boss."

. . . a small shop has always been more than merely an economic unit . . . the parallel to farming presents itself. The small farm has always been more than merely an economic unit. . . It offers values which cannot be strictly accounted for in pounds, shillings, or pence. There is independence. The owner is or appears to be his own master. His social position is . . . enhanced by not belonging to the wage-earning class.[29]

These reasons are all too often augmented by ignorance of the odds against the new retailer.

It is not difficult to enter into retailing. The public does not regard it as a type of activity calling for any high degree of technical knowledge. We all remember how successfully we played with toy cash registers as children and feel that successful merchandising needs only an average amount of intelligence and common sense. We meet merchants daily, and they do not impress us as being supermen. The result of this situation is a continual flow of hopeful and enthusiastic individuals into retailing, replacing another group of sadder and, we hope, wiser men.[30]

This unjustified optimism about the prospects for success [31] has often led completely inexperienced men to enter the field. Some studies have shown that half of the retailers surveyed had little or no previous experience in the trade.[32] But more

[29] Hermann Levy, *The Shops of Britain; A Study of Retail Distribution* (London: International Library of Sociology and Social Reconstruction, Kegan Paul, Trench, Trubner & Co.; 1947), p. 10. For a similar view, see Maynard and Beckman, p. 134.

[30] Willard L. Thorp, in an address, "Trend of Failures in the Distribution Field," quoted in a Bureau of Foreign and Domestic Commerce release, Business Information Section, October 1938. (As cited in TNEC Monograph No. 17, p. 82.)

[31] For a brief description of a number of studies demonstrating this unjustified optimism, see TNEC Monograph No. 17, pp. 81–86.

[32] E.g., more than half of the retailers surveyed in one study had little or no previous experience, and 12 per cent had no previous employment at all. R. G. Hutchinson, A. R. and M. Newcomer, p. 507. Another survey found that

than simple optimism is involved; economic necessity plays an important part. Even the inadequate income of a small retailer is better than none, and it may be a helpful supplement to other income. Many people enter retailing because they have lost other jobs; [33] many small, so-called "hole-in-the-wall" stores are opened within their proprietors' homes both to provide some income and to obtain wholesale discounts.[34] Just as unemployment causes some people to turn to subsistence farming, so it encourages others to open what they hope will be subsistence stores.[35]

A final reason for the willingness of so many to enter retail trade and for the survival of some of them is that they are encouraged and often subsidized by wholesalers seeking to increase their volume or to replace those retailers who have failed.[36] And the extent to which wholesalers in effect subsidize small retailers is surprising. Although most wholesalers increase their prices on small quantities, studies show that on small orders the wholesaler's margin is perhaps usually insufficient to meet his costs.[37]

---

half of all new grocers had no previous experience. R. S. Vaile, *Grocery Retailing with Special Reference to the Effects of Competition*, Studies in Economics and Business, No. 1 (Minneapolis: University of Minnesota Press; 1932), p. 16.

[33] One local study found that over half of the people opening groceries in 1930 in one area did so because they were unemployed and "had to do something." Vaile, p. 16.

[34] Another local survey found that in the period 1923–1926 two thirds of all independent groceries, 52 per cent of all confectionery stores, and 18 per cent of all meat markets were located within their proprietors' homes. R. G. Hutchinson, A. R. and M. Newcomer, p. 506.

[35] Although national business mortality statistics have been estimated only since 1940, they do seem to demonstrate this. In the somewhat depressed years of 1940 and 1941 new retail businesses with less than 4 employees totaled 96,000 and 109,000. In 1942 and 1943, when employment opportunities were plentiful, the comparable totals declined to 70,000 and 34,000. *Survey of Current Business*, July 1944, p. 13. However, wartime shortages of materials and labor probably were partly responsible for this decline.

[36] In one survey, for example, it was found that three meat wholesalers had a customer turnover on the average of every nineteen months. Howard C. Greer, "Customer Turnover Experience of Meat Packing Companies," *Journal of Business*, vol. III, no. 3, part 2, April 1933.

[37] One analysis of a food wholesaler, whose typical small sale of $24.37

Before we conclude this sketch of the retail field, a word of caution is in order. This somewhat extended description of the pathology of the small independent retailer should not be applied to all independent merchants. For there are hundreds of thousands of independent retailers who are strong, vigorous, and either able to meet the price competition of the newer forms of distribution or able to better them on other appeals. Since 1933 independents have maintained or increased their share of total retail sales.

Thus, in summary, the most obvious basis for political groupings in this field lies in the conflict between older and newer methods of distribution. This conflict is intensified by its correspondence to a conflict between large and small retail units. Yet the grouping together of independent retailers is made difficult by the broad range of size over which they extend, one end of which is marked by an extraordinarily large number of small stores with extremely short life expectancies. There are, however, significant differences in the breadth of size range for various kinds of business — groceries, for example, having an extremely large proportion of small shops with a high death rate, while the drug trade has few very small units and is marked by greater homogeneity in size and by a far higher life expectancy.

---

grossed him a margin of 97¢, showed that the variable cost of this sale was 95¢, leaving only 2¢ to cover his fixed expenses, although these were 55 per cent of his total costs. Six food wholesalers realized a net profit only on sales of $20 or more a week. Although only one third of their retailer customers bought $25 or more a week, these sales accounted for 91 per cent of sales volume but only 37 per cent of wholesaling costs. Donald R. G. Cowan, *Sales Analysis from the Management Standpoint* (Chicago: University of Chicago Press; 1938), pp. 134–135. A survey of a full service wholesale druggist showed that retailers' purchases of individual commodities averaged about two dollars per line. U.S. Department of Commerce, Bureau of Foreign and Domestic Commerce, Domestic Commerce Series No. 86, *Wholesale Druggists Operations* (Washington: GPO; 1934), p. 28. And 45 per cent of the sales of two drug wholesalers involved sales of less than one dollar per line, and 70 per cent involved sales of less than two dollars per line. National Wholesale Druggist Ass'n, Statistical Division, Bull. No. 12, June 1930. (As cited in TNEC Monograph No. 1, *Price Behavior and Business Policy*, by Saul Nelson and Walter G. Keim, Washington: GPO; 1940, p. 386.)

## B. WHOLESALE DISTRIBUTION

Wholesale distribution — the process undergone by a product between its manufacture and its arrival at a retail store — similarly is marked by antagonism and competitive warfare between older and newer methods of distribution. Here, too, the conflict is in part one of size. The wholesale organizations of the newer distributive media are substantially larger than their older competitor, the merchant wholesaler. In 1939 the average wholesaler had sales of only $233,000, while manufacturers' sales branches (with stocks) had sales of $682,000, manufacturers' sales offices (without stocks) $914,000, wholesale organizations of retail mail-order houses $1,238,000, and wholesale warehouses of retail chains $3,003,000.[38] Furthermore, since these wholesale activities of the newer media are but part of far greater corporate activities, a wholesaler may be threatened by a manufacturer or retail chain whose total size dwarfs its wholesale activities.

This clash between large- and small-scale organization is a

. . . struggle . . . for the control over the marketing machinery — over who shall perform the marketing functions . . . there are a large variety of unescapable marketing functions which must be performed by someone. These functions of marketing include assembling, buying, or purchasing; advertising and selling; grading, sorting, and standardization; transportation and delivery, storage, and warehousing; financing sales, keeping records, extending credit, and, above all, assuming the risks of marketing. . .[39]

This struggle to perform the wholesaling function is a relatively recent one, resulting from the rise of the new methods of distribution mentioned above — the department store, the mail-order house, the chain store, the supermarket — and also of a channel not previously mentioned, manufacturer owner-

[38] *1939 Census of Business*, vol. I, part 1, pp. 63, 69, 183; vol. II, p. 49. These figures somewhat overstate the average size of merchant wholesalers since some manufacturer-owned wholesale establishments were included with merchant wholesalers.

[39] TNEC Monograph No. 17, pp. 159–160.

ship and operation of wholesale (and sometimes retail) units. But it was not always so. There was a time when the merchant wholesaler, often in combination with functional middlemen,[40] was an essential and dominant link in the distribution of final products.

> . . . the traditional channels of distribution for manufactured goods . . . have been manufacturer to wholesaler to retailer, with some use of agents, brokers, and factors of various types. . . Indeed this traditional system of distribution was characteristic of American marketing until well into the present century. . .
> Wholesalers had enjoyed a rather large measure of control over marketing . . . from the earliest times. Direct descendant [sic] of colonial importers, they grew up with the country and waxed wealthy and powerful in their growth. It was the wholesalers who were the big businessmen of the early nineteenth century. . . These wholesalers were able to dominate the puny manufacturing industries of the early industrial revolution. They provided about the only means of disposing of the manufacturers' output. They had access to greater stores of capital and often were able to finance nascent manufacturers. Retailers were largely of the general store type and had to depend on wholesalers for such manufactured goods as they handled. Wholesalers kept pace in the changing patterns of trade from rural to urban markets, and from general line to specialty merchandising as long as such changes were slow. Thus, with the growth of cities, retail shops developed which were able to specialize in groceries, in drugs, in dry goods, in hardware, in shoes, and in clothing. Wholesalers followed or, perhaps more accurately, kept pace with these changes, and retained their dominant role in the marketing structure until well into the twentieth century. . .[41]

[40] The usual mark of a merchant wholesaler, who customarily performs a large number of marketing functions, is that he takes title to the goods involved. Merchant wholesalers are usually classified as either service (full-function) or as limited-function wholesalers depending on the range of marketing functions they perform. On the other hand, a middleman who does not take title and who usually performs much more limited functions, an agent or broker for example, is usually classed as a functional middleman. Maynard and Beckman, p. 314.

[41] TNEC Monograph No. 17, pp. 159–160. Agricultural commodities, too, were usually marketed through middlemen, although producers' coöperatives have sometimes played an important role. Maynard and Beckman, pp. 253, 367–372.

It is against this background of a historical predominance of the traditional distributive pattern of manufacturer to wholesaler to retailer that we examine the situation in 1939. Table II, based upon a combination of wholesale and manufacturing statistics, shows total retailer purchases from virtually all sources of supply. Since almost all consumer goods pass through a retail stage,[42] such an analysis provides our best measure of the wholesaling functions performed by different media and of the extent to which the once dominant merchant wholesaler has been displaced or bypassed.[43] Table II shows that the wholesaler, attacked from both sides, has lost ground both to the manufacturer who establishes his own wholesale outlets and to the retailer who purchases directly from manufacturers. The merchant wholesaler has not been routed: alone, he still made 41 per cent of all sales to retailers; together with functional middlemen (agents and brokers), assemblers, and

[42] In 1939 wholesalers made direct sales of 766 million dollars to household consumers and direct sales of 832 million dollars were made by manufacturers. Together, these total only 3.6 per cent of all consumer purchases from retailers and more direct sources. *1939 Census of Business*, vol. II, p. 122; vol. V, pp. 6–7. In addition, a small number of sales are made by farmers directly to consumers. Many of these sales are tabulated in the retail census under roadside stand sales.

[43] *Ibid.*, vol. V, "Distribution of Manufacturers' Sales," presents statistics about the first distributive stage undergone by manufactured or processed goods, but this presents an incomplete picture because it omits goods which do not pass through a manufacturing or processing stage and because not all of the transactions that it records as sales to manufacturers' own wholesale outlets result in the displacement of independent wholesalers, for more than one fifth of the sales of these outlets are made to independent wholesalers. *Ibid.*, vol. II, p. 122. Vol. II, "Wholesale Distribution," records these movements but omits manufacturers' direct sales to retailers. Consequently, Table II is based upon a combination of volumes II and V. It slightly overstates the role of independent wholesalers. While most of the product movements recorded in volume V as sales to manufacturers' own wholesale outlets appear in volume II, in the second distributive stage, as sales by manufacturers' outlets, a small proportion appear as sales by wholesalers. The Census Bureau states that, although the category of wholesalers is composed of "wholesale establishments . . . which are largely independent in ownership," it does contain some "subsidiary sales corporations of manufacturers set up to do a regular wholesale business. . ." But the great bulk of "wholesale outlets owned and operated by manufacturers . . . for the purpose of carrying stocks, selling, and delivering their products" are classified as manufacturers' own outlets. *Ibid.*, vol. II, pp. 31–32.

independent oil distributors, he commanded half of the field. But two new major channels of distribution have been opened. One, a backward extension of large retail enterprises, enables

TABLE II [a]

RETAILERS' SOURCES OF SUPPLY, BY TYPES OF OPERATION, 1939

| Type of operation | Sales to retailers (add 000) | Percentage of total sales to retailers |
|---|---|---|
| Total, all types: | $34,010,024 | 100.0 |
| Manufacturers' direct sales: | 9,840,990 | 28.9 |
| Manufacturers' sales branches or offices: | 4,088,857 | 12.0 |
| Manufacturers' sales to own retail stores: | 1,046,796 | 3.1 |
| Integrated petroleum bulk stations and terminals: | 2,324,904 | 6.8 |
| Independent petroleum bulk stations: [b] | 492,491 | 1.5 |
| Merchant wholesalers: | 13,918,001 | 40.9 |
| Agents and brokers: | 1,880,657 | 5.5 |
| Assemblers: | 417,328 | 1.2 |

[a] Computed from *1939 Census of Business*, vol. V, pp. 6–7; vol. II, pp. 49, 122. Note: this table assumes that *all* establishments engaged in wholesale trade had the same distribution by class of customer as did those reporting such data. Establishments doing 87.4 per cent of all wholesale business made such reports.
[b] Includes coöperative bulk stations.

retailers to bypass wholesalers and purchase directly from manufacturers; it carried about 29 per cent of the flow of goods to retailers. The other, a forward advance of large manufacturing or processing corporations, displaces independent wholesalers with manufacturer-controlled outlets and, if we include sales to manufacturer-controlled retail stores and sales of refiner-controlled oil distributors, made about 22 per cent of all sales to retailers. These two channels are part of what is called mass distribution, for they usually represent a substantial increase in scale of operation and are extensions of activity by firms which have already mastered either large-scale manufacturing or retailing. Mass distribution agencies, then, have captured half of the field, make half of all sales to retailers, and perform, or make unnecessary, half of the wholesaling function.

Although the merchant wholesaler has held his ground since 1939,[44] in the decade before that year his position had deteriorated rapidly. In terms of the distribution of manufacturers' sales, the proportion of marketing performed by wholesalers declined almost a fifth, while direct sales to retailers were increasing by more than a tenth, and sales through manufacturers' wholesale outlets increased by more than a third.[45]

Thus the independent, or merchant, wholesaler had been losing ground steadily. Most merchant wholesalers are service or full-function wholesalers, who, in addition to taking title to the commodities they handle, perform a full range of marketing functions.[46] It is the service wholesaler, then, who suffers most from the advance of the newer media. His economic response has been primarily defensive, for, although he has been the victim of vertical integration, he himself has engaged in comparatively little integration, vertical [47] or horizontal.[48] However, substantial differences in size do exist.

[44] His share of wholesale trade rose from 41 per cent to 42.3 per cent. *1948 Census of Business,* vol. IV, p. 12.

[45] *1939 Census of Business,* vol. V, p. 7.

[46] Limited-function wholesalers comprise voluntary group wholesalers, textile converters, export merchants, importers, industrial distributors, cash-and-carry wholesalers, drop shippers or desk jobbers, wagon distributors, and retailer-coöperative warehouses.

[47] This, like any other general statement about a field as large and diverse as distribution, is an oversimplification, for some vertical integration does exist. Many wholesalers — grocery, for example — process some merchandise; others order goods to be manufactured for them in accordance with their specifications and under their own labels; and a few even manufacture some of the goods they handle. This assumption of some of the functions of manufacturing strengthens the position of the wholesaler. Vertical integration in the other direction, however, often represents a deterioration of the wholesaler's position; generally, a wholesaler will not sell directly to household consumers unless he desperately needs the volume or succumbs to the importunities or blandishments of those who wish to buy at wholesale prices, or when, because of a disorganized retail structure, he can make sales at retail without offending his retailer customers.

[48] Census statistics on horizontal integration lump manufacturers' wholesale

Table III summarizes size variations among merchant wholesalers in the same manner as did Table I for independent re-

TABLE III [a]

WHOLESALE TRADE ANALYSIS BY SIZE GROUPS

| Size Group | Establishments | | | Sales | | |
|---|---|---|---|---|---|---|
| (Annual volume) | Number | Per-centage | Cumula-tive per-centage | Amount (add 000) | Per-centage | Cumula-tive per-centage |
| $2,000,000 and over: | 1,102 | 1.2 | 1.2 | $5,025,212 | 25.9 | 25.9 |
| $1,000,000 to $1,999,000: | 2,052 | 2.2 | 3.4 | 2,792,112 | 14.3 | 40.2 |
| $500,000 to $999,999: | 5,047 | 5.4 | 8.8 | 3,482,371 | 17.9 | 58.1 |
| $300,000 to $499,999: | 6,195 | 6.7 | 15.5 | 2,376,989 | 12.2 | 70.3 |
| $200,000 to $299,999: | 6,717 | 7.2 | 22.7 | 1,641,459 | 8.5 | 78.8 |
| $100,000 to $199,999: | 14,226 | 15.3 | 38.0 | 2,017,339 | 10.4 | 89.2 |
| $50,000 to $99,999: | 16,971 | 18.3 | 56.3 | 1,213,777 | 6.3 | 95.5 |
| $10,000 to $49,999: | 30,446 | 32.8 | 89.1 | 810,906 | 4.1 | 99.6 |
| Under $10,000: | 10,038 | 10.8 | 99.9 [b] | 58,382 | 0.3 | 99.9 [b] |

[a] *1939 Census of Business,* vol. II, p. 90.
[b] Rounding error.

tailers. It reveals variations fully as striking and as great as
those in the retail field. But, although there are many small
and often marginal wholesalers whose total volume is but a

outlets together with independent wholesalers. Insofar as these outlets supply
retailers or industrial consumers all over the nation, they are likely to be multi-
unit operations, e.g., the General Electric Supply Corporation. Despite their
inclusion, statistics on all wholesale organizations show that 68.2 per cent of all
wholesale establishments are single-unit operations and make 52.1 per cent of
all wholesale transactions. Only 11.9 per cent of all establishments are in organizations containing 25 or more units, and they make 18.8 per cent of all sales.
Furthermore, except in the case of the very large wholesale chains, mainly manufacturers' outlets, this horizontal integration did not advance significantly during
the period 1929–1939. *Ibid.,* vol. II, p. 29.

small proportion of all wholesale transactions, these small wholesalers enjoy larger incomes than do their retail counterparts. The typical small wholesaler has a volume about ten times as large as that of the small retailer. A small wholesaler with a volume of $50,000 has a gross margin of better than $10,000,[49] as compared with the gross margin of about $1250 received by his retail counterpart on a volume of $5000. Even though the wholesaler has greater expenses and a larger investment, his lot is less marginal. Furthermore, many small wholesalers make both wholesale and retail sales and so receive double margins on some sales.

Size ranges vary in different trades. Automobile wholesalers run well to the top of the scale, with those wholesalers who had a volume in excess of two million dollars accounting for 85 per cent of all wholesale automobile sales in 1939. General-line drug wholesalers with sales of more than one million dollars made 77 per cent of all wholesale drug transactions, but million-dollar volume general-line grocery wholesalers made only 34 per cent of all wholesale grocery sales.[50]

Thus, as was also true of retailing, the obvious economic conflict which might be expected to be transferred to the political sphere is the struggle between the older and the newer distributive media — a struggle which is also a conflict between large- and small-scale business organization. However, the greater size of typical wholesalers should make political grouping and action easier than it is for retailers.

[49] For wholesalers with a volume of between $50,000 and $100,000, operating expenses were 19.3 per cent of sales; for those with a volume of between $10,000 and $50,000, 21.4 per cent; and for those with a volume of less than $10,000, 26.0 per cent. *1939 Census of Business*, vol. II, p. 90. Consequently, an average margin of over 20 per cent seems to prevail.

[50] *Ibid.*, vol. II, pp. 90–94.

## Distribution: Its Economic Conflicts

Next we shall examine distribution's economic conflicts to determine the extent to which they become translated into politics. There are three basic forms of distributive conflict. The first, which I shall call horizontal competition, is the conflict among competitors of the same type, e.g., competition between two independent grocers. The second, which for want of a better term I shall call intertype competition, is the conflict among different methods of distribution, e.g., competitive struggle among a mail-order house, a chain variety store, and an independent hardware dealer. And the third is the conflict between different stages in the same line of distribution and can be called vertical struggle. An example of this is conflict over prices and margins between a refiner's bulk station and a filling-station operator.

### A. HORIZONTAL COMPETITION

Horizontal competition is the type of competition described in economic theory and usually stressed in economic studies. It is the competition among sellers and among buyers which characterizes the central institution postulated by economic theory, the market. With the construct of perfect competition, economic theory offers a full and internally consistent explanation of the operations of a market. Unfortunately, this explanation is precariously based on certain narrow assumptions — those which are most nearly approximated in such exchanges as agricultural commodity exchanges or stock markets. They are not as valid for modern industrial and commercial activities.[1] Briefly put, they require that the market deal in standardized or homogeneous commodities and that it contain numerous buyers and sellers each of whom knows all pertinent facts and rationally calculates his self-interest and no one of whom is large enough to affect market operations significantly. Prices and quantities are the only important data, and no one buyer or seller can appreciably influence a market price — instead, he adjusts his operations to a price determined by the market.

Now this theory and its derivative methods of analysis explain much of horizontal competition; much of it is price competition. Customers may "shop around," may look for lower prices; retailers and wholesalers do compete on the basis of price; and, even if the "higgling" process of the classical market does not operate constantly and directly, no prices are immune to changes in the conditions of supply and demand. Nevertheless, it has been generally recognized for some time

[1] Note how frequently classical economists demonstrate their theorems with illustrations borrowed from agricultural or stock exchanges. Indeed, Schumpeter goes so far as to say, speaking of Marshall and Wicksell, that "if we look more closely at the conditions . . . that must be fulfilled in order to produce perfect competition, we realize immediately that outside of agricultural mass production there cannot be many instances of it." Joseph A. Schumpeter, *Capitalism, Socialism, and Democracy*, 2nd ed. (New York and London: Harper & Bros.; 1947), pp. 78–79. Elton Mayo, in an attempt to explain Ricardo's limited conception of economic activities, makes much of the fact that Ricardo's "practical" experience was confined to seven years in a stockbroker's office. *Social Problems of An Industrial Civilization* (Boston: Division of Research, Graduate School of Business Administration, Harvard University; 1945), pp. 38–39. And Drucker comments that ". . . the model of the 'trading economy' . . . was developed by Ricardo who gave to nineteenth century economics its basic concepts and terms, its major tools, and above all its attitude and mood. Ricardo was a stockjobber, and he constructed his model of economic activity in his own image. No other business could have furnished so good a model of a trading economy as the stockjobber, who is the perfect 'economic man in the market.' But none seems as ill-suited to serve as the model for an industrial economy." Peter F. Drucker, *The New Society* (New York: Harper & Bros.; 1950), p. 53.

that, because of the limited validity of the assumptions which underlie it, the concept of perfect competition is an inadequate analytical tool. It is especially deficient for the analysis of distributive markets because they so little resemble those postulated by classical economic theory.

Professor Chamberlin's theory of monopolistic competition is an attempt to construct a theory of value based upon more valid assumptions. He rejects any theory of perfect competition because actual competition is always streaked with elements of monopoly: first, buyers or sellers are often few enough in number so that one has an appreciable control over supply or demand and hence over price; second, products are sufficiently differentiated so that a seller has some control over price.[2] Both elements exist in most distributive markets. The number of buyers and sellers in any market is limited by a variety of factors. While the concept of a market is a rather indefinite one, if a market be defined in terms of an appreciable cross-elasticity of the products offered for sale by various sellers, then most retail markets have a limited number of sellers. The effective horizontal competition confronting a grocer is limited by such factors as location, convenience, habit, and personal ties between retailer and customer. He therefore possesses some monopoly power; he has some control over the prices he charges, for they are not precisely fixed by the market, as they would be under conditions of perfect competition. Similarly, in wholesale markets a buyer or seller often can appreciably influence prices, because of size or fewness of number.

Chamberlin's second monopoly element — product differentiation — is even more obviously a characteristic of distribution.[3] Most consumer goods are trademarked or otherwise dif-

[2] Edward Chamberlin, *The Theory of Monopolistic Competition*, 5th ed. (Cambridge, Mass.: Harvard University Press; 1946), pp. 7–8. His analysis is based upon a definition of monopoly as a "control over the supply, and therefore over the price."

[3] *Ibid.*, pp. 7–10, and chs. IV, V. Much of TNEC Monograph No. 1, *Price*

ferentiated and, at least to some consumers, these differentiations are important. This means that manufacturers command a degree of monopoly power and that many retailers possess a partial monopoly control — for example, a dealer with the only Ford franchise in his town, or a dress shop with an exclusive territorial agency. Furthermore, even dealers selling goods bearing the same trademarks are really selling differentiated products. One grocer sells Wheaties for cash over the counter; another sells Wheaties plus delivery, plus credit, and plus a friendly chat or titillating bit of neighborhood gossip. Two druggists both sell Bayer's Aspirin, but one surrounds it with a gloomy but dignified atmosphere of musty crinoline and old lace, and the other a garish atmosphere of jukeboxes and teen-age chatter.

Thus the whole field is pervaded with elements of monopoly, but this does not mean that the economic theory and analysis of monopoly applies, for these monopoly elements are limited by competitive forces. Most markets contain a mixture of monopolistic and competitive factors, and "the two forces are complexly interwoven, with a variety of design, throughout the price system. . ."[4]

Actual prices no more approximate purely competitive prices than the actual course of a twin-screw steamship approximates the course which would be followed if only one propeller were in operation. Pure competition and pure monopoly are extremes, just as the two courses of the ship, when propelled by either screw separately, are extremes. Actual prices tend toward neither, but towards a middle position determined with reference to the relative strength of the two forces in the individual case.[5]

Again distribution affords an excellent demonstration of

*Behavior and Business Policy*, by Saul Nelson and Walter C. Keim (Washington: GPO; 1940) is a discussion of nonprice competition — which is a reflection of product differentiation — in the field of distribution.

[4] Chamberlin, p. 3.

[5] *Ibid.*, p. 64. His "pure" competition is that which is free of monopoly elements even though it may lack the perfection in other respects which characterizes "perfect" competition. *Ibid.*, p. 6.

Chamberlin's thesis. None of its monopoly elements is absolute. The protection afforded a grocer by location, habit, and friendship is limited. Any relative rise in his prices will cause some of his customers to walk or drive further to other stores. Moreover, differentiations of product are always relative; accordingly, the protection they afford a distributor from competition is limited.[6] A Ford dealer sells to some customers who are convinced of the inherent superiority of Fords, but he also sells to many customers who are shopping for a cheap car and who compare the prices of Fords, Chevrolets, and Plymouths. And even an ingratiating grocer who offers credit and delivery will find that an increase in his prices will cause some of his customers to shift to a surly, cash-and-carry grocer.

Furthermore, these monopoly elements are limited by vertical relationships and by intertype competition. The price charged and the supply offered by our Ford dealer are subject to control by the manufacturer. And chain-store competition limits the freedom of independent grocers and druggists in setting their prices.

Consequently, it is out of a mixture of elements of both competition and monopoly that Chamberlin constructs his theory of monopolistic competition, a theory which seeks to explain, and to provide analytic tools for the study of, most markets. The core of this theory is his examination of how both individual and group equilibrium is achieved in a market containing both competitive and monopoly elements.[7] Given cost and demand curves, a determinate solution is possible. The use of his theoretical tools should enable one to determine the trends operative in a given market and to determine the equilibrium prices, volumes, and product qualities — i.e., those prices, volumes, and products which would result were all variables held constant.

[6] "Differentiation implies gradations, and it is compatible with *perfect* monopoly of one product that control stop short of some more general class of which this product is a part, and within which there is competition." *Ibid.*, p. 65.

[7] Chamberlin, pp. 74–100, 110–116.

But one assumption which does not hold for most distributive markets is crucial to the determination of these firm and market equilibria. This assumption is "that any adjustment of price or of 'product' by a single producer spreads its influence over so many of his competitors that the impact felt by any one is negligible and does not lead him to any readjustment of his own situation"; [8] or, in other words, the assumption that the relevant market contains so many buyers, or sellers, that no one buyer, or seller, feels that his actions will have a significant effect on others and so cause a reaction. But most distributive markets do not fall within this large-group case, as Professor Chamberlin himself acknowledges. Most retailers, wholesalers, and distributing manufacturers function in markets in which they compete significantly with but a few other firms. Hence each seller, or buyer, must allow for the reactions of his close competitors to his own price policies.

Almost any general class of product divides itself into subclasses . . . Similarly, most kinds of retail groups fall into certain quality or price classes, and these into subclasses . . . any individual seller is in *close* competition with no more than a few out of the group, and he may seek to avoid price competition for the very reason given as applying to small numbers — that his cut will force those in *closest* competition with him to follow suit.

Similar considerations may hold, even though the larger grouping does not fall readily into distinct subdivisions. Retail establishments scattered throughout an urban area are an instance of what might be called a "chain" linking of markets . . . the market of each seller is most closely linked . . . to the one nearest him. . . Under such circumstances subgroups cannot be distinguished. Were an area to be marked off arbitrarily, stores at its border would compete with those on the border of the adjoining area more than with those in other portions of the area in which they were placed. Classes of custom are often indistinct, and shade into each other in a similar way. . . The result is then a network of markets so intricately interwoven that, even though it is certainly not one, it defies subdivision which stops short of the individual seller. Where this is the case, considerations

[8] *Ibid.*, p. 83.

relative to small numbers hold even though the "group" be large, since each seller is in close competition with only a few others.[9]

When the effective market in the eyes of the participants is one of these small subgroups, as it usually is in distribution, then the theory of monopolistic competition no longer applies.[10] Prices and volume are determined by the way in which individual firms estimate the reactions of their immediate competitors and may range from those levels which would prevail under conditions of monopolistic collusion to those levels which would prevail under conditions of open price competition. What A does depends on his estimate of what B's reaction will be and upon B's present policy, and vice versa. Such an interdependency of policies is covered by the theory of oligopoly, which admits of no determinate solution in the absence of institutional data about reaction patterns.[11] Such an oligopolistic market is indeterminate, for it has neither the high degree of atomisticity present in both pure competition and the large group case of monopolistic competition, nor its complete absence in the case of monopoly, which make them determinate, given consumer tastes, prices of materials, and technology.

Thus economic theory does not explain a crucial feature of horizontal competition in distribution — the relations among sellers who must take each others reactions into account. Here is a fruitful field for the tools of sociology and psychology, for it is a field governed both by custom — even by mores — and by almost inscrutable personal interrelationships most akin to those established over a poker table.[12] About the more personal relationships among few competitors we know very little.

[9] *Ibid.*, pp. 102–104.

[10] Robert Triffen, *Monopolistic Competition and General Equilibrium Theory* (Cambridge, Mass.: Harvard University Press; 1949), p. 25.

[11] Kenneth E. Boulding, *Economic Analysis* (New York and London: Harper & Bros.; 1941), pp. 607–608.

[12] Little wonder that John von Neumann and Oskar Morgernstern seek to cast light on this phase of economic activity by studying the strategy and nature of similar interrelationships in games such as poker. *Theory of Games and Economic Behavior*, 2nd ed. (Princeton: Princeton University Press; 1947).

But where, in an attempt partly to escape the uncertainties of these interrelationships and partly to avoid price competition, custom has been allowed to govern relations among competitors, at least the *modus vivendi* becomes apparent. The prevalence of retail "price lines" is such a custom. Sellers of women's dresses, for example, avoid some of the uncertainties of oligopolistic competition by confining their prices to certain generally accepted price lines, such as $10.95, $12.95, $14.95, $16.95, $18.95, and $19.95. Uniform and conventional markups or margins also prevail in many trades.

We also have some knowledge of the way in which these competitive interrelationships are resolved when they are subjected to group controls. The literature on trade associations abounds in examples of ways in which distributors have tried to end competitive uncertainties. They have supported "coöperative," or nonprice, competition by education, exhortation, personal contacts and solicitation, group discussion, persuasion, watchfulness, threats of reprisal, dissemination of trade, price, and bid statistics, codes of ethics or "fair practice" rules, price agreements, establishment of resale price maintenance, buying out "chiselers," boycotts, and a host of other devices.[13] While such activities are important, the question of who should exercise academic sovereignty over the relations within trade associations — the economist, sociologist, or political scientist — is moot. Although some political scientists have studied the internal operations of trade associations,[14] I shall not examine this important feature of distribution.

Are the tools of political analysis, then, of any value in studying horizontal competition? The first and most general answer is that politics explain but little here. Politics arise primarily

---

See also John McDonald, *Strategy in Poker, Business and War* (New York: Norton; 1950).

[13] TNEC Monograph No. 18, *Trade Association Survey*, by Charles A. Pearce (Washington: GPO; 1941) pp. 46–63, 71–92.

[14] E.g., Oliver Garceau, *The Political Life of the American Medical Association* (Cambridge, Mass.: Harvard University Press; 1941).

from interrelationships of *groups*, but my definition of horizontal competition limits its existence to one *within* a group. Competition among sellers of a similar type does not provide a basis for grouping, unless some of the sellers can be meaningfully differentiated from the others. Consequently, we do not find one group of independent retail druggists reacting politically against another group of independent druggists. A political struggle between independent grocers and chain grocers — which we do find — arises, of course, from intertype, rather than from horizontal, competition. And a group of independent druggists pressing for political aid in their dealings with manufacturers would be an example of vertical conflict. In both of these last two types of conflict, as we shall see shortly, there is a basis for grouping, and we may expect politics to be of greater importance.

This is not to say that politics is of no importance at all. Politics relates to horizontal competition in two ways. First, insofar as politics subsumes the administration of legislation, it sets the frame within which horizontal competition takes place. It does not determine what competitors will do, but it sets limits on what they may do legally. Regulations governing standards of weights and measures, quality standards, mislabeling, and false advertising limit the alternatives open to competing distributors. And the Federal Trade Commission has tried to define and prevent "unfair methods of competition," thereby limiting the range of legal horizontal competition, as well as of intertype and vertical conflict.[15] This regulation is essentially the enforcement of minimum standards of business conduct, purging the market of dangerous nostrums, and curbing overenthusiastic advertising claims. Both types of regula-

---

[15] These activities are authorized by the Federal Trade Commission Act. The Clayton Act, on the other hand, has little relevance for horizontal competition. Its provisions regarding exclusive dealing arrangements and tying contracts refer to vertical conflicts, and its provisions forbidding price discrimination have been almost exclusively interpreted so as to apply to intertype competition. See Fainsod and Gordon, pp. 493–494.

tion are necessary to maintain effective and socially desirable markets in an economy containing many gullible consumers, but they are seldom of major importance in shaping competitive interrelationships.

The Sherman Act, on the other hand, has substantially limited the range of legal options available to competitors. Its greatest impact, at least until recently, has been on collusive restraints of trade,[16] which have also been attacked by the FTC as "unfair" methods of competition. It has usually been illegal for competing distributors to agree on price or volume.[17] Although it is difficult to detect and prove the existence of such agreements,[18] and although most distributive markets are so small that they usually are neglected by the Antitrust Division and the FTC,[19] the deterrent effects of the fear of possible governmental action cannot be measured by the number of actions brought. The sight of a police patrol car in a rear vision

[16] Fainsod and Gordon, pp. 456, 533–557.

[17] This has not invariably held true. For a while the Appalachian Coals case, *Appalachian Coals, Inc. v. United States*, 288 U. S. 344 (1933), appeared to extend the "rule of reason," thus making the legality of price and output agreements a matter for judicial determination, but the Madison Oil Case, *United States v. Socony-Vacuum Oil Co.*, 310 U. S. 150 (1940), again made *all* agreements on price and volume illegal.

[18] For an account of the difficulties involved in securing legal proof of price and output agreements, see TNEC Monograph No. 16, *Antitrust in Action*, by Walton Hamilton and Irene Till (Washington: GPO; 1940). It is probable, however, that, with the American Tobacco Case (*American Tobacco Co. v. United States*, 66 Sup. Ct. 1125) in 1946, the amount and nature of the evidence required to prove such conspiracy has been rendered easier to obtain. "Parallel action based upon acknowledged self-interest within a defined market structure is sufficient evidence of illegal action." Eugene V. Rostow, *A National Policy for the Oil Industry* (New Haven: Yale University Press; 1948), p. 135. In his discussion of this case (pp. 123–144), however, Rostow fails to emphasize that the Court examines the nature of the competition as well as the market structure. See Edward S. Mason, "Current Status of the Monopoly Problem in the United States," *Harvard Law Review*, vol. 62, no. 8, June 1949, pp. 1265–1285.

[19] A listing of 82 FTC or Antitrust Division actions brought against distributive groups accused of exercising controls over price, production, or terms of sale from 1920 to 1940 is to be found in TNEC Monograph No. 21, *Competition and Monopoly in American Industry*, by Clair Wilcox (Washington: GPO; 1940), pp. 280–285. Significantly enough, less than a quarter of these actions involved horizontal competition, most of them being concerned with intertype competition.

mirror slows many more speeders than are actually arrested. A few cases will illustrate the types of activity declared illegal. In one case the FTC ordered a retail trade association to "cease and desist" from attempts to maintain uniform drug prices by the publication of frequent appeals and exhortations in its trade paper.[20] In two other cases it ended direct price agreements among retailers.[21] In another case it forbade a retail association to "persuade" wholesalers to boycott a price-cutting retailer.[22] And in yet another case an exceptionally ambitious trade association tried to fix and maintain uniform prices at every level of distribution, setting manufacturers', importers', wholesalers', and retailers' prices. This was done by organizing wholesalers', manufacturers', and importers' boycotts of price-cutting retailers, and retailers' and wholesalers' boycotts of manufacturers or importers who failed to set prices agreeable to the organized retailers.[23]

In addition, organized competitors may attempt to use governmental sanctions to enforce codes of group ethics — codes which often control or even eliminate price competition. The administration of both the NRA and the FTC Trade Practice Conferences illustrate ways in which distributors may limit competition through administrative regulation. Such limitations are sometimes important but usually are concerned primarily with intertype competition.

The second aspect of horizontal competition of concern to

[20] *New York Pharmaceutical Conference, Inc.*, 11 F. T. C. 446 (1928).

[21] *National Retail Tea & Coffee Merchants Association, Inc.*, et al., 40 F. T. C. 226 (1945). *Retail Coal Merchants Association*, et al., 34 F. T. C. 543 (1942).

[22] *Milwaukee Jewish Kosher Delicatessen Association*, et al., 34 F. T. C. 1 (1941).

[23] *National Retail Liquor Package Stores Association, Inc.*, et al., 43 F. T. C. 379 (1947). The comprehensiveness of such industry-wide price controls is unusual in this country, but is strongly reminiscent of the controls over British drug distribution from manufacturer to consumer by the Proprietary Articles Trade Association. See Ewald T. Grether, *Resale Price Maintenance in Great Britain* (Berkeley: University of California Press; Publications in Economics, vol. XI, no. 3; 1935), pp. 257–334.

government, hence involving politics, is that which exists when physical force is employed. No government can tolerate force as a method of ordering competitive relationships.[24] Such methods are uncommon but not unheard of. Indeed, to take an extreme case, attempts of New York slaughterhouse groups — unions in this case — to prevent the importation of slaughtered and dressed poultry from Newark and Philadelphia produced ten murders in five years. These unions also tipped over trucks, filled truck engines with emery dust, and fed competitors' chickens with a mixture of sand, gravel, and plaster of Paris, with easily imaginable results.[25] Not even governmental officials were immune from intimidation.[26] These activities are but one example of what the Wickersham Commission found to be a frequent phenomenon — reliance upon racketeers to police or eliminate competition.

The racketeer exacts tribute from his immediate victims, and in some cases the matter ends there. . . But many racketeers do not end here. Greater gains can be realized by the racketeer and less resistance will have to be overcome by him if the racket can be made profitable . . . to its immediate victims. This is frequently feasible, since most fully developed rackets take in an entire line of business in a given locality, so that it may be possible for the racketeer, in

[24] "A distinctive feature of the state's rules which are called law is that they have force behind them. A distinctive feature of the state as an organization is that it organizes and uses force and that it insists on having a monopoly of force." A. D. Lindsay, *The Modern Democratic State*, vol. I (New York & London: Oxford University Press; 1947), p. 197.

[25] Temporary National Economic Committee, *Hearings on Investigation of Concentration of Economic Power*, 75th Cong., 3d Sess. part 7 (Washington: GPO; 1939), pp. 2876–2877. (Hereafter referred to as TNEC Hearings.) The power of the cutters' union was so great that its members were able to earn full pay for a thirty-hour week and so also take on a profitable side line by performing circumcisions afternoons, thereby producing one of the most improbable examples of the joint use of economic resources on record. *Ibid.*, pp. 2869–2870.

[26] "I went up into the market at Sixteenth Street, went into one of these large warehouses and a man asked me immediately if I would like to have a bodyguard. . . I asked him why. He said, 'Well, these big crates have a way of tipping over on people that we don't want around here. . .' " Testimony of Leroy Peterson, former NRA Code Administrator for the New York City poultry industry, *ibid.*, p. 2868.

return for tribute paid him, to bring about monopoly or semimonopoly conditions. When this is done, not only can the toll levied by the racketeer be passed on to the immediate victim's customers, but in some cases it may be possible for the immediate victim himself to benefit financially, provided effective price fixing can be maintained by the racketeer. . .

In this possibility of forcible suppression of competition is to be found one important reason why rackets tend to make especially rapid headway in lines of business having numerous small and actively competing units, where it is difficult to avoid so-called "cutthroat competition" which keeps all but the most efficient units at the starvation point. Open price-fixing agreements are forbidden by law, and probably would not be lived up to if made; but the racket may provide an effectively policed method of bringing about noncompetitive conditions.[27]

This acceptance of a racketeer's force in order to end an almost Hobbesian state of competitive war [28] is similar in nature to competitors' appeals for governmental sanctions to control or eliminate horizontal competition. Often, however, violence is but a small part of a campaign waged on many fronts. The primary significance of the use of physical force, then, is that it reveals the intensity of some competitive wars, the importance which the participants place on their endangered interests, and the loyalties which group standards of business ethics command.

One example suffices to indicate the varieties of fronts on which competitive campaigns can be waged. During the 1930's milk distribution in Detroit and Wayne County was marked by frequent competitive battles in which most distributors, both independents and affiliates or branches of national firms, were hurt by the price-cutting of a few independent dealers. Frequent violence marked this struggle; in less than four years fourteen creameries and milk plants were bombed.[29] But this

[27] U. S. National Commission on Law Observance and Enforcement, *The Cost of Crime*, Report No. 12 (Washington: GPO; 1931), p. 410.

[28] For an example see Sheldon Glueck, *Crime and Justice* (Boston: Little, Brown, and Co.; 1936), pp. 21–23.

[29] TNEC Hearings, part 7, p. 3232.

was only a small part of the struggle; economic methods were widely used. They included price wars in which the majority faction undercut the price-cutters and the issuance of low-price "fighting brands" by national distributors.[30] Economic power was used. A large manufacturer of dairy equipment was persuaded not to deal with a leading price-cutter.[31] Frequent and ingenious recourse to the facilities of government was had. Legislation was sought to set minimum retail prices for milk.[32] Health inspectors suddenly decided that one low-price dealer's warehouse required almost constant inspection, and they on occasion decided that many of the milk cans arriving from farmers merited rejection.[33] At another time this same maverick dealer found that one of his milk licenses had been revoked because of his failure to buy his milk from a certain association of milk producers and that a petition of bankruptcy had been entered against him.[34] In their efforts to secure favorable governmental actions, the milk distributors' association won the support of powerful allies, such as the milk producers and the consumers, by "knocking" the purchasing, labor, and sanitation practices of the price-cutting firm.[35]

Finally, as is also true of labor disputes, it is sometimes difficult to differentiate between physical and nonphysical coercion. Take, for example, the complaint of a price-cutting service station:

. . . a large automobile caravan . . . [of] members of the Stark County Retail Gasoline Dealers Association and others, drove into the Red Head track-side gasoline station . . . blocking the driveways with forty or fifty cars and trucks.

Twenty-, fifty-, and hundred-dollar bills were flashed in payment of one-gallon purchases or less. Numerous services were requested, all with the obvious plan of tying up the station. When these "cus-

[30] *Ibid.*, pp. 2832–2833.
[31] *Ibid.*, p. 2841.
[32] *Ibid.*, p. 2833.
[33] *Ibid.*, pp. 2837–2838.
[34] *Ibid.*, pp. 2837, 2840.
[35] *Ibid.*, pp. 2848, 3231.

tomers" ran out of service requests they still refused to move away from the pumps. Of course, this caused a general blockade of traffic, extending for several blocks, preventing the regular trade from getting gasoline.

This . . . movement was the result of the Red Head being unwilling to enter into price collusion with its competitors to raise and peg gasoline prices. . .[36]

These, then, are the two aspects of horizontal competition in distribution in which politics plays a role. In sharp contrast to the other two types of competition or conflict, here the role is a limited one, primarily because the nature of horizontal competition makes grouping difficult.

### B. INTERTYPE COMPETITION

Horizontal competition is stressed in economic theory as the mechanism which promotes economic progress by inducing lower costs and prices. In fact, however, it has been less conducive to economic betterment and material progress than has a second and more dynamic type of competition which is often overlooked and seldom stressed in the static framework of economic theory. This competition I call, somewhat clumsily, intertype, and define it as the competition between different methods of distribution. It is really a special application to distribution of what Schumpeter calls the process of "Creative Destruction."

Capitalism . . . is by nature a form of economic change and . . . never can be stationary. . . The fundamental impulse that sets and keeps the capitalist engine in motion comes from the new consumers' goods, the new methods of production or transportation, the new markets, the new forms of industrial organization that capitalist enterprise creates. . . The opening up of new markets, foreign or domestic, and the organizational development from the craft shop and factory to such concerns as United States Steel illustrate the same process of industrial mutation . . . that incessantly revolu-

[36] Text of an advertisement in the Canton *Repository*, June 26, 1939, as read in TNEC Hearings, Part 7, pp. 8979–8980

tionizes the economic structure from within, incessantly destroying the old one, incessantly creating a new one. This process of Creative Destruction is the essential fact about capitalism. . .

. . . it is still competition within a rigid pattern of invariant conditions, methods of production and forms of industrial organization in particular, that practically monopolizes attention. But in capitalist reality as distinguished from its textbook picture, it is not that kind of competition which counts but the competition from the new commodity, the new technology, the new source of supply, the new type of organization . . . — competition which commands a decisive cost or quality advantage and which strikes not at the margins of the profits and the outputs of the existing firms but at their foundations and their very lives. This kind of competition is as much more effective than the other as a bombardment is in comparison with forcing a door, and so much more important that it becomes a matter of comparative indifference whether competition in the ordinary sense functions more or less promptly; the powerful lever that in the long run expands output and brings down prices is in any case made of other stuff.[37]

Within distribution the agents of "Creative Destruction" are the chain store, the mail-order house, the department store, and the supermarket.[38] It is the competition of these new media, and not horizontal competition, that has played a creative role, introducing technological advances and reducing costs. And it is also intertype competition that has frequently performed

[37] Schumpeter, pp. 82–85. See also Adelman, who says that what has enabled progress has been "the repeated and massive injection of new products, methods, and sources of supply; these have prevented patterns of market control from freezing into place. Progress . . . is both the cause and the result of competition. . ." M. S. Adelman, "Effective Competition and the Antitrust Laws," *Harvard Law Review*, vol. LXI, no. 8, September 1948, p. 1301.

[38] "In . . . retail trade the competition that matters arises not from additional shops of the same type, but from the department store, the chain store, the mail-order house and the supermarket. . ." Schumpeter, p. 85. In addition, innovations in the form of new products sometimes have a marketing reflection in the form of new distributive media. The marketing channels for automobiles, trucks, tires, and gasoline, for example, resulted from the creation of one general type of product, and to the older distributors each is a new competitor for the consumer's dollar. Such competition, however, while significant in national totals and trends, is usually not acutely enough felt by any one older channel to cause political repercussions.

another duty usually assigned to horizontal competition — protecting the consumer from monopolistic exploitation. The older channels of distribution often failed to do this. The markets in which the wholesaler dealt, both in his purchases and in his sales, were the most competitive, but even these were often dominated by powerful wholesalers. Despite the idyllically competitive picture assumed by those who decry supposed modern trends toward monopoly, in the "good old days" retail markets were often monopolistic. Although the Sherman Act was passed in response to a fear of industrial concentration, "the most effective monopoly of the time was the small retailer — the general store at the crossroads — whose customers were as dependent on this single source of supply as the desert inhabitant on his oasis. Even the small town provided similar local monopolies in many of the specialized fields where the market could support only a single store." [39]

The consumer was left to the mercy of the local merchant, and it was usually a newer form of distribution which released him from his thralldom. The basic causes of his release were great technological changes. The development of transportation and of manufacturing produced urbanization, which broadened the scope of horizontal competition and, more important, created the department store, which challenged the older general and specialized stores by offering a greater range of selection at lower prices. Similarly, advances in transportation and communication permitted the development of the mail-order house, which freed the rural dweller from much of his dependence on the local general store. "The farmer's only friends are God and Sears-Roebuck." [40] The stories of the chain store and of the supermarket are similar. The automobile made the consumer more mobile, enabling him to range further in the pursuit of price reductions. At the same time, new methods of organiz-

[39] Willard L. Thorp, Foreword to Part II, TNEC Monograph No. 17, p. 157. Also see A. A. Berle, Jr., "Investigation of Business Organization and Practices," *Plan Age*, September 1938, p. 186, and Adelman, *Harvard Law Review*, p. 1296.

[40] Adelman, *Harvard Law Review*, p. 1296.

ing distributive functions, involving the integration of retailing with wholesaling, the application of new merchandising principles, and the institution of centralized management, produced retail stores that emphasized high volume, fast turnover, and lower prices. Thus it has usually been intertype competition which has played a creative role, offering broader ranges and producing lasting price reductions.[41]

Such economic changes can be expected to have political reflections. In intertype, in contrast to horizontal, competition, the economic bases of conflict permit and encourage grouping of the sort required for effective political actions. We find similar stores, sharing common methods of operation, objectives, and standards of business ethics. More important, they share a *common enemy*.

Here, for example, are some independent druggists. They have learned, consciously or otherwise, to avoid the uncertainties of horizontal price competition with uniform markups or margins and to base competition on service and other intangibles. Location usually assures each druggist a relatively secure market. Then their comfort and security is shattered by the intrusion of chain drugstores, who rely on price competition, lowering their prices by reducing their markups and by purchasing at lower costs. They advertise their lower prices and may dramatize them by using leaders (goods sold below net purchase cost plus average cost of doing business) and loss leaders (goods sold below net purchase cost). They may cut deeply into the volume of each independent druggist, whatever

---

[41] "Lasting" because they were based on reductions in the cost of retail distribution. For the purposes of my subject it is sufficient to say that these reductions reflect the economies of larger-scale retail operations, taking place on both the selling and purchasing ends. For brief discussions of these advantages, see Maynard and Beckman, pp. 143–144, and G. A. Domisse, *The Regulation of Retail Trade Competition; An Economic Approach* (New York: Colonial Printing Co.; 1939), pp. 19–22. For a more detailed analysis and suggestions of further sources, see Twentieth Century Fund, *passim*. The Fund's conclusions were that the chain store, and presumably the other new methods of distribution, have "brought widespread improvement of methods and lowering of costs and prices throughout retailing." *Ibid.* pp. 344–345.

his locational advantage. Thus are created the economic conditions of conflict.

It is only natural that the independent druggists, probably already joined together for social or business purposes, would tend to group together to combat a common enemy who threatens their economic security. The likelihood of this grouping is enhanced by other forces. The chains may be owned and operated by "outsiders" — New Yorkers, Wall Street, Jews, Easterners, damyankees, or any other group especially obnoxious to the parochialism of the region. And the aggressors employ "unfair" methods of competition and are downright immoral in their business practices. They violate precepts that have been accepted by the independents because of custom and the inspirational literature and speeches of trade associations, not to mention self-interest. These outsiders "chisel," violating customary markups. They may sell below cost, which no ethical dealer ever does, the argument runs. They are deceiving the customer, since the loss "must" be made up by higher margins elsewhere. They may further deceive him by promoting private brands, which clearly are not as reliable as nationally-advertised brands. Finally, grouping is made even more likely by the nature of the distributive process, which almost insures that any aggrieved group will find allies. Should our retail druggists be laggards, it is likely that the wholesalers, themselves suffering from the incursions of the same enemy, will spur them to action.

Thus intertype competition tends to produce bases for political grouping. The firmness of these bases and the strength and cohesion of these groups will be examined later in our study of the "fair-trade" acts, the Robinson-Patman Act, and chain-store taxes. That the economic struggle between channels of distribution has often become a political battle in which organized groups sought political redress of their economic woes has been recognized by many observers,[42] but it has never been analyzed in detail.

[42] "The battle ground is as much political as economic." Thorp, *American*

Two last points remain. First, although our discussion has been centered on the retail level, the impact of new distributive media has been as severely felt at the wholesale level, where wholesalers and functional middlemen have as much cause as do independent retailers to lick their wounds and to combine in order to seek political redress.

The final point is that it would be a mistake to regard distributive trade associations as purely political groups, for they undertake a host of activities.[43] Many of these are economic, such as trade promotion, technical research, statistical and advisory services. And independent merchants may coöperate to achieve some of the efficiencies of the newer channels, e.g., voluntary chains and coöperative warehouses. Many of their other activities, however, are political. Trade association executives, when reporting to governmental agencies, are not likely to overstate their political role, yet, in response to a Department of Commerce survey, "government relations" was the most common activity reported by retail and wholesale trade associations. About four fifths of them had performed this function, and about half of them described it as a major activity.[44] Much, if not most, of this political activity was concerned with intertype competition.

In addition, most associations engage in a third type of activity which is also in part a response to the impact of intertype competition. Over three quarters of them described themselves as engaging in the control of trade practices, and almost one half reported it to be a major activity.[45] This, however, is an

---

Economic Review, p. 84. See, e.g., Fainsod and Gordon, pp. 595–608; TNEC Monograph No. 17, pp. 159–166; John H. Cover, "Changing Distribution Channels, The Initiative Taken by Distributors Themselves," American Economic Review, vol. XXIX, no. 1, part 2, supplement, March 1939, pp. 104–105; Burton A. Zorn and George J. Feldman, Business Under the New Price Laws (New York: Prentice-Hall; 1937), pp. 24–27, 46–57, 275–277.

[43] See TNEC Monograph No. 18, pp. 21–26, 378–383, for a listing, by rank of frequency, of activities undertaken by trade associations.

[44] Ibid., pp. 378–383.

[45] Ibid., pp. 380–381, 383.

activity which does not fall neatly under either politics or economics. It is clearly economic in that its subject matter is business practices. Yet these activities are also political. Many of
the NRA codes and some of the marketing legislation of the
1930's were the application of governmental sanctions to regulations which had been first issued as trade association rules.
Furthermore, these controls are often of questionable legality
and so become the concern of governmental agencies. Finally,
they involve the organization and use of power, and ultimate
decisions about power tend to become political. In short, these
activities lie at the very heart of the mixture of politics and
economics which characterizes our political economy in a
world which unfortunately cannot be as easily compartmental-
ized as can academic disciplines.

Be that as it may, it here suffices to examine the general
content of these controls. Some dealt with competitive relations
among members of the association: i.e., the policing of horizontal competition. But, in an interesting verification of my con-
tention that the nature of intertype competition renders it more
likely to produce group cohesion, most of these controls were
designed to protect the association's members from intertype
competition.[46] Control of trade practices to limit either intertype or horizontal competition is equally likely to cause the
displeasure of the FTC, yet of the twenty-eight actions brought
by this agency against distributive associations from 1915 to
1933, eighteen involved intertype competition, three involved
both types, and only four were concerned exclusively with horizontal competition.[47] A series of FTC cases illustrates the usual

[46] "In the wholesale and retail trades, associations have concerned themselves
largely with the preservation of the traditional channels of distribution." TNEC
Monograph No. 21, p. 257.

[47] *FTC Decisions*, vols. I–XVII, which cover the period from March 16,
1915, to June 18, 1933. The three remaining cases involved distributive groups
which were combining or conspiring to perform other illegal acts. All twenty-
eight were actions in which the FTC issued cease-and-desist orders. I have
chosen this time period because after 1933 the NRA, chain store taxes, the
Robinson-Patman Act, state fair-trade acts, and the Miller-Tydings Amendment were all pinch-hitting for the trade associations in protecting the older

pattern of group attempts to limit or recoup losses of business to newer methods of distribution, usually chains.[48] Facing a common enemy, wholesalers and independent retailers designate themselves and their method of distribution as "legitimate" and mobilize their forces. Their weapon is their economic power, their strength lies in their numbers, and their strategy most frequently is to cut the enemy's supply lines. They pool their economic power to attack his relations with either his suppliers or his customers. When fighting a retailer, they induce manufacturers not to supply him; [49] in the case of a manufacturer selling directly to retailers, they refuse to buy from him.[50] In either case, the weapon is the same — some form of boycott.[51] Distributive groups have often been quite

---

distributive channels. Even during this later period, from June 1, 1935, to October 1, 1939, of forty-eight FTC complaints and Department of Justice actions in the field of distribution, twelve involved intertype competition, and nineteen horizontal competition. TNEC Monograph No. 18, p. 394.

[48] For examples of infinite variations within a single general pattern, see *Wholesale Saddlery Ass'n,* 1 F.T.C. 335 (1919); *McKnight-Keston Grocery Co., et al.,* 3 F.T.C. 87 (1920); *Wholesale Grocers of El Paso,* 3 F.T.C. 109 (1920); *Atlanta Wholesale Grocers,* 4 F.T.C. 466 (1922); *Southern Hardware Jobbers' Ass'n;* 4 F.T.C. 428 (1922); *California Retail Fuel Dealers' Ass'n, et al.,* 9 F.T.C. 405 (1925); *Mid-West Retail Coal Ass'n, et al.,* 10 F.T.C. 135 (1926); *Arkansas Wholesale Grocers' Ass'n, et al.,* 10 F.T.C. 155 (1926); *Wisconsin Wholesale Grocers' Ass'n, et al.,* 10 F.T.C. 409 (1926); *Northwestern Traffic & Service Bureau, Inc., et al.,* 11 F.T.C. 1 (1926); *Atlanta Wholesale Confectioners' Ass'n, et al.,* 11 F.T.C. 102 (1927); *Wholesale Grocers' Ass'n of New Orleans, et al.,* 11 F.T.C. 415 (1927); *So. California Laundry Owners' Ass'n,* 17 F.T.C. 20 (1932); *So. N. Y. Candy Distributors' Ass'n,* 20 F.T.C. 360 (1935); *Wyoming Valley Jobbers' Ass'n,* 21 F.T.C. 244 (1935); *N. Y. State Wholesale Confectioners' Ass'n,* 22 F.T.C. 607 (1936).

[49] E.g., *California Retail Fuel Dealers' Ass'n, et al.,* 9 F.T.C. 405 (1925).

[50] E.g., *Atlanta Wholesale Confectioners' Ass'n, et al.,* 11 F.T.C. 102 (1927).

[51] There are some ingenious exceptions. In one case, local merchants, suffering from mail-order competition, made the discovery, unfortunately since shared with breakfast cereal manufacturers, that small children can be transformed into ruthless and determined allies. These merchants induced the proprietor of the local motion picture house to have "mail-order catalog days," during which children would be admitted upon the payment of a catalog and cash prizes would be offered for the oldest or newest catalogs. The catalogs were then destroyed. *Chamber of Commerce of Missoula, Montana, et al.,* 5 F.T.C. 451 (1923). In three other cases, groups of lumber retailers effectively buried their mail-order competitors in paper work by a campaign in which the dealers and their cousins and their sisters and their aunts all wrote seemingly authentic

frank about this, even though they risk the displeasure of the FTC or the Antitrust Division.[52] Their calls to action are often precise and clarion.

Boycott them? Why certainly. . . . They are criminals without the law, a menace to commerce, society and the peace of the world. Boycott them by all means, fair or foul. . . . Don't buy their goods, use their goods, or miss a chance to advise your friends to give like treatment.[53]

Even when associations are aware of the legal dangers of open boycotts, their methods, however subtle and disguised, are still basically those of the boycott. A retail druggists' association, for example, carefully avoided direct boycotts or threats; instead, in a "Distributor Plan," it gently but meaningfully "advised" manufacturers to sell only through traditional channels.

The Conference believes that direct sale . . . to either retailer or physicians is contrary to the generally accepted theory of merchandise distribution. Moreover, the Conference believes that direct selling to retail dealers . . . at terms equal to or better than those offered to legitimate service jobbers is unfair discriminatory and demoralizing to the trade as a whole.

We are unalterably opposed to granting special terms and discounts to the chain drug and department stores. . . . We believe that with total retail pharmacist outlets of 51,000 we are entitled to that

requests for detailed estimates of kind, quality, and prices of lumber and building materials, and for catalogs, printed matter, and special information. *Botsford Lumber Co., et al.*, 1 F.T.C. 60 (1918, 1919); *St. Lawrence Lumber Co.*, 1 F.T.C. 325 (1919); *J. H. Patterson Co.*, 1 F.T.C. 363 (1919).

[52] "There is nothing unethical in joint endeavor, as such, but when directed to the injury of a competitor or the compulsion of a business concern to do that which it otherwise would, in its own interest, refrain from doing, it comes fully within the settled principles of restraint of trade." M. V. Watkins, *Public Regulation of Competitive Practices — Business Enterprise* (New York: National Industrial Conference Board; 1940), p. 229. Such a boycott may be the subject of action under either the Sherman Act, as a restraint of trade, or the Federal Trade Commission Act, as an unfair trade practice.

[53] An article in *Trade Register*, February, 1922, listing manufacturers who sold direct to retailers under the heading "List of Undesirables and Malefactors of Great Wealth." *Arkansas Wholesale Grocers' Ass'n, et al*, 10 F.T.C. 155 (1926) at 162–163.

degree of protection against the inroads this type of competition has made. . .[54]

The association printed in its official organ a list of those manufacturers and wholesalers who had agreed to its Distributor Plan and had received Conference courtesy cards. Then the point was driven home to even the most obtuse manufacturer or wholesaler when his salesmen were not even accorded interviews by retailers unless the salesmen presented courtesy cards.

Perhaps the retail coal trade best shows how fear of FTC or antitrust action led legally sophisticated associations to change the form of the boycott but not its substance. One naïve association simply blacklisted and boycotted producers who sold to "snowbirds" (purchasers, shippers, or producers of coal which does not flow through traditional channels).[55] A more subtle association helped publish a "Coal Dealers Blue Book," which listed all producers and wholesalers but identified snowbirds with a special code number. The association also published lists of snowbird shipments under the names of the shippers in its trade paper and elsewhere in the same issue advised its numbers not to deal with snowbirds. Finally, it wrote snowbird producers and jobbers saying simply that it was association policy not to deal with snowbirds.[56] Two other associations became quite indirect. They combined and incorporated as a service bureau which ostensibly sold commercial information to retail dealers. When its subscribers reported snowbird shipments, the bureau traced the shipments and then wrote a letter to the shipper concerned. On its face the letter simply asked for information, but it also noted that the bureau had "subscribers" in seven states. In addition, it frequently sent shippers lists of "The Only Equipped Retail Coal Dealers" in towns in which snowbird retailers were located.[57] Obviously this pro-

---

[54] *New York Pharmaceutical Conference, Inc.*, 11 F.T.C. 446 (1928) at 450.
[55] *California Retail Fuel Dealers' Ass'n, et al.*, 9 F.T.C. 405 (1925).
[56] *Mid-West Retail Coal Ass'n, et al.*, 10 F.T.C. 135 (1926).
[57] *Northwestern Traffic & Service Bureau, Inc., et al.*, 11 F.T.C. 1 (1926).

gram was effective only insofar as it was, or threatened, a boycott.

Now this emphasis on the boycott is significant in two respects. First, because of judicial readiness to apply the Sherman Act and the Federal Trade Commission Act to loose agreements and reluctance to apply them to single large firms,[58] the rules of the game governing intertype struggles tend to aid the mass distributors because of their greater individual size. It is legal for a single firm to use its economic power, to refuse to buy or sell in an attempt to induce or deter actions by another firm,[59] in a way that is illegal when done by a group of firms. Thus a large retail chain is granted a weapon denied its competitors when they act together, and only by acting together can they be effective.

The second point of significance about this tendency to use the boycott is that is reveals quite clearly one facet of this conflict. A boycott resembles a strike or a lockout in that it indicates a state of mutual dependency; hence intertype competition tends to raise, and often to run concurrently with, vertical conflict.

### C. VERTICAL CONFLICT

The third general type of conflict is the one which has been most neglected by economic theoreticians.[60] Here we shift our attention from conflicts on the same plane of distribution to

[58] "Explanation of the contrast lies partly in legal tradition, partly in judicial psychology. Long-established doctrines of conspiracy were more clearly applicable to loose agreements than to mergers. . . A more probable basis lies in the differing effects on established property relationships consequent on successful government attack. Dissolution of an important trust, to be effective, may require an economic upheaval in the industry concerned; termination of a contract or dissolution of a trade association is a relatively simple matter." Fainsod & Gordon, p. 535. See also pp. 460–473, 533–552.

[59] The exercise of this power is not unlimited. The terms of the settlement resulting from its use are now limited by the Robinson-Patman Act; and, until the passage of the Miller-Tydings Amendment, the exercise of this power by a manufacturer was limited when its purpose was resale price maintenance.

[60] This neglect was in part recently corrected with J. K. Galbraith's penetrating and well-written *American Capitalism; The Concept of Countervailing*

the vertical struggle between different levels of distribution, between manufacturer and wholesaler, wholesaler and retailer, or manufacturer and retailer.

Once again our starting point in defining the role of politics will be the analysis of the classical economists. For our purposes the significance of their theories is that they contain an unconscious, contradictory, but illuminating dualism.[61] On the one hand, they believed that society was characterized by a natural harmony of interests. Each man pursued his own self-interest, but, through the mechanism of the impersonal market, this was transmuted into the interest of all. Since economic activities were controlled by the impersonal market, men were free of all but material limitations; since under *laissez-faire* the market was virtually identified with society itself, men were subject to only minimal social restraints. Men lived and worked in natural harmony with their fellows. Yet, on the other hand, classical economics was also a theory of artificial harmony, a theory of the way in which the total product was divided among interdependent yet opposing factors of production, a theory of rent, profits, and wages, a theory of power relations. It was, as Marx pointed out, a theory of economic classes. Indeed, it was almost a theory of irreconcilable class conflict, for whatever one class gained was at the expense of the other classes.[62] Such a society, as Bentham saw, could be held together only if an artificial harmony were imposed upon it.

Economic theory has viewed the relationships between levels of distribution primarily as relationships between buyer and

---

*Power* (Boston: Houghton Mifflin; 1952). See pp. 27–75, 115–181. While my approach has been conducted independently (this study was first submitted as a doctoral dissertation and filed in Harvard's Widener Library in 1951), and while I cannot share his apparent belief that the mere existence of countervailing vertical power almost automatically promotes the public interest, there are many obvious similarities in our treatments of vertical power.

[61] For penetrating discussions of this dualism, see George H. Sabine, *History of Political Theory* (New York: Henry Holt; 1937), pp. 657–661, and Lindsay, pp. 136–146.

[62] "The interest of the landlord is always opposed to the interest of every other class in the community." Attributed to Ricardo by Sabine, p. 659.

seller, i.e., in terms of the market mechanism. In a market these vertical relationships are defined by objective, material factors. The pivotal datum is price, which is determined by the interaction of conditions controlling supply and demand. Since no one buyer or seller is large enough, or in a strategic enough position, to influence price, no participant stands in any significant relationship to any other. Power is completely absent. Each participant is free from the power or influence of any other, although narrowly limited by material circumstances. While few distributive markets are as devoid of imperfections as this, most do considerably control and channel economic activities. Material conditions of supply and demand are of great importance, especially over time, in defining vertical relationships. Yet the existence of imperfections, by loosening the grip of material determinism and enabling group efforts to influence economic activities, makes our economy a political one.

The very errors of classical analysis best reveal the role of politics. Briefly, they are three in number. First, the classical economists grossly minimized the necessity for rules of business conduct. Second, although they dealt with the process of combining factors of production, they failed to appreciate the probability of organization and grouping. Organization is usually necessary to produce new products and apply new techniques, and grouping may enable men to increase their economic rewards. Such organization or grouping necessarily creates power. Third, not correlating their two analyses of harmony, the early economists failed to see that conditions of mutual dependency, with concomitant power relations, limit the market mechanism. All three errors open the door to politics.

Economic theory usually fails to recognize the extent to which operations even in a fairly perfect market are enabled and channeled by legal regulation. Common law has long played an important role in supporting and protecting market competition.[63] Effective operation of the market requires regulation of

[63] See Watkins, pp. 19–28.

such matters as weights and measures, enforcement of contracts, minimum health standards, monopoly practices, deceitful diversion of patronage, misappropriation of trade secrets, and malicious interference with business relations or operations.[64] Even when buyers and sellers are small in scope, their relations on a personal basis, and the channels of distribution simple, there is need for rules of the game. When marketing conditions change, this need increases. For example, the rise of large manufacturing concerns and retail firms has produced major inequalities of bargaining power in many vertical relationships, although older rules assumed substantial equality. Increased scale and scope of marketing operations have reduced the role of custom and increased the need for rules. Newer media have often shattered older forms and customs of marketing, further adding to the uncertainties of vertical relations. These and other changes create a need for either the extension of old rules to cover new situations or the formulation and acceptance of new rules. As was also true in horizontal and intertype competition, the effects are political when they involve the administration of existing economic regulation, the group determination of standards of economic behavior, or direct political pressures for the enactment of new regulatory legislation.

Now, the classical explanation of distribution as a series of markets omits consideration of power. The typical distributive market, however, is imperfectly competitive. Each imperfection partially frees distributors from market constraints. To the extent that they are thus freed, they have some bargaining power over those with whom they deal. A manufacturer who has created consumer preference for his brands enjoys a bargaining advantage in his dealings with distributors. A dealer who benefits from consumer habit and from location is strengthened in his relations with wholesalers. Monopolistic and oligopolistic elements in horizontal competition add uncertainties

[64] *Loc cit.*, and Fainsod and Gordon, pp. 444–448.

to vertical relationships and cause their outcome to rest in part on relative bargaining strengths. Furthermore, the increase in size associated with mass distribution has added to the importance of bargaining power. The relations between A & P and a small salmon packer are hardly those contemplated in the concept of a perfectly competitive market.

It is apparent that a principal factor differentiating vertical conflict from horizontal and intertype competition is that it is so directly a power conflict.[65] Power relationships among horizontal competitors occasionally are significant, but this power usually is narrowly limited. Lasting power relations require organization,[66] but organization is difficult, sometimes legally dangerous, and its effects often limited by intertype competition. This latter type of competition is almost devoid of power relationships. With the exception of such haphazard, indirect, and double-edged devices as price wars, there are almost no direct power relationships among different channels. The primary weapon of economic power, the boycott, is directed at a third party and occurs in vertical relationships. In the plane of

[65] At best, power is an elusive concept. Nowhere is the imprecision of the social sciences, and the complexity of their subject matter, better demonstrated than in the difficulty involved in defining such an obvious and basic factor as power. For a bibliography, see Harold D. Lasswell and Abraham Kaplan, *Power and Society* (New Haven: Yale University Press; 1950), pp. 285–286. It is not my purpose, nor, alas, is it within my competence, to produce a full definition and classification of power. For the purposes of this study, however, the broad category of power, or *social* power, to differentiate it from control over external nature, always involves control of other men. This means that power is always a two-sided human relationship in which both consent and constraint are important, although variable elements. See Carl J. Friedrich, *Constitutional Government and Democracy*, rev. ed. (Boston: Ginn & Co.; 1946), pp. 16–19; Franz L. Neumann, "Approaches to the Study of Political Power," *Political Science Quarterly*, vol. LXV, no. 2, June 1950, pp. 161–180. Although all kinds of power are interrelated, I choose to regard economic power as that relationship in which the consent is based on economic motivations and/or the constraint is based on economic sanctions. Political power is defined by its relation to government and is manifested when consent is to or by governmental agencies, and/or constraint is exercised by or on governmental bodies.

[66] "Without common objectives there can be no power. Enduring common objectives engender organization. All more stable power is therefore based on organization and the control of organization." Friedrich, p. 17.

vertical conflict, however, power relationships are direct, obvious, and important to the extent that the market is imperfect.

Vertical power becomes more apparent when we adopt the second approach of the classical economists. It will be remembered that, in addition to their market analysis, they also regarded production as a *process*. Distribution is a process in much the same sense. Just as production is the transformation of raw materials, labor, and capital into finished goods, so distribution is the transformation of finished goods in the producer's hands into final products in the consumer's hands. Just as mutual dependency characterizes relations among the factors of production, so does it characterize relations among the stages of distribution. The degree of dependency has increased greatly since the late nineteenth century. The very essence of the newer marketing media is their integration of a series of marketing functions which formerly were executed by separate firms. This integration, as we have seen, has been executed from both ends of the distributive chain. Both manufacturers and retailers have acted on the premise that distribution is a process, and have organized it as such, much in the manner that different phases of the manufacturing process are more and more conducted under integrated control and organization. They apply principles of "mass distribution" much as manufacturers apply those of mass production. The older system of distribution, on the other hand, resembles the nonintegrated, Balkanized women's garment industry in which gray goods are often made by one firm, converted by another, cut by another, and assembled and sewn by yet another. In the distribution of some products, such as shoes and tires, manufacturers now perform even the retailing function. Some retail food chains perform all marketing functions and even do some manufacturing and processing.

The reasons for this integration are diverse. There are the efficiencies of mass distribution, an obvious factor in the growth of mail-order houses, department stores, chain stores, and supermarkets, all of which have introduced economies of scale and of uniform and centralized management. And integration from the manufacturing end often results from the development of new products. The last seventy-five years have seen the introduction of many mechanical devices which require considerable capital for their manufacture, intensive efforts for their sale, demonstration and instruction in their uses, and special services to maintain them. Their distribution is apt to be a unified, integrated flow; otherwise they will be difficult to sell.[67] Indeed, any new product may create for its producer the problem of finding marketing channels. If none are available, he has to encourage their creation or provide his own. In either case, they are likely to be integrated and under his control. Finally, integration is a general policy of many large corporations who try to free themselves from the limitations and uncertainties of their environment. Here integrated marketing is but a part of a broad program of vertical and horizontal integration and control. Most major oil refiners, for example, develop and protect their retail markets by integrating and controlling marketing, just as they protect and develop their sources of supply by integrating and controlling production.

Marketing functions also have often been radically shifted. The crucial function of selection, the choosing of one product from many similar or even identical products, was once performed by the independent wholesaler who decided which line or brand of commodities to carry.[68] Now, with the prevalence of nationally advertised brands, the consumer does much more of the selecting. This increases the dependence of distributors on manufacturers, for they desire to carry popular brands. Large retailers also do much selecting, for many consumers accept the retailer's private brand, buying All-State tires or

[67] Hence the prevalence of exclusive dealing arrangements and other signs of an integrated distributive flow in such products as automobiles, farm equipment, sewing machines, and vacuum cleaners. For a fuller discussion, see Watkins, pp. 210–211.

[68] For a discussion of the importance of this function, see Domisse, pp. 15–16.

Ann Page jam without knowing, or caring, who manufactures them. This makes the manufacturer and middleman, if any, dependent on the retailer.

These conditions of dependency and control, revealed by a process analysis, vitiate much of the market analysis of distribution's vertical conflicts. Process analysis reveals power relationships, but power is incompatible with the classical market. There never was absolute equality of bargaining power on opposite sides of distributive markets, but such dominance as did exist was that of the wholesaler. This relative dominance at the mid-point of the distributive flow sharply broke it into two phases, preventing contact between producer and retailer. This structure has now been shattered in many trades. Great increases in the size of either manufacturers or retailers have changed much of distribution from a flow through a series of largely autonomous markets to a single movement dominated by either manufacturer or retailer. Dominance by a manufacturer often reflects the shifting of the selective function to the consumer, for many manufacturers compete more for the patronage of the consumer than for that of the wholesaler and wish to control wholesale and retail levels, since their competitive success is determined at the retail level. A filling station proprietor limited to the sale of Texaco products is largely but an agent of the Texas Company, and his relations with his jobber are not those of a free market. In other channels a large retailer may be dominant and exercise the selective function. His volume may be so great, and his consumer acceptance so strong, that he orders goods to be made under his own specifications and his own label. Manufacturer and middlemen may become almost agents of the retailer.

Furthermore, the impact of intertype competition on the older marketing channels heightens their mutual interdependence. The retailer looks to his wholesalers for aid, and the wholesaler becomes increasingly dependent on his retailers and suppliers. A small manufacturer may be forced to choose sides, to decide either to ally himself with the traditional channels, or to sell only to large retailers.

Finally, power has multiplied in many of the newer marketing channels. Power is a two-sided relationship, and organization tends to breed counterorganization. Dominance by one end of the distributive chain often promotes grouping at the other end, for those subordinated to economic power will naturally tend to organize in attempts to create and use economic or political power.[69] The analogy of the distributive to the manufacturing process applies. What the classical economists overlooked in their analysis of production was the almost inevitable creation of class or group consciousness, although one by no means as simple and monolithic as that described by Marx. Owners or managers, and workers, perceived the similarities of their interests and tried to organize. This organization bred enough power to alter radically the market mechanism. The organization of one productive factor encouraged the organization of another. Thus the organization of capital made the organization of labor more necessary and its advantages, to labor, more apparent. A similar development has occurred within distribution. Reeling from the impact of newer marketing media and from the economic power of large corporate concerns, smaller distributors have become conscious of their group interests. They, in turn, have tried to organize and to employ economic and/or political power. This group consciousness sometimes, as in the case of retail druggists, becomes quite intense.[70]

[69] ". . . power on one side of a market creates both the need for, and the prospect of reward to, the exercise of countervailing power from the other side." Galbraith, p. 120.

[70] "The prime issue in the conflict within the channels of distribution is where dominance will rest. In the horse-and-buggy period . . . wholesalers tended to be the dominating factors. . . Toward the end of the last century dominance often began to shift towards manufacturers. . . More recently, the large-scale retail types, the department, mail order, and chain systems, and organized groups of individual merchants have asserted themselves. . . It is commonly overlooked that these major groupings typically are highly class conscious in their attitudes and objectives. In other words, there is an organ-

In conclusion, power has come to rival economic factors as the governing element in the vertical relationships of distribution. Manifestations of this power will be examined in later chapters.

---

ized, not a haphazard, struggle going on in the channels of distribution." Ewald T. Grether, "Changing Distribution Channels; The Specific Effects of the Robinson-Patman Act," *American Economic Review*, vol. XXIX, no. 1, part 2, supplement, March 1939, p. 105.

## The Distribution of Groceries

Since it is impossible to describe all trades in detail, if we are to analyze and describe the economic bases of political actions in the light of the analytic approaches developed in the preceding chapter, I must necessarily select a few marketing channels which will best illustrate the specific institutional content of the whole field. I have chosen the grocery, drug, and automobile trades as the best illustrations of the conflicts creating demands for political action and of the power structures which condition the success of these demands. Horizontal competition occurs in all three trades. Intertype competition has been important in the first two; the last is itself a new method of distribution, but there is no intertype competition. As for vertical power structures, in the automobile trade the manufacturer is dominant; in the other two trades the older marketing channels, with their more balanced power structure, still predominate but are modified by the power of large retailers and of groups of retailers. Finally, the grocery trade was the major concern of the framers of the Robinson-Patman Act and of those who advocated chain-store taxes, while the drug trade was the principal concern of fair-trade legislation. The marketing of automobiles has occasioned little special legislation.

Groceries are the largest trade. The nation's half million retail grocery or combination grocery and meat stores comprise 28 per cent of all retail units and make about 24 per cent of total retail sales. There are about 17,000 grocery wholesalers, 7 per cent of all firms engaged in wholesale activities, who make about 6 per cent of all wholesale transactions.[1]

Horizontal competition has had few political consequences and has provided little basis for grouping. There has been some uncertainty in competitive interrelationships, which has invited the establishment of group codes or agreements, but for many reasons such agreements were difficult if not impossible. The great number of retail firms and ease of entry make difficult the achievement and maintenance of price agreements. An annual birth rate of about 10 per cent means that a retail group has constantly to recruit new members. And a high mortality rate means that many marginal grocers are constantly tempted to chisel on prices.[2] Finally, that such a high proportion of grocers have failed in other occupations, are waiting to reënter other fields, or are only part-time grocers increases the difficulty of establishing group discipline. It is not surprising that there is little evidence of group control over competitive practices. Many of the same generalizations hold for wholesalers. Horizontal competition provided a poor basis for grouping, and there is little concrete evidence of explicit price agreements. The prevalence of uniform margins and discounts, however, strongly suggests common understandings or tacit agreements. Evidence of agreements among food manufacturers and processors is more apparent, but is outside the scope of this study.[3]

Political repercussions of intertype competition, on the other hand, have been obvious and important. Their extent reflects the economic impact of the newer methods of distribution. These newer media involve large-scale organization centered

[1] *1948 Census of Business,* vol. I, p. 1.02; vol. V, p. 0.02.
[2] Cf. Domisse, p. 42.
[3] E.g., the apparent agreement among the major meat packers allocating quotas of production. Arthur R. Burns, *Decline of Competition* (New York and London: McGraw-Hill; 1936), pp. 156–165.

at either end of the distributive chain, but by far the greater impact has resulted from the growth of retail chains. With some important exceptions, most large manufacturers and processors appeared contemporaneously with, or after, the establishment of large chains.[4] Consequently, most large producers have used existing channels of distribution. Some large firms do much of their own marketing, but their total impact has been much less than that of the chains.[5] Greater organizational development has marked the retail level because it offered the most fertile soil for technological improvements.

Innovations made in food distribution are even more important than those made in food processing. . . The most likely place to effect significant savings in food distribution is in . . . retailing. The retail margin is usually the largest single element in the cost of food distribution, and often it is larger than all other transportation and marketing costs combined. Because their operations have been primarily in this phase of distribution, the innovations made by the grocery chains probably have been more important from the standpoint of reducing food costs than those made by any other types of large-scale concerns.[6]

These improvements in efficiency, however, were not profit-

[4] "The food industries are among the last fields of enterprise to which corporate mass methods have been applied. There are several reasons for this, chief of which is the fact that the technological processes necessary for the preparation of food products have been until recently comparatively simple. With a few exceptions these processes did not lend themselves to, or at least did not particularly invite, the application of large-scale methods." TNEC Monograph No. 35, *Large Scale Organization in the Food Industries*, by A. C. Hoffman (Washington: GPO; 1940), p. 3.

[5] Large manufacturers and processors perform many distributive functions in the fields of meat packing, flour milling and baking, and fluid milk. In the first field, some of the economies of scale were those involving distribution. The combination of this with other motives led to the creation of manufacturer-operated distributive systems. In recent years only 6 to 8 per cent of sales were made to independent wholesalers. TNEC Monograph No. 35, ch. III. In fluid milk most of the economies of scale are those of distribution and have led to the creation of an almost entirely new — manufacturer-controlled — channel of distribution. See *ibid.*, ch. IV, and Irene Till, "Milk — the Politics of an Industry," in Walton Hamilton, *et al.*, *Price and Price Policies* (New York and London: McGraw-Hill; 1938), pp. 431–524.

[6] TNEC Monograph No. 35, pp. 156–157.

able until the consumer became mobile. While chain stores first appeared after the advent of large cities, they did not expand greatly until after the development of urban transportation. They then rapidly multiplied with the introduction of the automobile. Although the first chain, the Great Atlantic & Pacific Tea Company, opened its second store in 1859,[7] the introduction of new grocery chains and the growth of individual chains was very slow before 1900. Of the 315 grocery chains operating in 1928 and reporting historical data to the FTC or traced by it, only 17 were in operation by 1900. By 1914 the number had increased to 85 and by 1928, after a mushroomlike growth, to the full 315, despite absorption of 111 chains through merger and consolidation.[8] In 1929 there were 807 grocery chains with 4 or more units, and the average chain had 67 stores. These grocery chains were among the leading carriers of the general chain revolution in distribution, for their 54,000 stores were one third of all chain units, and they made 34.0 per cent of all grocery sales, while all chains accounted for only 20.3 per cent of all retail sales.[9]

Mobility enabled the consumer to reach the chain grocery store, but it took lower prices to bring him into the store. This was their major appeal,[10] and was stressed in advertising. Lower prices were often dramatized with leaders and sometimes with

[7] Maynard and Beckman, p. 169.

[8] FTC, *Chain Stores; Growth and Development of Chain Stores*, 72d Cong., 1st Sess., S. Doc. No. 100 (Washington: GPO; 1932), pp. 55, 80–81.

[9] Chains were even more successful among variety stores and automotive parts and accessories stores, making 90.1 per cent of sales in the former category. *1939 Census of Business*, vol. I, part 1, pp. 9, 63–64, 66–70, 179–182; and *1935 Census of Business*, vol. I, part 2, section 2, pp. 13–14.

[10] In one survey by far the most important reason given by consumers for patronizing chains was lower price. This was given in 28.1 per cent of the 4435 reasons given by 1496 persons. The second most important, wider selection of goods, was listed in 18.8 per cent of the reasons given. Theodore N. Beckman and Herman C. Nolen, *The Chain Store Problem* (New York and London: McGraw-Hill; 1938), p. 169. Also see FTC, *Chain Stores; Chain Store Price Policies*, 73d Cong., 2d Sess., S. Doc. No. 85 (Washington: GPO; 1934), *passim*, and especially pp. 89–104. The Commission stresses "the extent to which chains have made prices and price competition a central feature of their merchandising policies." *Ibid.*, p. xv. The Commission presents many statements

loss leaders.[11] The latter were also used as a retaliatory weapon in competitive battles.[12] The loss leader has been a symbol of the intertype price competition of the chains. Independents attack it as unethical and often, ignorant of chains' lower purchase costs, exaggerate its prevalence. The chains' price appeal, however, is more broadly based. Virtually all price comparisons have shown that chain stores do sell for less.[13] The FTC concluded that "on the average, chain stores can and do sell at prices which are somewhat lower than the prices charged by independent retailers or by cooperative retailers."[14] Its comparison of chain and independent grocery prices indicated that independent prices were about 6 to 8 per cent higher,[15] and this conclusion has been buttressed by many other surveys.[16]

Despite the independents' frequent claim that the lower selling prices of the chains are due primarily to the (unfairly)

---

of policy emphasizing price competition, e.g., the boast of a confectionery chain: "Prices are set so low at the start that we are not bothered by reducing prices to meet competition. . . We have no competition when it comes to price and quality; we meet it and beat it, and this applies to all kinds of competitors and all lines of merchandise. . ." *Ibid.*, p. 92. Usually, however, chains claim only to meet competition, but, since often they try to match any cut by any competitor, this means prices lower than those of most independent merchants.

[11] About 17 per cent of all grocery chains reporting such data admitted the use of loss leaders in 1928. FTC, *Chain Stores: Chain-Store Leaders and Loss Leaders,* 72d Cong., 1st Sess., S. Doc. No. 51 (Washington: GPO; 1932), p. 21. The losses averaged about 10 per cent. *Ibid.*, p. 49. In general, the smaller chains admitted to more frequent use of this device. *Loc. cit.*

[12] "When our store is given a hard run by competition, rather than simply cutting prices to meet competition, we prefer to shoot specials [loss leaders] into the town until the competitor gives up his warfare." Statement of a chain policy quoted in FTC, *Chain Store Price Policies,* p. 92.

[13] For a recent listing and description of price comparisons, see S. N. Silbert, "Are the Chains Really Cheaper?" unpublished thesis (A.B.), Harvard University, 1949. For a more readily accessible listing and criticism, see Beckman and Nolen, pp. 77–89.

[14] FTC, *Chain Stores: Final Report on the Chain-Store Investigation,* 74th Cong., 1st Sess., S. Doc. No. 4 (Washington: GPO; 1935), pp. 28–29.

[15] Its comparison of grocery prices in four cities showed that aggregated independent prices were 5.7 to 7.3 per cent higher. When prices were weighted by volume and the results averaged geometrically, independent prices were 6.4 to 10.5 per cent higher. *Ibid.*, pp. 29–30.

[16] Silbert, *passim.*

lower prices at which they buy their goods, the FTC's data on the grocery trade do not support this claim.[17] The Commission's comparison of purchasing and selling prices of chains and independents on a sample of identical goods showed that only about one fifth of the difference in retail prices was attributable to advantages in buying prices.[18] The other four fifths resulted from lower costs of chain retail and wholesale operations, from retail and wholesale operating economies inherent in high-volume, limited-service operations, and in the application of uniform principles of management and operation.[19]

If chain selling prices are lower because of unfair use of bargaining power, as is alleged by independents, then the measure of this use of power lies in the lower chain buying prices. There are two types of discount and allowance — invoice and special. The first includes ordinary trade, quantity, and cash discounts, together with some allowance of "free goods." In

[17] The FTC apparently did not appreciate the significance of its own data, for it erroneously concluded "that lower buying prices than are available to independents are a most substantial, if not the chief, factor in these lower [chain] selling prices." *Final Report*, p. 53. This conclusion is clearly in error.

[18] These buying prices reflect reductions resulting from the application of both regular quantity and/or functional discounts (those appearing on the invoice) and all special discounts and allowances. Independent prices are those paid by wholesalers when manufacturers sell to wholesalers, and those paid by retailers when manufacturers sell to retailers. In the same four cities in which the FTC had compared chain and independent selling prices, it found that from 6.2 to 45.3 per cent of the difference in selling prices was attributable to lower buying prices. When weighted by chain volumes, the proportion ranged from 3.0 to 20.5 per cent; when weighted by independent volumes, from 4.8 to 35.8 per cent. *Ibid.*, pp. 54–55.

[19] "The main elements of successful management in retailing are skill in buying, advertising, and merchandising, together with careful attention to all cost factors. One of the characteristics of mass retailing is that all these elements are centrally planned and carried out in the retail unit on a more or less standardized basis. . . Many independent retailers can and do match the chains in the skill with which they conduct their store enterprises. But . . . most of them do not. The business of the independent retailer is not large, and his earnings are necessarily small. He is nevertheless confronted with most of the problems of stock selection, merchandising, and expense control confronting the corporate chains. It is inconceivable that any very large percentage of the 300,000 independent grocers should have all of the requisite qualities possessed by the chain experts for meeting these problems." TNEC Monograph No. 35, pp. 65–66.

its investigation the FTC found that these discounts "were usually open to all buyers . . . and . . . that the invoice prices on identical merchandise showed a considerable tendency to be the same to all the wholesalers and chains in the same city. . ." [20] Chains simply took advantage of terms of sale open to all buyers. Performing wholesaling functions, they naturally received wholesale discounts,[21] and they took quantity discounts on their large orders.[22] Accordingly, if invoice terms of sale reflect manufacturers' estimates of their savings from large sales or from being relieved of some marketing functions — and this is the justification of quantity and trade, or functional, discounts — then the lower invoice prices paid by chains reflected the savings in manufacturing and distribution costs they enabled and the marketing functions they performed or made unnecessary.[23] In general, manufacturers' cost savings apparently at least matched the invoice discounts granted large buyers.[24]

[20] FTC, *Final Report*, p. 57.

[21] Grocery chains usually bypass wholesalers. Even in 1928 about 90 per cent of their purchases were made directly from manufacturers, growers, or agents. FTC, *Chain Stores; Sources of Chain-Store Merchandise*, 72d Cong., 1st Sess., S. Doc. No. 30 (Washington: GPO; 1932), p. 15. Bypassing the wholesaler does not do away with all of his functions, but it usually does enable their rationalization, simplification, and abbreviation. One authority describes the costs of the bargaining transactions and ownership transfers of the wholesaler-retailer system as "nothing short of stupendous." TNEC Monograph No. 35, p. 67. Selling expenses usually amount to about a fourth of a wholesaler's operating costs. Beckman and Nolen, p. 49.

[22] A large buyer may use his bargaining power to win large quantity discounts, but he usually seeks special discounts rather than invoice discounts, which grant the same concession to any other large buyer.

[23] This probably attributes to manufacturers' discount policies, and to their cost accounting, a higher degree of rationality and precision than they actually possessed, at least in the days before the Robinson-Patman Act. Yet, experience under this Act appears to indicate, insofar as these discounts did fail to reflect actual cost differences, the error probably favored the independents. With the necessity for extension and refinement of cost accounting under this Act, many manufacturers have found their smaller sales are unprofitable. Edwin S. George, "Business and the Robinson-Patman Act: the First Year," in Benjamin Werne, ed., *Business and the Robinson-Patman Law: A Symposium* (New York: Oxford University Press; 1938), p. 62.

[24] It was the opinion of the economist in charge of the FTC chain-store

Consequently, if we are to find abuse of bargaining power, it will be reflected in special discounts and allowances. But these discounts are granted to wholesalers as well as to chains. In 1929 grocery chains received special discounts and allowances amounting to 1.89 per cent of their purchases. Wholesalers received similar concessions of 0.87 per cent, and retailer coöperatives 1.00 per cent. In 1930 the comparable figures were 2.02 per cent, 0.91 per cent, and 1.04 per cent.[25] This difference of 1 per cent is the maximum measurement of chain bargaining power.

Not all of even this small fraction can be attributed solely to power, for, while it may well be that power enables distributors to win special concessions,[26] there is also much economic justification for them. For example, the most frequent kind of concession, promotional allowances, is often made in return for specified services, such as special sales effort or featuring products in newspaper advertising and window and counter displays. A chain, because of its central control of many retail units, can usually perform these services better than its independent competitors can.[27] But there sometimes is no *quo* rendered for the *quid*. The FTC found that frequently manufacturers did not check on whether advertising allowances had actually been devoted to that use.[28] It seems clear that, while

---

investigation that "the allowances made by sellers for quantity have relatively seldom represented the full . . . savings in selling and delivery costs that were involved. . ." W. H. S. Stevens, "An Interpretation of the Robinson-Patman Act," *Journal of Marketing*, vol. II, no. 1, July 1937, p. 44. Also see my preceding footnote.

[25] FTC, *Chain Stores; Special Discounts and Allowances to Chain and Independent Distributors: Grocery Trade*, 73d Cong., 2d. Sess., S. Doc. No. 89 (Washington: GPO; 1934), p. 3. These percentages were computed from reports of manufacturers and processors.

[26] "Many manufacturers . . . explained that such [promotional] allowances were granted only when purchasers were sufficiently powerful to demand them." *Ibid.*, p. 61.

[27] "Other manufacturers informed the Commission that this type of allowance is restricted to chains on the theory that similar cooperation from jobbers would not be effective." *Loc. cit.*

[28] *Loc. cit.* E.g., in 1934 A & P received a special advertising allowance of

many, and probably most, allowances were justified by retailer services, many other allowances were only disguised price concessions and tributes to retailer power.[29] Similarly, other types of special concession,[30] usually economically justified, were sometimes simply indirect discounts.[31]

Thus, economic power plays a part in these vertical relationships, since, whatever their economic justification, these special discounts would not usually be granted in its absence. Its significance, however, should not be exaggerated. The differential

---

5 per cent on its purchases of about eight million dollars from General Foods. This amounted to a sizable sum — about $400,000 — yet A & P kept no records and made no reports of the extent to which it actually advertised General Foods' products. House Committee on Investigation of American Retail Federation, *Hearings on Investigation of the Lobbying Activities of the American Retail Federation*, vol. I, 74th Cong., 1st Sess. (Washington: GPO; 1935), pp. 434–435. (Hereafter cited as Patman Committee Hearings.)

[29] E.g., in 1935 Standard Brands bought "coöperation service" from five firms, paying for $299,892 worth of this elusive service from A & P, but only $44,468 worth from Kroger, $11,600 from American Stores, $9,135 from National Tea, and $3,400 from First National. *Ibid.*, vol. IV, pp. 7–34. Although Standard Brands claimed that these were payments for services rendered, the great differences in payments strongly suggest that these were really bargaining concessions.

[30] After promotional allowances, the FTC found the most frequent special allowances to be in the form of special trade discounts, brokerage allowances, and special prices. *Final Report,* p. 60.

[31] There is some disagreement on whether these concessions were "usually" justified. E.g., see Joel B. Dirlam and Alfred E. Kahn, "Antitrust Law and the Big Buyer: Another Look at the A & P Case," *Journal of Political Economy*, vol. LX, no. 2, April 1952; M. A. Adelman, "Dirlam and Kahn on the A & P Case," *ibid.*, vol. LXI, no. 5, October 1953, and Dirlam and Kahn, "A Reply," same issue, and the literature cited in these articles. Adelman maintains that A & P's concessions usually reflected cost savings or services performed, but another student of the A & P case concludes that "many" of these concessions "could not be shown to reflect actual savings." Carl H. Fulda, *Food Distribution in the United States; the Struggle between Independents and Chains* (Association of American Law Schools; 1951, mimeographed), pp. 136–137. Much of this debate simply reflects inadequate cost accounting which makes it impossible to prove conclusively whether specific concessions were economically justified. While some concessions do have dubious economic justification, in general it appears to me that these concessions did reflect actual savings. E.g., in a field in which A & P was notorious for hard and vigorous bargaining, the FTC found that in 1936 sellers of fruits and vegetables received a somewhat larger return on sales to chains than on sales to independents. *Report on Distribution Methods and Costs* (Washington: GPO; 1944), Part I, pp. 140–142.

benefits chain power commands average only 1 per cent of their total purchases. Yet, so low is the average rate of net profit on sales — 2.63 per cent in 1929 [32] — that they are a substantial proportion of total net profits. In 1929 one hundred and eighty-four chains had net profits of $66,000,000 and bought slightly more than two billion dollars' worth of goods.[33] If their bargaining power gained them differential special concessions of 1 per cent on their purchases, then almost one third of their profits was enabled by economic power. All special concessions, including those also granted wholesalers, would account for over one half of total chain profits.[34]

These statistics, however, are so affected by one firm that they are somewhat misleading. Over one half of the special concessions reported were granted to A & P. In 1929 all other grocery chains received special concessions of only 1.35 per cent. Thus, despite their greater size and ability to perform special services, they enjoyed but a relatively small advantage over their independent competitors, who, it will be remembered, received concessions of 0.87 per cent. The giant A & P, however, won concessions of 2.37 per cent, or almost three times as great a percentage as that granted to wholesalers and almost twice that won by its chain competitors.[35] This was in large part the result of its vigorous and sharp buying tactics and not simply an automatic reflection of its great size and bargaining power, for there was little correlation between a chain's size

[32] Computed from returns of 184 grocery chains with total sales of two-and-one-half billion dollars, or about 90 per cent of total grocery chain sales. FTC, *Chain Stores: Sales, Costs, and Profits of Retail Chains*, 73d Cong., 1st Sess., S. Doc. No. 40 (Washington: GPO; 1933), pp. 61, 67, 70, 77.

[33] *Ibid.*, pp. 70, 72, 77.

[34] In 1934 A & P received special discounts and allowances of about $6,105,000 and brokerage fees of about $2,000,000. In the same year it paid a little more than $14,000,000 in dividends on its common stock. Patman Committee Hearings, vol. I, pp. 461, 485.

[35] FTC, *Special Discounts and Allowances: Grocery Trade*, pp. 40–43. In 1930 the advantage enjoyed by the A & P was almost as large. Although all chains received special concessions and allowances averaging 2.02 per cent, all chains other than A & P received only 1.59 per cent, while A & P secured 2.42 per cent.

and its success in winning special concessions. For example, the second largest chain, Kroger, with over a third as many units as the A & P, received concessions of only 1.17 per cent, or less than the average received by smaller chains.[36]

Thus, on the basis of evidence regarding identical commodities, the gains economic power can command are narrowly limited. But there are other ways in which bargaining power can be used. Chain buyers undoubtedly also use their power to seek more favorable prices on private brands.[37] Since the pricing of these special orders is not as much limited by traditional discount policies and by manufacturers' fears of offending other distributors, bargaining and bargaining power probably have greater influence on the terms of trade.

Having indicated the scope of economic power, let us see how it is used. The bargaining process can involve intangible personal relationships and usually is private, but we do have the results of the FTC's investigation.

There were interviews with 129 manufacturers in the grocery group, 76 of which admitted that preferential treatment in some form was given. Thirty-three . . . stated positively that threats and coercion had been used by chain-store companies to obtain preferential treatment. . .

In 23 of the 33 instances, threats and coercive measures were employed and resulted in securing the concession demanded. Of the 10 cases where the manufacturers refused to accede to chain buyers, 5 were demands for brokerage and 5 for concessions of various other kinds. A number of manufacturers reported that due to their unwill-

[36] And C. F. Smith Co., with 618 retail units and reported purchases of $3,825,000, received concessions of 0.61 per cent, while MacMarr Stores, Inc., with 1,394 units and purchases of $4,314,000 gained 1.62 per cent. James Butler Grocery Co., with 1,066 units and purchases of $5,571,000, received 0.67 per cent, while National Grocery Co., with 782 units and purchases of $5,286,000, was granted 2.09 per cent. *Ibid.*, pp. 40–41.

[37] A private brand is differentiated from manufacturers' brands, which are often nationally advertised and available to all channels of distribution. A chain-store private brand may be defined "as a commodity sold by the chain only through its own stores under its own distinctive mark of identification." FTC, *Chain Stores: Chain-Store Private Brands*, 72d Cong., 2d Sess., S. Doc. No. 142 (Washington: GPO; 1933), p. 2.

ingness to accede to such demands, they had not only lost some regular customers, but had been unable to sell others making the demands. . . . One or two manufacturers, stating that coercion had been employed to force the cutting of prices, said that if the customer has a large order and demands a cut price, the company often is required to meet the demand or lose the business to its competitors.[38]

Thus frequent use of power did characterize vertical relationships within this new channel of distribution. Yet this power needs to be examined further before it can be condemned. Power exists in many nongovernmental institutions, such as the family and the church. Ultimately, however, the decision of what types of power will be tolerated, and within what limitations, is usually a political decision in that the arena of final decision is political. This decision is based upon the purposes or consequences of the exercise of the power in question.

The power of chains is a function of size and is expressed in bargaining as a threat, explicit or implied, not to buy. Its results are not as simply expressed. Some consequences are clearly beneficial. The FTC reported that one chain, probably the A & P, "is usually successful in buying under the list price because of its keen knowledge of the markets . . . it will frequently play the market of one State against the market of another . . ." [39] Despite the Commission's implied criticism, this activity is desirable. Even in imperfect markets it operates in the direction of more workable competition,[40] tending to equalize prices in different markets, an especially useful role in the case of perishables, where frequent gluts and shortages make the equalization of supply and demand difficult.[41]

Since it is desirable that prices reflect costs, this power is

[38] FTC, *Final Report*, pp. 24–25.

[39] *Ibid.*, p. 25.

[40] That type of competition which, although operating in imperfect markets, will most nearly produce the results of perfect competition. See John M. Clark, "Toward A Concept of Workable Competition," *American Economic Review*, vol. XXX, no. 2, part I, June 1940, pp. 241–256.

[41] TNEC Monograph No. 35, p. 104.

also beneficial when it wins price concessions which reflect savings in manufacturers' sales, advertising or production costs. Otherwise economic resources will be allocated and organized less efficiently. Threats to patronize other sources of supply or to manufacture products themselves fall into the same general pattern. It is desirable that chains seek their cheapest source of supply.

Furthermore, a powerful buyer may intensify competition in the markets in which he buys. While monopoly, *per se*, tends to increase prices, the tendency of monopsony is to reduce prices.

A limited degree of monopoly ("substantial bargaining power"), on one side of the market, can be of great service in maintaining competition on the other. A strong, alert buyer, large enough so that the loss of his patronage is not a matter of indifference, constantly on the watch for a break which he can exploit by rolling up the whole price front, able to force concessions first from one and then from all, and followed by other buyers, can collapse a structure of control or keep it from ever coming into existence.[42]

Of course, whether these lower buying prices are transformed into lower selling prices will depend on the effectiveness of the horizontal and intertype competition confronting the monopsonistic buyer in his selling markets.

Was this power, beneficent in so many ways, abused? The evaluation of the "fairness" of bargaining practices is a somewhat delicate task, and the outcome depends upon the value system of the commentator. Nevertheless, this is not a hopelessly relativistic task, for we do have some fairly well accepted criteria. To begin, at the time of its investigation there was little that was illegal in those exercises of power discovered by

---

[42] Adelman, *American Economic Review*, p. 1300. This, of course, is an example of Galbraith's "countervailing power." However, this beneficent result of chain power can easily be exaggerated. Dirlam and Kahn show that most of the markets in which A & P bought were marked by fairly effective competition among sellers and that A & P seldom significantly influenced the prices of groceries supplied under seriously monopolistic conditions. *Journal of Political Economy*, April 1952, pp. 121–129.

the FTC. It was quite legal for a chain to threaten to seek other sources of supply and actually to do so.

The "threats" and "coercion" used consisted of statements or intimations that unless the manufacturer would grant . . . special concessions in price, the chain would either buy the goods elsewhere, proceed to manufacture its own, or conduct its stores so as to discourage therein the sale of the recalcitrant manufacturer's goods. If it be admitted that the chain has a legal right to adopt any or all of these policies, it seems to follow that it has a right to announce its intention of doing so. . . . If an attempt should be made to outlaw the use of such "threats" and "coercion" without also removing the existing legal right to do the things threatened, it would be abortive and ineffective. For it is the manufacturer's recognition that the chain, with its tremendous purchasing and distributing power, may do those things and not the "threat" of the chain to do them that is the real inducement for granting the special concession.[43]

Chain threats to buy elsewhere or to do their own manufacturing are legal as individual acts, and their consequences are not undesirable so long as chain power is effectively checked by horizontal or intertype competition. If a seller can find alternative buyers among other chain buyers and in other channels of distribution, the power of any one chain buyer is effectively restrained.[44] When one approaches the FTC's findings in this light, the "coercion" they describe raises few legal or ethical questions.

Paraphrasing its summary of interviews in reverse; [45] of 129

[43] FTC, *Final Report*, p. 49. However, it would not be legal for a group of independent concerns, even though its total size were far less than that of the chain, to act in a similar manner. This would be regarded as a boycott, or as the threat of one, and, as such, clearly illegal as either an unfair method of competition under the Federal Trade Commission Act or as a conspiracy or combination in restraint of trade under the Sherman Act. Thus, as we have seen before, existing legislation, and its interpretation, strongly aids the newer methods of distribution insofar as they involve corporate concentration.

[44] The FTC produced no evidence to indicate collusion among grocery chains. A high degree of competition appears to mark their buying, as well as their selling, activities. However, as we shall see shortly, chain power can be used to cause economically unjustified discrimination among buyers and so have undesirable consequences.

[45] Cf. FTC, *Final Report*, pp. 24–25, and above pp. 68–69.

grocery manufacturers, 53 did not have to give any special concessions to chains in order to win or keep their trade. Of the remaining 76, 43 granted concessions relatively willingly, since no threats were employed. Of the remaining 33, 10 were unwilling to grant the concessions demanded, apparently because they could sell their output elsewhere. The last 23, who granted concessions after being threatened with loss of business, apparently did so in the belief that they would gain more thereby than they could by selling to other buyers. In this light, assuming effective horizontal and intertype competition, the FTC's findings reveal buying tactics which are sharply competitive but hardly reprehensible on either ethical or economic grounds. This competitive safeguard seems to operate even in rather extreme cases. The FTC cited a manufacturer who had gradually increased his sales to one chain until they totaled 40 per cent of his output. The chain "then suddenly demanded larger concessions, which the manufacturer was forced to grant or else have its [sic] production curtailed to that extent." Here its power probably enabled the chain to reduce its buying prices unfairly and to an uneconomic extent in the short run. But these consequences were temporary, for, "as a result of this experience the manufacturer built up a trade with small jobbers to avoid being forced to make concessions." [46] The existence of competitive alternatives prevented this power from having permanently undesirable consequences.

And competitive alternatives in a chain's buying markets are based on effective retail competition. A chain must meet the competition both of other chains and of other channels. Able independent merchants have always competed effectively with chains and in the late 1920's prodded them out of an incipient lethargy by introducing a new kind of retail operation.

Some of the older grocery chains . . . had a rather rude awakening . . . when the supermarket . . . was introduced. For them it was a new experience to find themselves consistently undersold. . .

[46] FTC, *Final Report*, pp. 25–26.

The effect on them, however, seems to have been salutary from the public standpoint. Most of the larger chains were quick to adopt the new idea themselves. . . As a result of this newer technique of retailing with its emphasis on low prices, competition and rivalry between the chains on the selling end seems to be keener today than at any time in the past ten years.[47]

It is only when competitive safeguards become less effective, or are interfered with, that chain buying practices become legally, as well as ethically and economically, questionable. It appears that A & P has sometimes passed beyond merely vigorous buying and has tried to disadvantage its competitors unfairly and so weaken competition. The FTC questioned the legality of some of its buying practices insofar as these put A & P in a position to control or substantially affect its competitors.[48] And one of the assumptions of the successful Sherman Act prosecution was that some of A & P's buying practices were illegal insofar as they represented a systematic attempt to coerce suppliers into giving it discriminatory discounts in order to disadvantage its competitors.[49] While there is much debate about this case and the soundness of the position of the Antitrust Division and of the courts,[50] whatever offenses did occur lay in the restraints on horizontal and intertype competition

[47] TNEC Monograph No. 35, p. 103.

[48] FTC, *Final Report*, pp. 27–28, 49–50. In these cases A & P operated through its subsidiary, Atlantic Commission Co. (Acco).

[49] "The buying power of A & P was so to use its power as to get a lower price on its merchandise than that obtained by its competitors. . . It used its large buying power to coerce suppliers to sell to it at a lower price than to its competitors. . . The purpose of these unlawful preferences and advantages was to carry out the avowed policy of A & P to maintain this two-price level which could not help but restrain trade and tend toward monopoly. Furthermore, to obtain these preferences, pressure was put on suppliers not merely by the use but by the abuse of A & P's tremendous buying power." *U.S. v. Great Atlantic and Pacific Tea Co.*, 173 F. 2d 79 (1949), at 82, 88.

[50] See Adelman, *Harvard Law Review; Journal of Political Economy;* "The A & P Case: A Study in Applied Economic Theory," *Quarterly Journal of Economics*, vol. LIII, 1949, pp. 238–257; "The Great A & P Muddle," *Fortune*, December 1949; Dirlam and Kahn, *Journal of Political Economy;* "Price Discrimination in Law and Economics," *American Journal of Economics and Sociology*, vol. II, April 1952, pp. 300–301; and Fulda, pp. 128–142.

and not in the mere exercise of vertical power. Although it is most difficult to differentiate between acceptable albeit vigorous bargaining for price concessions and unfair attempts to disadvantage competitors, the remedy lies in the policing of trade practices and not in efforts to eliminate or frustrate vertical power *per se*.[51]

Furthermore, there are other restraints. Power, as we have noted, is a two-sided relationship, involving consent as well as constraint. In other words, a degree of interdependency characterizes vertical relationships.

It is of some significance . . . that most of the chains manage to retain more or less permanent connections with those from whom they buy. Criticisms against the mass buyer come more often from those who do not sell to them than from those who do. It is, after all, to the advantage both of the mass buyers and of their suppliers to retain semipermanent and more or less amicable relationships. Generally speaking, the mass buyer today places less emphasis on trying to drive shrewd bargains here and there, and more on building up steady sources of supply on a price basis which insures their permanence.[52]

Finally, chains are checked by manufacturers. The size and the control over supply possessed by many manufacturing and processing concerns grants them sufficient power to balance, with varying outcomes, the power of chains.[53] But what thus appears as a power struggle on the vertical plane appears as competition on the horizontal plane, for the vertical power generated by a retailer or manufacturer depends on his competitive success in winning the support of consumers. In this

[51] Of course, were a chain to achieve such a size as to dominate any market, then it might be difficult for it to exercise its vertical power without seriously handicapping its competitors. Here size, rather than unfair trade practices, might have to be attacked. Even Acco, which sold to the trade as well as to A & P, never reached this size. In the mid-1930's it never handled more than about 7½ per cent of any principal kind of fruit and vegetable. FTC, *Agricultural Income Inquiry, 1937* (Washington: GPO; 1938), part II, p. 95.

[52] TNEC Monograph No. 35, pp. 106–107.

[53] E.g., the struggle between the meat packers and the chains, both sides seeking to perform the wholesaling function. *Ibid.*, p. 20.

sense the power of the consumer — his freedom to choose — restrains the power of both manufacturer and retailer.

This proposition is illustrated by the example of brands. When a trade-mark or brand wins consumer acceptance, its owner commands vertical power. This power may enable a manufacturer to reduce wholesale and retail margins and even to control distributors' competitive practices.[54] Manufacturers' brands were the first to develop in groceries but never became as important as they did in some other fields. The great number of manufacturers and the relative ease with which a consumer can judge the alleged superiority of a brand probably explain this comparative lack of success.

Grocery chains have developed and pushed private brands in part because of competition. A private brand gives a chain an exclusive product, which may command some consumer loyalty, promote good will, and have some advertising value. It usually costs a chain less than does a nationally advertised brand because its manufacturer does not have to allocate any of his selling and advertising expenses to its production, and because he may utilize in producing it otherwise idle capacity. Accordingly, a retailer can price a private brand under the nationally advertised products he and his competitors carry. The FTC found that, although there were no significant over-all differences in quality,[55] private brands averaged about 10 per cent lower in price than standard brands sold by the same chain.[56] Most or all of this price difference resulted from lower purchasing costs.[57]

[54] Extreme examples of manufacturers' power over retail and wholesale competition are to be found in a number of patent cases. At one time control of the patent covering an antiknock ethyl fluid enabled Standard Oil of New Jersey to control wholesale gasoline prices. *Ethyl Gasoline Corp., et al. v. U. S.*, 309 U. S. 436 (1940). See also *U. S. v. Univis Lens Co., Inc.*, 316 U. S. 241 (1942).

[55] FTC, *Private Brands*, pp. 17–19.

[56] *Ibid.*, pp. 92–95, 99–102.

[57] Because the markup on private brands is usually about the same as, or slightly higher than, that on standard brands. However, the evidence is a little confusing. Reports on markup policy were received from 95 grocery chains

Private brands also have important effects on vertical relationships, and, indeed, it is often for this reason that they are adopted and their sale promoted. Just as the possession of a strong brand enables a manufacturer to exert considerable power over distributors, so its possession by a retailer gives him power over manufacturers. Owning the brand, the retailer controls its specifications, and the manufacturer may become little more than his agent. If he has difficulty in promoting competition for his orders, he may do his own manufacturing, thereby entering into direct competition with manufacturers.[58] Thus private brands enable retailers to lessen their dependence on the manufacturer: i.e., reduce his power over them. Some of the statements of chain policy gathered by the FTC reveal an explicit recognition of the use of the private brand as a tool in a vertical power conflict.

Once a national brand is firmly established, the retailer's original profit margins are frequently reduced. The manufacturer often feels that his advertising expense warrants the raising of wholesale costs. The retailer often finds he must carry the article although the profit margin is less.[59]

We are opposed in principle to the advertising and promotion of nationally known brands . . . because such policies tend to give the national brand increased consumer prestige and place control of

---

operating 26,710 stores. Chains containing 21.0 per cent of these stores said they applied a higher markup to private brands, chains with 52.6 per cent of these stores the same markup, and chains with 26.5 per cent of these stores a lower markup. *Ibid.*, pp. 61–63, 125. But a comparison of the gross profits made on private and standard brands indicated that grocery chains actually applied a higher markup to their own brands. This comparison covered the leading brands sold by 59 grocery and combination grocery chains operating 13,955 stores. It showed that these chains realized a gross margin of 23.1 per cent on private brands, compared with 19.0 per cent on those competing standard brands with the highest markup and 17.8 per cent on those with the lowest markup. *Ibid.*, pp. 68–74.

[58] In 1930 manufacturing grocery chains manufactured 9.8 per cent of the goods they sold and these products constituted 5.2 per cent of total grocery chain sales. The comparable figures for combination grocery chains were 13.2 per cent and 12.1 per cent. FTC, *Chain Stores: Chain-Store Manufacturing*, 73d Cong., 1st Sess., S. Doc. No. 13 (Washington: GPO; 1933).

[59] FTC, *Private Brands*, p. 10.

an increasing amount of retail business in the hands of a limited number of powerful national advertisers.[60]

We have found from long experience that the manufacturer of standard brands has very often made unreasonable demands of us, especially if the product has become sufficiently advertised.[61]

What we find, then, is a complex interlocking of all three planes of conflict or competition. Vertical power has important consequences on horizontal and intertype competition at the weaker end of the distributive chain. A manufacturer's power may enable him to control retail competition. A retailer's power may enable him to prevent competition among manufacturers from having any benefit for the consumer. On the other hand, vertical power is limited by competition at the dominant end of the distributive chain. In addition, it is checked by power at the other end of the distributive channel. This vertical conflict may produce competition between retailer and manufacturer for consumer patronage: e.g., competition between standard and private brands. Here the power of both manufacturer and retailer may be checked by their joint subordination to the consumer's power — his power to choose.

Thus the rise of newer marketing media has profoundly altered distributive structures of power. These media, being applications to marketing of principles of large-scale organization — "mass distribution" — necessarily inject new foci of power. But power existed before their arrival. The task is not to avoid power and to destroy all institutions which possess it, but to evaluate its consequences and to attack its abuse. Yet concentrations of power can be dangerous. The objective of public policy, then, is an *economic* balance of power. It is not power *per se* which is to be feared but an imbalance of power. Just as the Founding Fathers added strength to the inherently weaker, so they believed, executive and judicial branches to enable them to balance the inherently stronger legislative

[60] *Ibid.*, pp. 109–110.
[61] *Ibid.*, p. 110.

power, so the creation of power by retailers may add a desirable balance to the distributive power structure.

Only this approach, I suggest, makes understandable our conclusion that retailer power in this trade can and does have generally desirable results and that the injection of this power was necessary to smash traditional and uneconomic discount structures. If one adopts the older belief that all economic power is dangerous and that economic activities can and should be channeled completely by impersonal market forces, then the methods of the chains are incompatible with their results.

To complete our analysis, we must now examine the reactions of other participants in the trade. We shall take up in order the three major groups affected by the rise of the chains — independent retailers, wholesalers, and manufacturers.

Independent retailers were, of course, directly hurt by chain competition, which by 1929 had captured over one third of their market. Their reaction was in part economic. The high proportion of very small proprietors who scarcely eke out an existence should not obscure the many thousands of grocers who are quite successful. Many grocers heightened their non-price appeals, improving their services, enlarging their selection, stressing quality or unusual commodities, and advertising or displaying their goods to better advantage. Others tried to match the chains on their own terms, reducing costs, lowering prices, and stressing higher turnover. Some formed retailer coöperatives, others joined wholesaler-sponsored voluntary chains, and a few patronized cash-and-carry wholesalers. And it was independent merchants who first appreciated the possibilities of the supermarket and developed it.

That growth of grocery chains came to a virtual standstill after 1929 [62] is partial evidence of the success of these efforts, although it is possible that chains had already won most of the

[62] Grocery chains made 38.5 per cent of all grocery sales in 1929 and 39.8 per cent in 1949. *1929 Census of Business*, vol. I, part 1, p. 71; *Survey of Current Business*, October 1949, and July 1950, pp. S–8, S–9.

consumers to whom price was a dominant consideration.[63] Restrictive legislation, as we shall see later,[64] did not seriously hamper the chains. In general, however, independents have been unable to match the chains in efficiency. Although it was independents who first developed the supermarket, their very success caused many of them to open more units and become chains themselves. Furthermore, after an initial aloofness, grocery chains opened supermarkets and soon were predominant in their development.[65]

Voluntary chains and retailer coöperative warehouses were a direct economic reaction to the success of chains.[66] Arising in the 1920's, they attempted to secure for independent grocers many of the advantages of chains. They were designed to preserve individual store ownership and yet permit retailers to copy many chain methods, to purchase in wholesale lots, to apply mass pressure for special concessions, to advertise collectively, to promote private brands, and to apply uniform principles of retail management and operation. These two kinds of coöperative chain have been moderately successful, although their growth since 1929 has been slow.[67] In 1939 and 1948 they

[63] One poll listed the following, in order of decreasing frequency, as the principal reasons given by consumers for patronizing independent stores: convenient location, pleasing personality, better quality, lower price, credit, wider selection of merchandise, and delivery. Beckman and Nolen, p. 169.

[64] Chapters VI, VII.

[65] Even in 1939, before many chains had completed programs of supermarket expansion, of 1447 grocery and combination grocery stores with sales of more than $300,000, 1183, or 82 per cent, were chain units, making 81 per cent of all sales made by units of this size. *1939 Census of Business*, vol. I, part 2, pp. 671–672, 679–680.

[66] For a fuller description, see FTC, *Chain Stores; Coöperative Grocery Chains*, 72d Cong., 1st Sess., S. Doc. No. 12 (Washington: GPO; 1932); Maynard and Beckman, pp. 192–201; Hector Lazo, *Retailer Cooperatives — How to Run Them* (New York: Harper & Bros.; 1937).

[67] The FTC estimated that in 1929 they numbered 395 and did a total retail business of between $600,000,000 and $800,000,000. *Coöperative Grocery Chains*, p. 14. (The 1929 Census did not separate these organizations from regular wholesalers. *1929 Census of Business*, vol. II, p. 43.) Ten years later they numbered 804 and had a wholesale volume of $824,000,000, which corresponds to retail sales of about one billion dollars. *1939 Census of Business*, vol. II, pp.

accounted for about three eighths of all general-line grocery wholesale volume.[68]

This limited success reflects in part the fact that coöperative chains have been unable to cut costs as much as have corporate chains. Operating on a voluntary basis, they have not matched the scale of operation of the corporate chains. In 1939 they achieved an average volume of about four times that of merchant wholesalers but less than a third that of the average corporate chain.[69] Consequently, they were able to win greater discounts than merchant wholesalers but unable to match those given chains. The invoice discounts of which they were able to take advantage ran from a fourth to a half of the difference between the invoice prices paid by wholesalers and those paid by chains.[70] And, probably handicapped by an inability to bind their members to a unity as close as that of a chain, they gained special concessions only slightly greater than those given to ordinary wholesalers, closing about one eighth of the gap between wholesalers and chains.[71]

Nor have coöperative chains matched the wholesale operating efficiencies of the corporate chains, although retailer coöperative warehouses have come close. The Census Bureau issues no statistics on total operating expenses of chain warehouses, but it does present payroll costs, which are usually over half of total operating expenses. In 1939 payroll expenses of retailer coöperative warehouses averaged only 3.7 per cent of sales, or the same ratio as that of the chains. The payroll ratio of voluntary group wholesalers was 6.4 per cent, only slightly less than the ratio of 6.7 per cent averaged by merchant wholesalers. The indicated annual turnover rate of chains, another

---

49, 59–60. In 1948 there were 846 with a wholesale volume of $2,216,000,000. *1948 Census of Business,* vol. II, p. 1.10.

[68] *1948 Census of Business,* vol. II, p. 1.10, and *1939 Census of Business,* vol. II, pp. 49, 59–60.

[69] *1939 Census of Business,* vol. I, part 1, pp. 179–182; vol. II, pp. 49–60.

[70] FTC, *Final Report,* pp. 56–57.

[71] FTC, *Special Discounts and Allowances; Grocery Trade,* p. 3.

index of operating efficiency, was 20.9, a figure which was not closely approached by the others. Coöperative warehouses had a rate of 9.8, voluntary groups 6.5, and regular wholesalers 7.4.[72]

Thus retailer coöperatives have been more successful than have voluntary groups in reducing wholesaling expenses. Yet they have been far less successful in membership and in sales. Despite wholesaling costs double those of the retailer coöperatives, in 1939 the voluntary groups enjoyed a volume more than four times as great — $663,000,000 as compared with $161,000,000.[73] The reasons lie in differences of organization. Retailer coöperatives grew out of informal buying groups of merchants who wished to take advantage of quantity or functional discounts. In a fully developed coöperative the group maintains a warehouse which reduces wholesaling costs by purchasing in large lots, denying or severely restricting credit, and partially or totally eliminating salesmen and other forms of sales effort. A voluntary group, on the other hand, is sponsored by a wholesaler, and the wholesale house remains under his ownership. While it tries to lower wholesale costs by concentrating buying power, its primary efforts are directed at improving retail operations. Its goals are uniform retail prices, the promotion of private brands, retail advertising, and uniform principles of retail management and operation. But the wholesaling gains of coöperatives are so great that it is doubtful that they are matched by the retailing gains of voluntary groups.[74]

[72] All statistics in this paragraph are computed from *1939 Census of Business*, vol. I, part 1, p. 183; and vol. II, pp. 49–60. It should be noted that chain statistics are based on all sides *billed* through chain warehouses. Actually, chain warehouses *handle* only about 70 per cent of the goods billed through them, yet the fact that a chain can eliminate warehousing is a part of its efficiency and should be reflected in these ratios.

[73] *Ibid.*, vol. II, pp. 49–60.

[74] Retailer coöperative warehouses had an operating expense ratio of 5.2 per cent in 1939, and voluntary group wholesalers one of 10.6 per cent. (*Ibid.*, vol. II, p. 49.) Since the latter try to make a profit, retailers in coöperatives buy their goods at prices at least 5 per cent lower than those paid by voluntary group members. But the difference between chain and independent retail oper-

Then why have voluntary groups been so much more successful? The answer lies in the difficulty of organization in this trade, whether for economic or political purposes. The problems of organizing either type of coöperative chain are considerable. As we have seen in Chapter I, many grocers are unable or unwilling to submit to the organizational discipline required in most other occupations. Entrance is easy, so the field provides a haven of sorts for those who have failed elsewhere and who may be only filling in time between periods of employment. Many groceries are part-time ventures of their proprietors, whose principal attention and energies are devoted elsewhere. Many are so small that they lack the capital to join a coöperative or to institute the improvements suggested by wholesalers sponsoring voluntary groups. Finally, high birth and mortality rates create a constant turnover in the ranks. However, a successful coöperative requires about forty retailers, and the requirements of a voluntary group are probably similar.[75] Thus organization of any kind is quite difficult, and it is understandable that the members of voluntary chains, perhaps a third of all independent grocers, run the larger, and probably better managed, independent groceries.[76]

Since organization is so difficult, a grocer naturally looks for leadership to his wholesaler, a larger and presumably more capable firm which often adopts an almost parental attitude toward retailers. The wholesaler frequently inseminates the proprietor-to-be with the desire to enter the trade, usually assists at the birth, nourishes the infant with credit, counsel, and en-

ating expense ratios is usually only 2 to 4 per cent, and groups could not expect to cut their ratio below that of the chains. (An FTC study found that in 1937 43 chains had an average ratio of 20.7 per cent, and 156 independent grocers one of 22.8 per cent. *Distribution Methods and Costs*, part 1, pp. 208–211.) And a survey of voluntary group members in 1934 showed that their retail prices were only 3.63 per cent lower than those of independent merchants not belonging to a voluntary chain. Charles F. Phillips, "Chain, Voluntary Chain, and Independent Grocery Store Prices, 1930 and 1934," *Journal of Business*, vol. VIII, no. 2, April 1935, p. 145.

[75] Lazo, pp. 57–59.
[76] Maynard and Beckman, p. 195.

couragement, may subsidize its early years, and, all too often, buries the dead. When this leadership is not proffered, then organization by retailers themselves is most difficult.[77] Although but 638 out of 3,424 general-line wholesalers sponsored voluntary groups in 1939, only 136 coöperatives had been formed.[78] As we shall see later, this tendency to look to the wholesaler for leadership carries over into politics.

In summary, supermarkets were soon taken over by the chains, and coöperative chains have adopted many of the weapons of corporate chains, lowered costs and prices, and sharpened their competition, but they have not matched fully the efficiency and the prices of the chains. Consequently, some nonprice factors must be included among the economic reasons for the relative success of independents in checking chain growth.

Many of the same factors which hindered their economic organization also hampered the political reactions of independent grocers. The difficulties of welding a cohesive body out of small, individualistic, and often incompetent or uninterested members are obvious. Such a group can offer a trade association but limited contributions in either energy or money. Organization of trade associations has been slow throughout retail trade,[79] but it has especially lagged in groceries. True, in 1939 the National Association of Retail Grocers (NARG), with 40,000 members, was the largest of all trade associations,[80] but it had enlisted but little more than a tenth of its potential

[77] "Eleven years ago, when the chains first started coming into —— , a number of grocers went to the different wholesalers and asked them what they would do to help meet the chain prices. They all gave the same answer; that they would do nothing. It is largely the wholesalers' fault that the chains have such a hold in —— . When they gave us that answer, 10 of us got together and put in $100 each to do some of the buying at wholesale ourselves." Statement of a retailer coöperative president, FTC, *Cooperative Grocery Chains*, p. 9.

[78] *1939 Census of Business*, vol. II, pp. 49–60. In 1948 there were 635 groups and 211 coöperatives. *1948 Census of Business*, vol. IV, p. 1.10.

[79] Of 1,311 trade associations tabulated in a TNEC study, only 85 were in retail trade. TNEC Monograph No. 18, pp. 407–409. Yet of the nation's 3,942,000 operating businesses, 1,690,000 are in this field.

[80] TNEC Monograph No. 17, p. 165.

membership, for in this same year there were about 350,000 independent grocers. The National Association of Retail Druggists (NARD), on the other hand, had recruited 52 per cent of its constituency.

Difficulty or ease of organization is in part a function of size. A merchant's volume is a rough index of the money, energy, interest, and ability his association can tap.[81] It is the larger merchants who join.[82] Size alone, however, is not enough to explain success or failure. The NARG could have had 40,000 members in 1939 by tapping only those grocers with annual volumes of $30,000 or more, while the NARD had to include many druggists with sales of less than $20,000 in order to reach its membership of 28,000. Ease of entry also plays an important role. So long as it is easy to enter the grocery trade, it will be marked by a high proportion of incompetent or apathetic proprietors, which makes more difficult the organization of those alert, energetic grocers who wish to make a permanent career in this field. Retail pharmacy offers a striking contrast. Entry is difficult, since the man who opens a drug store must himself be a registered pharmacist or have sufficient capital and volume to hire one. In effect, entry is limited by licensing, and there is much more group cohesion. Most proprietors are full-time druggists.

Lack of cohesion among grocers is illustrated by the relative absence of effective group action in the control of trade practices. The records of the FTC and of the Antitrust Division

---

[81] Note the analogies to labor organization, where it has been highly skilled workers who were the first to organize, while most marginal workers are still unorganized.

[82] E.g., the NARD contains but 52 per cent of all independent druggists, but its members make over 75 per cent of all independent retail drug sales. Of 11 retail trade associations in the apparel and general merchandise line, only one reported a coverage of between 50 and 75 per cent of its membership potential, and three claimed a coverage of between 25 and 50 per cent. But when their coverage was measured by the volume of total business conducted by their members, then three associations reported a coverage of between 50 and 75 per cent, and two a coverage of between 25 and 50 per cent. TNEC Monograph No. 18, pp. 413, 416.

disclose almost no actions against retail grocers — impressive, if negative, evidence of the barriers to unified action.[83]

The position of the wholesaler in the competitive struggle with chains is a peculiar one. Their gains are his losses, yet he rarely competes directly with them. Consequently, his economic reactions to chain competition usually occur in his dealings with retailers and manufacturers. He must try both to strengthen retailers and to induce manufacturers to patronize only the older distributive media. Some wholesalers did sponsor voluntary groups, but, as we have seen, these groups had only a limited success.

The wholesaler is often equally frustrated in attempts to induce manufacturers and processors to market their products only through traditional channels. Unable to control his retailers, he cannot match the chains in special promotions, advertising, and the like. Nor can he match the size of chain orders.[84] Consequently, he has been tempted to organize boycotts in efforts to coerce manufacturers into selling only to wholesalers. FTC and Antitrust Division records contain many examples of such boycotts, especially during the 1920's. The first step usually was the formation of a trade association, which designated "legitimate" and "illegitimate" channels of trade. The former were those which flowed through wholesalers; [85] the

[83] I have found only one FTC cease-and-desist order issued against a group of retail grocers, and the author of a TNEC monograph finds no antitrust actions. TNEC Monograph No. 21, p. 282. This does not, however, signify a total absence of group activity. California retail grocers induced manufacturers to enforce programs of resale price maintenance from 1907 to 1911, and thereafter engaged in sporadic attempts to secure uniform prices through group action. Lorenzo A. McHenry, "Price Stabilization Attempts in the Grocery Trade in California," *Journal of Marketing*, vol. II, no. 2, October 1937, pp. 121–128.

[84] In 1939 the average general-line grocery wholesaler not sponsoring voluntary groups had sales of $470,000, the average specialty-line wholesale grocer had sales of $157,000, and the average grocery chain had wholesale billings of $7,271,000. *1939 Census of Business*, vol. I, part 1, p. 183, and vol. II, p. 49.

[85] E.g., one association stated that one of its principal objects was "to bring about a better feeling, a better working understanding, a better cooperation with the manufacturers, the wholesale grocers and the retail grocers. . . We contend that the most economic and most efficient way to market food products

latter were those in which chains bought directly from manufacturers or in which "illegitimate" jobbers, such as coöperative warehouses, did not retain the usual wholesale margin. Pressure was put on manufacturers who sold to chains or to "chiseling" jobbers. This took the form of "white lists," which urged the support of manufacturers who had agreed to sell exclusively through "legitimate" channels,[86] of blacklists, which listed direct-selling manufacturers and urged that they be boycotted. [87] Within this general pattern many variations occurred. Wholesalers promised to "push" a manufacturer's products in return for a promise to use only the traditional channels.[88]

---

is through the three channels we have mentioned. . ." *Arkansas Wholesale Grocers' Ass'n., et al.,* 10 F.T.C. 155 (1926) at 162.

[86] E.g., one association urged its members to "stand by the manufacturer that is working exclusively with the wholesaler. . . How can you expect the manufacturer to stick to you if you don't stick to him? It is a case of 'you scratch my back and I'll scratch yours.' Be loyal to those who are loyal to you. You can reduce to the minimum the articles carried for those manufacturers who are giving the 'double cross' to the wholesale grocers. You know who those manufacturers are." *Ibid.,* at 163–164.

[87] E.g., one association listed manufacturers who sold to chains, and elsewhere it referred to "deadhead" articles. "Many of these articles are NATIONALLY ADVERTISED STAPLES whose manufacturers patronize every possible channel of distribution and who care not a fig if their distributors suffer injustice and the loss of an earned and deserved compensation.

"Now is the time and *now the opportunity to clean all such articles out of stock and . . . to favor the goods which 'pay their fare' and to favor those manufacturers who favor you.* . . The trade is united, it is on the defensive, courageous action is the need of the hour! To temporize means eventual surrender!" *Ibid.,* at 163.

Another trade association publication, referring to Procter & Gamble, which had just begun direct sales to large retailers: "Instead of eliminating the jobber . . . they merely cheapen and insult him. In other words, with scant courtesy and meager notice they literally kicked you out the back door. Now they are looking over the field of carnage in an effort to find a few with warped and blunted consciences and who may have had padding in their pants and didn't feel the jolt. Of these they propose to make 'sub-jobbers' to whom they can now and then throw a crust and pass on their cast-off clothes. Will you fall for it? The thought is ghastly. The fetid odor of such a monstrous proposition is so offensive that I wonder their representatives are treated with common courtesy." *Missouri-Kansas Wholesale Grocers' Ass'n., et al.,* 9 F.T.C. 153 (1925) at 160.

[88] In one case the FTC found that "the Postum Cereal Co., refused to sell the so-called irregulars upon the understanding that respondent members would

They spied on wharves, docks, freight stations, and terminals to detect direct sales and then threatened to boycott the erring manufacturers.[89] They helped organize a retail association and sought to elicit its support.[90] Finally, they pushed rival products in order to coerce a recalcitrant manufacturer.[91] Not all boycotts arose out of intertype competition. Some were used in vertical bargaining in attempts to improve terms of sale and to increase discounts.[92]

These measures did not help much in meeting chain competition. They were illegal, and large manufacturers were far from helpless in such struggles. However, they do indicate how relatively easy it was for wholesalers to organize. It is clear that, because of greater size, ability, and interest, wholesalers are capable of more effective group organization and action than are retail grocers. Although a prevalence of territorial and specialized associations hampered it, the leading national wholesale grocers' association had enlisted about half of its potential membership in 1939.[93] And state and regional wholesalers' associations similarly were far more successful than were those of retail grocers.[94] Thus, although their total numbers do not

---

urge their salesmen 'that Post Toasties be pushed in preference to other corn flakes.' " *Wisconsin Wholesale Grocers' Ass'n.*, et al., 10 F.T.C. 409 (1926) at 418.

[89] *Wholesale Grocers' Ass'n. of New Orleans*, et al., 11 F.T.C. 415 (1927).

[90] *Arkansas Wholesale Grocers' Ass'n.*, et al., 10 F.T.C. 155 (1926) at 171.

[91] In an attempt to punish Procter & Gamble, salesmen of four competing wholesalers worked together with a Peet Brothers salesman to induce a retailer to buy Peet products. *Missouri-Kansas Wholesale Grocers' Ass'n.*, et al., 9 F.T.C. 153 (1925) at 164–165.

[92] *St. Louis Wholesale Grocers' Ass'n.*, et al., 7 F.T.C. 1 (1923); *Wisconsin Wholesale Grocers' Ass'n.*, et al., 7 F.T.C. 489 (1924); *North Dakota Wholesale Grocers' Ass'n.*, et al., 9 F.T.C. 266 (1925).

[93] In 1939, when there were 2,786 general-line grocery wholesalers not sponsoring voluntary groups, the National American Wholesale Grocers' Association claimed about 1500 members. A few of them, however, were specialty-line wholesalers. The National Food Brokers' Association had about 1000 members and a potential membership of 4000. TNEC Monograph No. 17, p. 165; *1939 Census of Business*, vol. II, pp. 49, 55–57.

[94] While only 2 retail grocers' associations out of 8 reporting such data covered more than half of their potential membership, 7 out of 14 wholesalers' associations did so. Only 5 out of 14 wholesale groups failed to include more

compare with those of the retail grocers, it may be expected that their political influence, depending as it does on organization, will be out of proportion to their numbers.[95]

Finally, manufacturers, too, reacted economically and politically to the chains. Since they stood in a vertical relationship to chains, their reactions differed considerably from those of distributors. To a manufacturer, the first consequence of chains is a desirable one: another buyer has entered his market, another distributive medium is available to him. Consequently, he does not share the almost instinctive abhorrence and fear which is the first reaction of retailers and wholesalers. Furthermore, since few food products have stable retail prices, the manufacturer has no obvious reason to dislike chain emphasis on low prices or loss leaders and discriminatory local pricing. Even the sharp tactics of chain buyers and special chain discounts may be accepted as part of the cost of utilizing this marketing channel, just as advertising and sales effort are part of the cost of the older channels.

Thus there is no necessary alliance between manufacturers and independent distributors. Many small manufacturers may find that the best solution of their marketing problems calls for the exclusive use of either the chains or the older agencies. Those who choose the latter course will thereby ally themselves with the wholesalers and retailers, but others will choose the chains. Most large manufacturers cannot afford to confine

---

than a fourth of their potential, but 5 out of 8 retail groups failed. And the members of 15 out of 16 reporting wholesalers' associations made over 75 per cent of the sales made within the trade represented by the association. Only 3 out of 7 retail associations reported similar coverages. Furthermore, since these reports unfortunately include liquor as well as grocery retailers (and beverage and tobacco as well as grocery wholesalers), and since liquor dealers are unusually well organized, these statistics overstate the degree of organization among retail grocers. TNEC Monograph No. 18, pp. 412–416.

[95] In 1939 there were 2786 general-line, merchant wholesalers not sponsoring voluntary groups, 11,791 specialty-line wholesalers, and 4016 grocery and food brokers and agents, as compared with 346,987 independent proprietors of food stores of all kinds. *1939 Census of Business*, vol. I, part 2, p. 671; vol. II, pp. 49, 55–57, 59.

themselves to one channel. To dispose of their output, they have to use both channels unless they establish their own marketing agencies. Nor is it easy, let alone legally advisable, to coerce manufacturers into using only the traditional channels. A small manufacturer may react by selling only to chains. A large one cannot afford to limit his sales. He may consider this antagonism simply as one of the costs of selling to chains and may expand advertising and sales effort to overcome independents' opposition.

Thus any alliances between manufacturers and distributors are limited ones. There is, however, some occasion for the pursuit of common purposes. While only a few grocery manufacturers would willingly ally themselves with independents in order to cripple chains or to eliminate loss leaders or discriminatory local pricing, most would join in a movement to restrict chain bargaining power, for this would reduce the cost of distributing through chains. It is precisely this sort of limited participation which they contributed to the campaign to control politically the channels of distribution.

# The Distribution of Drugs

Although it is a much smaller segment of the national marketing system,[1] drug distribution bears many similarities to the grocery trade. Until the 1920's the great preponderance of drugs and toiletries flowed through the usual channel — manufacturer–wholesaler–retailer. After World War I independent wholesalers and retailers were threatened by the rise of drug chains which had applied the principles of mass distribution and had reached considerable size.[2] By 1935 chain drugstores were making 25.7 per cent of all drug sales.[3] This success resulted largely from their low prices, for they were even more successful than were grocery chains in this respect, underpricing independents by about 15 per cent.[4] Most of this difference in selling prices was due to efficiency of retail and wholesale operations and to a concentration on high volume items.[5] And

[1] In 1939 the nation's 57,903 drugstores, about 3.27 per cent of all retail units, made sales of slightly over one-and-a-half billion dollars, or about 3.72 per cent of all retail sales. *1939 Census of Business*, vol. I, part 1, p. 57.

[2] In 1939 the average drug chain had 14.3 units and sales of $1,385,000. The average chain drugstore had sales of $97,000, as compared with $22,000 for the average independent store. *Ibid.*, vol. I, part 2, pp. 671–672, 679–680.

[3] As compared with 38.8 per cent won by grocery chains. *1935 Census of Business*, vol. I, part II, sect. 2, pp. 13–14.

[4] The FTC found that on an unweighted basis independents charged prices from 9.8 per cent to 12.4 per cent higher than those charged by chains. When a geometric average of weighted prices was taken, then independent prices were from 17.5 per cent to 22.7 per cent higher. FTC, *Final Report*, pp. 30–31.

[5] Only a small proportion of the difference in selling prices resulted from

they were more successful than grocery chains in gaining special discounts and allowances, receiving concessions amounting to 5.2 per cent of their purchases, while drug wholesalers received only 1.1 per cent.[6] Moreover, they have been relatively successful in promoting private brands, thereby augmenting their vertical power.[7] Finally, chains sometimes employed loss leaders and frequently used leaders.[8]

Thus far, the bases of conflict appear similar to those prevailing in the grocery trade. In brief, this similarity would lead us to expect intertype conflict between chains and independents— a conflict centering first on the existence of the chains and then on loss leaders and buying practices. One would also expect some friction between chain and manufacturers over chain buying practices.

This similarity also extends to vertical relationships within the older channel of distribution. The wholesaler, formerly relatively dominant, since a few wholesalers stood between many manufacturers and many retailers, was weakened by the vertical expansion of both manufacturers and retailers. One would expect the wholesaler to dominate his retailers. In 1939 the average general-line wholesaler had a volume of $1,224,000, in comparison to the average druggist's sales of $22,000.[9] The druggist is quite dependent on his wholesaler. He has more skill, interest, and capital than the average grocer, but his pecul-

---

advantages in buying prices. When computed on an unweighted basis, it ranged from 5.7 per cent to 13.5 per cent; when weighted by chain weights, from 5.3 per cent to 17.4 per cent; when weighted by independent weights, from 3.9 per cent to 18.3 per cent. *Ibid.*, pp. 55–56.

[6] *Ibid.*, p. 58. These figures indicate a somewhat greater chain buying advantage than that discovered by the FTC in its survey of four cities (Note 5, above).

[7] In 1930, 17.3 per cent of their total sales were of private brands. FTC, *Private Brands*, p. 32.

[8] 16.5 per cent of reporting chains admitted using loss leaders in 1928. In one week 27 out of 98 chains employed leaders, the loss averaging 14 per cent. FTC, *Leaders and Loss Leaders*, pp. 21, 40, 47.

[9] The average specialty-line wholesaler of drugs and drug sundries, however, had an annual volume of only $119,000. *1939 Census of Business*, vol. II, pp. 50, 52.

iar stock requirements usually necessitate an intimate dependency on his wholesaler, for he must carry from five thousand to eight thousand different items.[10] His turnover in most of them is slow, and he must make frequent purchases in small lots — transactions which achieve only a dubious wholesale status by being called "1/12 of a dozen lots" or "1/6 of a dozen lots."[11] Accordingly, he depends on the full-service wholesaler, who maintains a large stock, makes frequent deliveries, and extends credit.

If these similarities to the grocery field exhausted a description of the drug trade, we might expect that druggists were largely unorganized, incapable of sustained group action, and that they usually followed the lead of the wholesalers. That this is not so and that the course and outcome of group conflicts differ so widely from those in the grocery trade point up the significance of the differences between the two trades.

Let us begin with the retail druggists. Here the crucial fact is a homogeneity and group cohesion so notably lacking among grocers. There are three major reasons for this. First, there is far less size variation among druggists. In 1939 the bulk of independent drugstores had volumes of between $10,000 and $50,000. Within this range lay 63.6 per cent of all druggists, accounting for 67.4 per cent of all sales, while only 34.5 per cent of all independent food stores, making 52.6 per cent of all independent food sales, fell within this range. 61.3 per cent of the independent food stores had a volume of less than $10,000, and 30.1 per cent of independent food sales were made by stores with sales of more than $50,000.[12] It is possible to speak of *the* typical independent druggist with some accu-

---

[10] A study of seven independent drugstores showed that six carried between 4500 and 8200 different items. U.S. Department of Commerce, Bureau of Foreign and Domestic Commerce, Domestic Commerce Series No. 90, *Cost, Sales, and Profits in the Retail Drug Store* (Washington: GPO; 1934), pp. 110–111.

[11] A survey of a drug wholesaler revealed that retailer purchases averaged only about $2.00 per line. Domestic Commerce Series No. 86, *Wholesale Druggists' Operations* (Washington: GPO; 1934), p. 28.

[12] *1939 Census of Business*, vol. I, part 1, pp. 671–672.

racy, whereas it is necessary to speak of the typical marginal grocery store — a "Mama, Papa, and Rosy store" [13] — the typical medium-sized full-service grocery store, and the typical large-volume self-service grocery. This means that most druggists are engaged in much the same *type*, as well as size, of operation. They share the same problems to much the same degree.

A second reason for greater group cohesion is that retail pharmacy is a chosen occupation. Most druggists have undergone some training in preparation for a lifetime career. Entry tends to be limited to those who have some training and sufficient capital to carry a large stock. This again is in contrast to the grocery trade, which attracts a high proportion of the incompetent, the misfit, and the unemployed.[14] And a mortality rate which is only from a half to a third of that for grocers enables greater stability and cohesion.[15]

Finally, a third reason is that most druggists, being registered pharmacists, share an important bond and tend to regard themselves as professional men rather than as merchants. Thus to the ties of economic interest are added those of a profession — ties which usually cause those so united to share a feeling of exclusive superiority. Such a fusion of economic and professional bonds, as the American Medical Association demonstrates, can produce an unusually cohesive economic group with a strong sense of group purpose. It also tends to produce a

[13] This happy phrase for the small home store was developed by NRA administrators. Kenneth Dameron, "Retailing Under the N.R.A., I," *Journal of Business*, vol. VIII, no. 1, January 1935, p. 8.

[14] "Perhaps the most logical reasons for the drug trade showing the best relative position [in terms of mortality rates] are the capital requirements of the trade, educational requirements for dispensing prescriptions, and the general expansion of merchandise lines carried by drugstores. At the other extreme grocery stores have high turnover of stock and therefore require little capital. No special knowledge of merchandise is believed to be required in the operation of a grocery store, and it is a trade that attracts the unthinking on the basis that 'everyone must eat' and therefore the business is sure to be successful." A. E. Boer, p. 54.

[15] See above, Chapter I.

conviction that their services should not be evaluated under solely economic criteria and that, accordingly, they should be protected from the rigors of the market.[16]

This cohesion has characterized retail druggists for many years. The NARD, the politically most powerful of all retail associations, was organized in 1898. By 1906 it was powerful enough to enforce a "Tri-partite Agreement" among drug manufacturers, wholesalers, and retailers. This agreement established uniform retail prices through manufacturers' sales contracts binding distributors to specified resale prices. Manufacturers were induced to sign contracts by a well organized program of blacklists, white lists, and boycotts by wholesalers and retailers. While this scheme was held to be a violation of the Sherman Act, and the NARD and the National Wholesale Druggists' Association (NWDA) were perpetually enjoined from continuing these practices, the scope and success of the Tri-partite Agreement do attest to the high level of organization achieved by both wholesalers and retailers, although the NARD was the principal force behind the agreement.[17] And the NARD and other druggists' organizations were prominent in the political campaign for resale price maintenance legislation from 1914 on.[18] Even in the absence of formal organization, group consciousness and joint action mark the druggists. In the late nineties druggists adopted a code word "pharmocist," which could be so marked on prescription copies that the original prescription price could be ascertained and matched when refilled by a second druggist. While the NARD may have been

[16] Cf. TNEC Monograph No. 1, p. 352.

[17] *Jayne, et al., v. Loder,* 149 Fed. 21 (1906). For a brief discussion of the case, see Claudius T. Murchison, *Resale Price Maintenance* (New York: Columbia University Studies in History, Economics and Public Law, vol. LXXXII, no. 2; 1919), p. 98. For a brief analysis of the decree issued, see FTC, *Report on Resale Price Maintenance* (Washington: GPO, 1945), pp. 36–38. (Hereafter cited as FTC, *RPM*.)

[18] The NARD was one of the most influential forces behind the foundation of the American Fair Trade League, and, of the 143 associations listed as supporting the Stevens Bill, by far the largest group — 28 per cent — were druggists' associations. See FTC, *RPM*, pp. 39–59.

instrumental in the adoption of the code, it speedily dissociated itself from any responsibility for the practice. Yet in 1929, thirty years later, most druggists still honored code prices.[19]

This cohesion has had important consequences throughout the trade. Price competition has usually been avoided without arousing consumer antagonism, for a customer is peculiarly helpless in his drug purchases: he is seldom capable of intelligent judgment about the prices and qualities of drugs and usually is equally ignorant about toiletries and related products. Indeed, a low price may be a competitive disadvantage if it is substantially below the price of similar products.[20] In the absence of intertype competition there is a strong tendency toward price uniformity, price lines, and relatively high retail margins.

Here, too, the interrelations among horizontal, intertype, and vertical competition and conflict are complex. Retail emphasis on nonprice competition has combined with consumer apathy to cause manufacturers similarly to stress nonprice competition. The unusual cohesion of retail groups has made the boycott a powerful weapon, and retailers' vertical strength has been enhanced by their influence over consumers. In his drug purchases the consumer often asks the druggist's advice, and that fact that the druggist is a white-coated professional man, a registered pharmacist, renders the customer susceptible to suggestion. Thus the retailer is often in the peculiarly strategic position of selecting which one of several competing articles will be bought.[21] This power of selection makes boycotts most

[19] Seventy-one out of eighty-six retail druggists said they matched the price, and two said they used the code price if it was higher than their own price. FTC, *Open-Price Trade Associations*, 70th Cong., 2d Sess., S. Doc. No. 226 (Washington: GPO; 1929), pp. 48–49.

[20] E.g., a large drug chain failed to achieve a satisfactory level of sales for its private brand of aspirin when priced at 19 cents, in comparison with prices of between 59 and 75 cents charged for manufacturers' brands. It then raised its price to 49 cents and expanded its volume substantially. TNEC Monograph No. 1, p. 351.

[21] A survey of 5457 Cleveland housewives showed that 36.3 per cent said their druggists frequently suggested brands other than the one for which they

effective and causes manufacturers to compete for the support
of retailers as well as of consumers. This competition is reflected in high retail margins [22] and increases in normal margins
through such devices as "free goods" [23] and special allowances
and discounts. Manufacturers may also provide demonstrators [24] or pay commissions or "PM's" [25] to drug clerks.

Some manufacturers may try to offset retailers' power by
extensive advertising, using it not only as a weapon of horizontal competition but also as a tool in vertical relations. Others
may accept retailers' power and try to harness it by such inducements as those just described. Sometimes the tribute paid
to retailer power reaches major proportions, such as the payment of $25,000 to the NARD by the Pepsodent Company in
order to be reinstated in the good graces of the retail druggists.[26] Such special inducements, however, require a sizable
staff of sales representatives and may tend to displace the
wholesaler. But the general-line wholesaler is not easily displaced. As we have already seen, the stock requirements of a

---

had asked. Of these, 56.1 per cent (or 20.8 per cent of the total) said they
frequently accepted these suggestions. *NARD Journal*, Oct. 3, 1935, pp. 1154–
1155.

[22] E.g., the *NARD Journal* abounds in such advertisements as this: "Remember dealers make a higher percentage of profit on Pepsodent dentifrice than on
any of the 7 leading advertised brands." March 4, 1937, pp. 338–339.

[23] These usually take the form of offering, for example, one free article with
the purchase of every dozen of the same articles or the gift of a different product
which the manufacturer wishes to introduce.

[24] Salespeople paid by the manufacturer to "demonstrate," i.e., to sell, the
manufacturer's products to consumers in the retail store. In effect, the manufacturer thereby meets some of the retailer's payroll.

[25] Payment by the manufacturer of special sales commissions to the retailer's
employees on their sales of the manufacturer's products. This could almost be
described as a manufacturer's bribe to push his products rather than those of
his competitors. The origin of the initials — PM — is uncertain. They may stand
for "push money" or "post mortem." The latter term refers to dead stocks on
hand at the end of the year, which the retailer gets off his shelves by paying
clerks special commissions on their sale. See U.S. NRA, Division of Review,
Work Materials No. 57, "Restriction of Retail Price Cutting with Emphasis on
the Drug Industry," by Mark Merrell, E. T. Grether, and Sumner S. Kittele,
p. 12. (Hereafter cited as NRA Work Materials No. 57.)

[26] For a fuller discussion of this example, see Chapter VIII.

retailer make him dependent on his wholesaler for frequent delivery and usually for credit. Few other organizations can match the range of stock carried by a general-line wholesaler. Retailers who buy from voluntary group wholesalers, retailer coöperative warehouses, and cash-and-carry wholesalers, and even many chain drug stores, must patronize a general-line wholesaler for some purchases. He has the largest average volume of wholesalers in all trades, and his sales dwarf even those of the average manufacturer of drugs and toiletries.[27] Furthermore, many wholesalers do much manufacturing themselves, producing a variety of products from their own formulae, from those of physicians who purchase from them, and from the American Pharmacopoeia. Finally, the fact that their numbers are so few enables them to organize cohesive and strong trade associations.[28]

The power and strength of the general-line wholesaler has produced a stable discount schedule and a fairly high wholesale margin. Despite his strategic position and his strength, however, he has been increasingly replaced by manufacturers' wholesale outlets. He can perform many services for the manufacturer, such as the anticipation of demand and the allocation of supply, but, carrying so many thousands of lines, he cannot sufficiently focus his attention to offer the many special concessions, allowances, services, and personal contacts which manufacturers desire in their competition for the favor of the retailer. A large manufacturer therefore may establish his own wholesale outlets in order to contact retailers and to tap their power. Despite the danger of incurring the wrath of the powerful wholesalers, many large manufacturers [29] have undertaken

[27] In 1939 the average general-line drug wholesaler had sales of $1,224,000, and the average drug and toiletry manufacturer had sales of $262,000. *1939 Census of Business*, vol. II, p. 50; vol. V, pp. 18–19.

[28] The coverage of the NWDA is indicated by the fact that in 1938 it had 213 active full-service wholesaler members. FTC, *RPM* (1945), p. 149. In 1939 there were 297 general-line wholesalers. *1939 Census of Business*, vol. II, p. 50.

[29] It was primarily the larger manufacturers who sold through their own wholesale outlets. The average manufacturer's sales office or sales branch had

the laborious and expensive chore of supplying directly about 58,000 drugstores rather than simply selling to 297 wholesalers who cover almost every retail outlet, thereby demonstrating the value they place on personal contact with retailers and their high evaluation of retailer power. In 1939, while general-line wholesalers were the largest single source of supply for all retailers, selling them 46 per cent of their supplies, retailers bought 19 per cent of their supplies from manufacturers' wholesale outlets, 15 per cent from specialty-line wholesalers, and 17 per cent directly from manufacturers.[30]

Thus distribution by manufacturers is an important alternative marketing channel; it is in intertype competition with wholesalers. Unlike the channel opened by grocery chains, however, this medium is an extremely costly one, its operating expense in 1939 being about double that of general-line wholesalers.[31] It has directly increased distributive costs and also has unnecessarily duplicated marketing facilities.

All the factors — horizontal, vertical, and intertype — thus far discussed have increased distributive margins. Indeed so powerful have retailers and wholesalers been that a retail margin of 33⅓ per cent — equivalent to a markup of 50 per cent on cost — and a wholesale margin of 16⅔ per cent have been traditional. Although this retail margin has been reduced by competition on many fast-moving items, the full margin has long been a watchword among druggists and one of the major

---

a volume of $867,000, and the manufacturer's total sales might be substantially greater. *Ibid.*, vol. II, pp. 52, 54. The average drug manufacturer had sales of only $262,000.

[30] *Ibid.*, vol. II, pp. 49–57, 122–132; vol. V, pp. 18–19. Most direct sales were to chains and other large buyers.

[31] In other words, 26.5 per cent as compared with 13.0 per cent for general-line wholesalers. This contrasts with the grocery trade, where manufacturers' outlets, with an operating ratio of 11.5 per cent, almost match the 9.5 per cent ratio of general-line wholesalers and better the 14.1 per cent ratio of specialty wholesalers. *Ibid.*, vol. II, pp. 50–55. Drug manufacturers' high ratios probably result from an inability to spread costs, which tend to be fixed by the size of the area and the number of druggists served, over a sufficiently large number of product lines, since specialty-line wholesalers had the same ratio.

objectives of the NARD.[32] Manufacturers have been forcefully acquainted with the desire of organized druggists for a 33⅓ per cent margin. Boycotts and the pushing or burying of products have vividly demonstrated the intensity of this desire and the great influence of druggists over consumers.[33] Since consumers usually are not price conscious, manufacturers are often willing to grant such margins, especially since uniform margins may enable them to avoid price competition among themselves.

The simplest way for a manufacturer to guarantee a margin is to fix the retail, "resale," or "list" price of his item. Since he directly controls his price to wholesalers, he has now determined the combined wholesale and retail margins. The retail price is usually printed on the item's container, but this does not make it legally enforceable.[34] The most effective method of enforcement is to sign contracts with distributors or to refuse to sell to price-cutting distributors. These actions have usually been held illegal, but the persistence with which manufacturers have nevertheless attempted to control resale prices is another tribute to the power of retail druggists. It also demonstrates the complex interrelations among the different planes of competition and conflict. Here retailers have used vertical power over manufacturers to induce them, in turn, to use *their* vertical power over retailers to control horizontal competition among retailers.

Attempts to maintain resale prices on drugs began in California as early as the 1870's. The primary pressure on manu-

[32] E.g., see the convention address of its president in 1935: "The principle that 33⅓ per cent margin . . . is necessary is just as old as the National Association of Retail Druggists, and the cornerstone upon which the association was founded. I have presented it at every meeting that I have been privileged to address; at every audience with any manufacturer; at every gathering of associates. . ." FTC, *RPM*, p. 212. Also see pp. 131–135 for examples of the ways in which the NARD has stressed this margin. For some years it was the first item of the Association's platform.

[33] For some examples of retailer boycotts and promotions, see below, Chapter VIII.

[34] *Bobbs-Merrill Co. v. Strauss et al.*, 210 U.S. 339 (1908); and *Bauer et Cie. v. O'Donnell*, 229 U.S. 1 (1913).

facturers was at first that of wholesalers.[35] After the creation of the NARD in 1898, the movement to force manufacturers to maintain resale prices became national in scope, and retailers became the primary force behind the movement. The initial program, as we have seen, ended with the outlawing of the Tri-partite Agreement in 1907. Meanwhile, the NARD had per-suaded manufacturers to adopt resale price maintenance con-tracts together with a serial numbering of products to enable enforcement of the contracts — a program first developed by the Miles Medical Company in 1903 or 1904. At the NARD Convention in 1904 twelve of the largest drug manufacturers agreed to the plan.[36] When this plan was declared illegal in 1911,[37] druggists persuaded many manufacturers to announce resale prices and then refuse to sell to wholesalers or retailers who did not observe these prices. In 1919 the Supreme Court appeared to sanction this method[38] but later held refusals to sell illegal if they implied an agreement to suppress competition among retailers.[39] Despite these decisions and vigorous enforce-ment by the FTC until the NRA,[40] drug manufacturers still tried to enforce resale prices, and many successfully pursued refusal-to-sell policies.[41]

[35] Grether, *Price Control*, p. 83.
[36] FTC, *RPM*, pp. 128–129.
[37] *Dr. Miles Medical Co. v. Park & Sons Co.*, 220 U.S. 373.
[38] *U.S. v. Colgate & Co.*, 250 U.S. 300.
[39] *U.S. v. A. Schrader's Son*, 252 U.S. 85 (1920); *Frey & Son v. Cudahy Packing Co.*, 256 U.S. 208 (1921); *FTC v. Beech-Nut Packing Co.*, 257 U.S. 441 (1922).
[40] In the first five years following the Beech-Nut case, 71 complaints charging illegal use of resale price maintenance schemes were issued by the FTC. Watkins, p. 100.
[41] E.g., see the letter of a manufacturer to a state druggists' association: "For a period of 4 years now, we have steadfastly refused to sell anyone who cuts below these minimums. . . In your State . . . we have recently eliminated a number of wholesalers, further restricting our distribution so that we are in a position to control all phases of our business."
Another manufacturer selling to druggists said: "Although we had no con-tract with retailers or wholesalers, prior to the enactment of the Tydings-Miller Act in the various States, both those retailers and wholesalers understood that products bearing the Sheaffer name were sold under a price-maintenance policy

Thus, once again, the vertical power of retailers, group organization and cohesion at both retail and wholesale levels, and consumer ignorance and inexperience have all combined to maintain relatively high margins. Indeed, despite the rise of some intertype competition, actual wholesale and retail margins in the late 1930's approximated the 16 per cent and 33⅓ per cent traditionally demanded.[42] The same factors that produce high margins have also encouraged so much advertising and other sales expense that there is little correlation between manufacturing cost and retail price. It is notorious that many patent medicines selling for a dollar or more cost only a few cents. This is also true of many preparations which, although bearing brand names, are standard pharmaceutical formulae, and which can be made by a pharmacist for as little as one tenth of their *wholesale* price.[43]

The size of retail margins of course proves nothing about net profits; a margin is meaningless until applied to a sales volume.[44] But it does offer an enticing prospect for anyone who believes he can reduce distribution costs. It is little wonder that the drug trade was one of the first lines entered by chains. What is surprising is that they have had such a limited success, for drug chains have many advantages over their grocery counterparts. They undercut independent prices more deeply, and in

---

and if that price-maintenance policy were violated, we would immediately stop shipment of Sheaffer products to the violator." FTC, *RPM*, pp. 129–130.

[42] Actual margins were about 15 per cent and between 30 and 35 per cent. TNEC Monograph No. 1, pp. 404–405.

[43] For a list of such preparations, see Grether, *Price Control*, pp. 95–96. Among the examples he gives, quoting a paper presented at a retail druggists' association meeting, are: elixir phenobarbital, costing $2.50 a pint to buy at wholesale and 35¢ to make; ephedrine inhalant, $17.00 a 1000 cc. and 80¢; solution ephedrine and epinephrine, $28.00 a 1000 cc. and $3.80; and Fehlings solution — copper A, $1.00 a pound and 10¢.

[44] For the average independent druggist, with sales in 1939 of $22,000, a 33⅓ per cent margin would yield only a gross profit of about $7,300 out of which to meet all expenses, including his own compensation and that of 2.6 employees. (Employment data based on *1939 Census of Business*, vol. I, part 1, pp. 87–89.)

special concessions and allowances they have secured a buying advantage over independent channels far greater than that won by grocery chains.[45] Finally, like the grocery chains, they conduct their wholesale and retail activities more efficiently than do independents.[46]

Why, then, have drug chains had less success in winning trade away from independents? Private brands shed some light on this question. The drug trade appears to offer unusually promising opportunities for their development. Most drugs and toilet preparations are made to formulae; quality is easily standardized; and, by branding many thousands of items, a chain could extend its prestige to cover products where the consumer might be unfamiliar with any other brands. Yet in 1930 drug chains had a lower proportion of private brand sales than did combination grocery chains,[47] although the latter sold many nonbranded commodities, such as meats, fruits, and vegetables. The reason for this relative failure is that drug chains, in contrast to grocery chains, did not use private brands as a weapon of vigorous price competition. Although private brands cost them far less than standard brands, they did not price them below standard brands as often as did grocery chains.[48] Instead, they retained this difference in cost by more

[45] Some drug chains received allowances which, when expressed as a percentage of sales, dwarf those received even by the A & P. In 1930, for example, the Liggett chain received special allowances and discounts amounting to 13.69 per cent of its purchases from reporting manufacturers, as compared with 2.42 per cent for the A & P in the same year. FTC, *Chain-Stores: Special Discounts and Allowances to Chain and Independent Distributors — Drug Trade*, 73d Cong., 2d Sess., S. Doc. No. 94 (Washington: GPO; 1934), pp. 68–69.

[46] In 1939 all drug chain warehouses met a payroll amounting to 4.28 per cent of warehouse sales. The comparable percentage for general-line drug wholesalers was 7.57 per cent, and for specialty-line wholesalers 11.15 per cent. *1939 Census of Business*, vol. I, part 1, p. 183; vol. II, p. 50. And retail chain drug stores benefit from the efficiencies of high-volume operations.

[47] Private brand sales were 17.3 per cent of drug chain sales and 18.1 per cent of combination grocery chain sales. FTC, *Private Brands*, p. 32.

[48] Drug chains with 51.3 per cent of all chain units reported pricing private brands below comparable standard brands, and those with 12.4 per cent of all units priced private brands higher than standard brands, while grocery chains

than doubling their margin on them, retaining an average margin of 63 per cent (or a markup of 170 per cent!)[49] These extremely high margins indicate that drug chains use private brands primarily to enable the cutting of prices on standard brands.

In general, it seems that drug chains lowered prices only enough to gain a firm niche. They then reduced the vigor of their price competition, content with shallow price cuts which are matched by some independents, while the grocery chains have, whether willingly or not, transformed their lower costs into lower prices. Some of this relaxing of price competition may be due to a lack of aggressiveness and to a natural desire to enjoy the profits resulting from large retail margins. But there are other, probably more important, factors at work. Consumer ignorance and apathy (because drugs are but a small proportion of total consumer budgets) condition retail markets and trade channels. They blunt the appeal of lower prices, causing chains to turn to nonprice competition, raising their operating costs. As a result, drug chains, despite their many operating and buying advantages and their high margins, are less profitable than grocery chains.[50] Of course, it may be that they have misgauged consumer reactions and that more aggres-

---

containing 83.3 per cent of all chain groceries priced private brands below standard brands. *Ibid.*, pp. 65–67.

[49] This averaged 62.0 per cent on drugs and 63.2 per cent on toiletries. Their margins on standard brands with the highest markup were 33.6 and 38.9 per cent. On standard brands with the lowest markup, their margins were 23.3 and 21.9 per cent. Grocery chains had a margin of 23.1 per cent on private brands, 19.0 per cent on standard brands with the highest markup and 17.8 per cent on those with the lowest markup. *Ibid.*, pp. 72–73, 81.

[50] The FTC's study of the operating results for the years 1928, 1929, and 1930 of four leading combination grocery chains, including A & P, and of five leading drug chains, including Liggett and Walgreen, showed that while the drug chains had higher profit ratios in terms of sales, the grocery chains had a substantially higher profit expressed as a rate of return on business investment. The drug chains had operating profits amounting to 4.21 per cent of sales, as compared with 2.82 per cent for the grocery chains. But the drug chains showed a rate of return on their business investment of 11.73 per cent, as compared with 21.56 per cent for the grocery chains. FTC, *Miscellaneous Financial Results of Retail Chains*, pp. 14, 16.

sive tactics would be more profitable. Thus on the vertical plane chains have accepted the position of manufacturers, being generally content to sell standard brands and not to push vigorously their own brands, which are regarded primarily as a source of unusual profit rather than as a competitive weapon. In competition with independents, chains have minimized their intertype impact, tending to become horizontal rather than intertype competitors and turning increasingly to nonprice competition.[51]

Thus two kinds of intertype competition have failed to reduce prices substantially. But high margins continue to attract those who believe they can market more cheaply. Department stores have found that through quantity purchases and the promotion of private brands they can usually underprice both chains and independents. And some department store chains, notably R. H. Macy, and the department store trade association, the National Retail Dry Goods Association (NRDGA), have been of some importance in political struggles arising from the drug trade.

A greater impact, although for a limited period, was produced by another competitor, the cut-rate drugstore. For the most part born in the Great Depression, most cut-raters were small "pine-board" stores,[52] but some had spacious interiors and large prescription departments. Their common denominator, then, was not cheap fixtures and other "hole-in-the-wall" characteristics but deep price cuts on standard brands. Because chain price cuts were small and were matched by some inde-

---

[51] This is indicated by the fact that, in the period surveyed by the FTC, their operating expenses show constant increase. In 1922 drug chains had a ratio of operating expenses to sales of 31.45 per cent, in 1928 of 31.72 per cent, in 1929 of 33.33 per cent, and in 1930 of 34.17 per cent. FTC, *Miscellaneous Financial Results of Retail Chains*, p. 23.

[52] Small "hole-in-the-wall" stores, with a limited range of drugs and toiletries, in cheap locations, and furnished with simple, inexpensive fixtures. The term derives from their use of pine, rather than more expensive woods, for shelving and counters. For a fuller description, see NRA Work Materials No. 57, pp. 10–11, 47.

pendents, in the absence of resale price maintenance shallow price cuts of 10 per cent or sometimes even 20 per cent were quite frequent during the 1920's and 1930's. But the cut-rater slashed prices well below this level and usually used loss leaders. He could make deep price slashes because he often switched customers to high-margin private brands, because he carried only fast-moving items, because he spread his costs over a high volume of sales, and because he bought surplus stocks from distressed manufacturers or wholesalers. But, although it was the cut-raters who were the principal carriers of price competition during the 1930's, it was unlikely that they would permanently revolutionize trade channels. Most of their success was temporary; with the easing of the depression their sources of supply became more expensive and their lower prices appealed less. Furthermore, since much of their success was personal — based on their aggressiveness, their ability to find distress goods, their skill in undercutting clumsier and more bureaucratic chains and in shrewdly conducting dramatic price wars — rather than organizational, it could not be permanent. It was a symptom of the weaknesses of existing marketing media rather than an indication of new efficiencies in organizing marketing functions.

This completes our survey of the bases of conflict in this field. It seems that one of the strongest political drives will be that of retailers and wholesalers seeking to protect their margins. They can do this most easily by seeking legislative permission for them to compel manufacturers to guarantee margins. So strong are druggists that we may expect manufacturers to accept subordination to them. In intertype conflict we find even more striking variations from the grocery trade. Because it is the cut-rate stores who offer the greatest competitive challenge, it cannot be a form of organization which is attacked, but rather the methods used. Since the cut-raters also challenge chains, who have accepted the *status quo*, we will find the chains allying themselves with the NARD. Here the attack may be focused directly on the methods of the interlopers — loss leaders and low margins — or vertical power may be used to attack these methods. The passage and consequences of the Miller-Tydings Amendment will illustrate these political reactions.

# V

## The Distribution of Automobiles

In the marketing of automobiles intertype competition is virtually nonexistent, so we confront only the interrelations of horizontal and vertical competition and conflict.[1] In the last chapter we saw how the vertical power of retailers could control horizontal relations among both retailers and manufacturers. Here we will see how manufacturers' vertical power conditions competition among retailers. We will also see how this power causes retailers to organize in order to develop counterpower and the forms this retailer power takes.

Automobile sales account for a substantial proportion of total retail sales. In 1939 the nation's 33,609 new-car dealers made sales of almost five billion dollars, or 11.4 per cent of total retail sales. They are large retailers, having in this same year average sales of $143,000 and hiring 9.4 employees.[2] Yet, despite their size, the central fact about their vertical relations has been manufacturer dominance. There are several reasons for this dominance. The dealer's resources are microscopic when compared with those of his manufacturer. The Big Three — General Motors, Chrysler, and Ford — who make 95 per cent

---

[1] Some chains of automobile dealers do exist, but in 1939 they accounted for only 2.7 per cent of all sales made by dealers of new cars. *1939 Census of Business*, vol. I, part 1, pp. 63–64.

[2] *Ibid.*, vol. I, part 1, p. 57.

of all cars, are among the nation's very largest corporations. This dominance, moreover, has historical roots. Automobiles were first retailed by manufacturers' agents, who accepted them on consignment. From 1900 to 1920 the agent gradually assumed more responsibilities and performed more functions, finally becoming an independent dealer. But his independence has never become as full as that of most merchants, and in some respects he is still primarily a manufacturer's agent.[3] Furthermore, ever since the first sellers' market waned in the early 1920's, manufacturers have concerned themselves with retail problems. It is the dealer who makes the ultimate sales upon which rests the success or failure of the whole manufacturing process. He is the only direct contact the manufacturer has with the public. Consequently, dealers are one of the manufacturer's principal competitive weapons, and he has a vital stake in their volume, service, quality, and sales practices. Since automobile sales usually require considerable sales effort, service, demonstration, and postsale service, manufacturers check on the performance of these tasks and in order to insure satisfactory performance usually forbid dealers to carry competing products.

In short, because the manufacturer wants supervisory control over retail operations and because he finds retailers who are willing to accept these conditions, he exercises much vertical power. This dominance is facilitated by the fact that he sells to most of his dealers either directly or through his own wholesale outlets.[4] The cancellation provisions of dealer con-

[3] For a description of this historical development, see FTC, *Report on Motor Vehicle Industry*, 76th Cong., 1st Sess., H. Doc. No. 468 (Washington: GPO; 1940), pp. 106–114.

[4] 1939 Census statistics on the distribution of manufacturers' sales combine data on the sales of motor vehicles, motor vehicle bodies, parts and accessories, and automobile trailers, so that an analysis of the distribution of only automobiles is impossible. In 1935, however, of manufacturers' total distributed sales of motor vehicles (including trucks as well as automobiles), 41.1 per cent were direct factory sales to retailers, and 22.7 per cent were sales to retailers through manufacturers' own wholesale branches. 31.8 per cent were sales to independent wholesalers or jobbers. *Ibid.*, pp. 36–37.

tracts [5] reflect this dominance. Until recently contracts could be terminated at will by either party on the serving of a notice of from one to three months, and until the late 1930's no notice or one of but ten or fifteen days was necessary.[6] It is this ability to cancel a contract — really a franchise — that gives a manufacturer his power. While either party may cancel, this is an unequal power. Without a contract, a dealer ceases to be a retailer of new cars. While a manufacturer wishes to create enough dealerships for full territorial coverage and for maximum sales, no one dealer is essential, and there are many would-be dealers, usually drawn from the ranks of used-car dealers, available to replace those whose contracts have been terminated.[7] Cancellation is legal, being authorized by a contract which the dealer has voluntarily signed.[8] This weapon need not be unsheathed; threats or hints of revocation can be equally effective. A manufacturer has other weapons, such as discrimination or delay in deliveries or the establishment of other dealerships in the same area, but cancellation is the principal source of his power.[9]

[5] Contracts between a manufacturer and either a dealer or distributor. Most contracts are signed directly with dealers. Those signed with distributors usually also cover the dealers — often called "associate dealers" or "sub-dealers" — served by the distributor. Thus a manufacturer's control over associate or sub-dealers is as close, although not as direct, as that over direct dealers. *Ibid.*, pp. 115–116.

[6] *Ibid.*, pp. 123–125, 147–149.

[7] Manufacturers require their field representatives to maintain lists of prospective dealers so as to enable the prompt exchange of franchises. *Ibid.*, p. 148.

[8] "While there is a natural impulse to be impatient with a form of contract which places the comparatively helpless dealer at the mercy of the manufacturer, we cannot make contracts for parties or protect them from the provisions of the contracts which they have made for themselves. Dealers doubtless accept these one-sided contracts because they think the right to deal in the product of the manufacturer, even on his terms, is valuable to them; but after they have made such contracts, relying upon the good faith of the manufacturer for the protection which the contracts do not give, they cannot, when they get into trouble, expect the courts to place in the contracts the protection which they themselves have failed to insert." *Ford Motor Co. v. Kirkmyer Motor Car Co., Inc.*, 65 Fed. (2d) 1001. For similar judicial interpretations of these manufacturer–dealer contracts, see FTC, *Motor Vehicle Industry*, pp. 139–141.

[9] *Motor Vehicle Industry*, p. 149.

This power is an instrument of competition among manufacturers. The FTC's investigation of the industry describes the many ways in which this power was used. Its objectives fell into three broad, interrelated categories: insuring that the dealer has sufficient liquid capital, plant, and equipment to make him a vigorous, hardy competitor; the promotion of sales of accessories and services; and the maximum sale of new cars.

The first goal is understandable enough. Effective retail selling requires a wide stock of cars, a number of demonstrators, sufficient equipment to provide a broad range of services, a convenient location, and sufficient space to show and store cars. Since these necessitate a substantial investment, a manufacturer insists that his dealers possess ample capital. Usually a dealer contract contains such requirements, and during its life, the FTC's investigation showed, there is frequent pressure on dealers to increase their financial commitments. These demands took a variety of forms.[10] Manufacturers frequently required a dealer to invest a certain amount of capital. They often required that profits be left in the business until the capital was built up to a specified amount. Similar requirements about the size of a retailer's premises, the adequacy of his automobile and parts stock and of his service and repair facilities, the size of his sales and service force, and the amount of his advertising appropriations were often included in contracts.

When such provisions are in the contract, a market relationship exists between manufacturer and retailer, and power plays but little part. The manufacturer is seeking to recruit a sales force — his dealers. For the price he bids — the retail margin — he demands a certain amount of capital and equipment. The dealer-to-be, it can be assumed, has weighed the returns likely to accrue to him from the investment of his capital and labor in the various opportunities available to him. Free to accept or reject the bid, he is striking a bargain. But when the dealer

[10] For examples of the pressures used, and the various forms of demands made, see *Ibid.*, pp. 151–172.

has committed his capital and entered the business, a power relationship unites manufacturer and dealer. It is then that a manufacturer's threat to cancel the franchise takes on meaning, for the dealer is no longer a free participant in a market process. He has committed himself deeply. His firm's name is now associated with that of his manufacturer, and it is not easy to shift the capital he has invested in plant and equipment, let alone that invested in good will.

An examination of manufacturers' postcontract demands for increased investment in capital and equipment reveals the extent to which power underlies vertical relations. Now, some of these demands may well be for actions which are in the interest of both sides; because of his familiarity with markets across the nation, a manufacturer may know better what retail capital and equipment is necessary or desirable. Yet the FTC cites so many cases in which manufacturers coerced dealers to add to their capital, equipment, and services against both their stubborn opposition and their best interests as to indicate that in the early and middle 1930's, manufacturers often, if not usually, pressed dealers to increase their investment and expenses against their own wishes. That in so many cases dealers acceded, even at the cost of dangerously expanding their investment or expenses, is a measure of manufacturers' vertical power. A few examples will suffice to illustrate this use of their power.

Ford forced me to build present building which I doubt I will ever finish paying for.[11]

. . . I was informed . . . that I must obtain and maintain a separate used-car building and lot and engage a used-car manager. . . In order to retain my contract I purchased a two-story cement block garage . . . and developed a display lot. . . Then I engaged a manager at a substantial salary which experiment proved to be a failure. I carried on during 1937 and 6 months of 1938, but found that my overhead, resulting from maintaining two separate establishments,

[11] *Ibid.*, p. 161.

had become so excessive that I was obliged to close the used-car garage and carry on from my former place, as I had been doing for 16 years.[12]

I was practically forced to lease a building in March, 1937 on threat of cancellation of my contract.[13]

We were canceled out for a period of 90 days in April, 1937 until we had located larger and more expensive quarters. . .[14]

During the late twenties manufacturer used everything at its [sic] command to induce us to spend some $80,000 for a plant, which we foolishly did, after being assured that our contract and proposition would never be worse. However, before construction was completed, less than 4 months later, our direct contract was canceled. . .[15]

Dealers were also induced to purchase tools and other equipment and to increase advertising expenses.

. . . $7.50 on "6" cars and $10 on "8" cars are charged to the dealer for advertising on every car invoice. This must be paid and the money is supposed to be spent in his district. Although we are asked for suggestions as to how this money should be used, we cannot use this money as we see fit. . . We are not furnished a statement . . . showing where or how or how much was used.[16]

Have roadmen in dealer's place of business continually to sell such stuff and the dealer feels he cannot hold franchise without so-called cooperation with manufacturer.[17]

Contacted by zone man from branch to purchase picture machine, certain advertising programs, special tools, and accessories. Told we must cooperate on sales-promotion programs. If we refused . . . pressure was applied, asserting that we are "only" dealer not to have joined the program and manager would be informed of our unwillingness to cooperate.[18]

We were forced to buy a slide film machine, $100 truck rear axle

[12] Statement of a Chevrolet dealer. *Ibid.*, p. 162.
[13] Statement of an Oldsmobile dealer. *Ibid.*, p. 163.
[14] Statement of another Oldsmobile dealer. *Loc cit.*
[15] Statement of a Hudson dealer. *Loc cit.*
[16] Statement of an Oldsmobile dealer. *Ibid.*, p. 165.
[17] Statement of a Pontiac dealer regarding advertising and tools. *Ibid.*, p. 166.
[18] Statement of a Ford dealer. *Ibid.*, p. 168.

for display, and thousands of dollars of special tools which we didn't need or use.[19]

Advertising material . . . is shipped and billed to us, as well as picture films, without our consent.[20]

We have had a great deal of insistence from the manufacturer in buying numerous special tools, picture machines, picture films, and other similar commodities. . . We were threatened with cancellation at numerous times and the renewal of our contract was held up, we believe, to force the purchase of tools and equipment that we did not desire to buy.[21]

The second general use to which manufacturers put their vertical power was to induce dealers to stock and use only factory parts and accessories and to finance their wholesale purchases and retail sales through finance companies chosen by manufacturers. Their methods of persuasion were similar to those used to persuade dealers to expand their investments.[22] Their reasons for pursuing these policies reveal vividly some of the interrelations between vertical power and horizontal competition. While manufacturers promote the sale of their own parts and accessories in part simply because they receive a high rate of profit on their sale,[23] other reasons derive from competition. They also wish to deprive competitors of retail outlets, to assure satisfactory service to the buyers of their cars, and to lower retail prices (retail margins on other parts and accessories are higher than those on factory products).[24]

[19] Statement of another Ford dealer. *Loc. cit.*
[20] Statement of a DeSoto-Plymouth dealer. *Ibid.,* p. 170.
[21] Statement of another DeSoto-Plymouth dealer. *Ibid.,* p. 171.
[22] For examples, see *ibid.,* pp. 260–287.
[23] During six of the years between 1929 and 1937 the automobile divisions of General Motors made an average net profit of 24.85 cents on every dollar of sales in parts and accessories, as compared with only 7.18 cents profit on every dollar in sales of new cars. In the same period Chrysler made an average net profit of 17.3 cents per dollar on sales of accessories and parts, and only 6.6 cents on new cars. In the same years Ford lost 0.36 cents per dollar of sales of new cars but made 12.07 cents on every dollar of sales of accessories and parts. *Ibid.,* p. 1062.
[24] *Ibid.,* p. 1069.

This effort to gain a competitive advantage by lowering retail prices is more clearly demonstrated in the case of finance companies. The financing of a new car is an important part of most retail sales, for most new cars are sold on credit,[25] and financial charges are a significant part of the total purchase price.[26] Each of the three major manufacturers has virtually required his dealers to use a specified finance company.[27] In 1938 the three chosen finance companies did about 80 per cent of the field's wholesale financing and 75 per cent of its retail financing, the remaining business being divided among 375 relatively small finance companies.[28] Manufacturers have used their vertical power to reduce competition among finance companies, yet their reason arose out of competition among manufacturers. Their primary purpose has been to lower total retail prices on their cars.[29] The chosen finance companies impose

[25] About 60 per cent of retail new car sales involve installment credit. *Ibid.*, p. 920.

[26] They average about 4 per cent of the total purchase price of cars sold under a twelve-month installment credit plan, about 5 per cent under an eighteen-month plan, and about 8 per cent under a twenty-four month plan. (Since down payments cover only about one half of the total purchase price, these percentages are not to be confused with the rates of interest charged.) *Ibid.*, p. 959.

[27] Chrysler promoted the services of Commercial Credit Co., independently owned but bound intimately to it by contract; General Motors promoted its subsidiary, General Motors Acceptance Corporation; and Ford promoted Universal Credit Co., organized by Ford in 1928 but sold to Commercial Investment Trust Corporation in 1933. On May 27, 1938, the Antitrust Division filed indictments against manufacturer sponsorship of these finance companies. On November 15, 1938, consent decrees were obtained and entered with Chrysler and Ford. In 1939 General Motors was found guilty. A court of appeals affirmed the judgment and the Supreme Court denied further review. 121 F 2d 376; 314 U.S. 618; and 314 U.S. 710 (1941). The net effect of both criminal and civil proceedings was the highly legalistic one of allowing a manufacturer to use "exposition," "persuasion," and "argument," but not "coercion," in attempts to induce dealers to patronize the manufacturer's chosen finance company. See also *Ford Motor Co. v. U.S.*, 335 U. S. 303 (1948).

[28] FTC, *Motor Vehicle Industry*, p. 280.

[29] "There is probably no doubt that the General Motors Acceptance Corporation and Universal Credit Co. were organized . . . with the object of decreasing the cost to the public of financing time sales. This appears to be particularly true of Universal Credit Co. . . . the Ford Motor Co. has indicated that it does not desire to have any manufacturing economies that have been passed

somewhat lower financial charges,[30] which result at least in part from a policy of lowering profits, for they show a considerably lower rate of profit than do independent companies.[31]

Thus a competitive policy by manufacturers lessens competition among finance companies and tends to make this competition a question of power. Dealers, too, have some vertical power, for it is usually the dealer and not the customer who decides which company shall finance a sale. Accordingly, just as drug manufacturers increase retail margins in attempts to harness retailer power, so independent finance companies woo dealers with deeper retail margins, granting them so-called "loss reserves," bonuses, and "packs." When the chosen companies buy or finance installment contracts from dealers, they do not assume responsibility for losses. If a car is repossessed, it is given to the dealer for reconditioning and resale. If he fails to recover from its resale the unpaid balance and the costs of repossession, reconditioning, and resale, the loss is his. Since he bears this risk, he is entitled to share in the finance charges, i.e., to receive a premium — the dealer's loss reserve — in return for his assumption of responsibility. The independent companies, however, usually buy installment contracts outright with no recourse to the dealer, and no dealer participation in

---

on to the public in the prices counteracted by excessive financing expenses charged Ford purchasers." *Loc. cit.*

[30] In 1935, before the initiation of a so-called "6 Percent Plan" by General Motors, the total financial charges imposed by the General Motors Acceptance Corporation on twelve-month credit plans amounted to an implied annual rate of interest (not compounded) of 13.68 per cent. The comparable charges by factory-preferred finance companies were 16.80 per cent, and those by independent finance companies 17.88 per cent. In 1938, on twelve-month plans, factory-controlled companies imposed charges implying an annual interest charge of 11.16 per cent, as compared to 11.64 per cent for factory-preferred companies, and 12.12 per cent for independent finance companies. *Ibid.*, pp. 959, 968.

[31] In 1935, 1936, and 1937, respectively, factory-controlled finance companies made net profits amounting to 6.95 per cent, 5.65 per cent and 5.56 per cent of their total capital employed. Factory-preferred companies had comparable profit rates of 8.92 per cent, 7.92 per cent, 6.47 per cent, while the averages for *all* finance companies were 9.16 per cent, 9.44 per cent, and 7.86 per cent. *Ibid.*, p. 947.

finance charges is economically justified. Yet, because of the power of dealers, independent companies offered them a so-called dealer's loss reserve, and the chosen companies offered them a loss reserve greater than was necessary to protect against repossession losses.[32] In addition, independent companies paid dealers' bonuses out of regular finance charges and allowed dealers to add a "pack" to regular finance charges.[33] Thus independents in effect resorted to commercial bribery in order to overcome the vertical power of manufacturers.

This conflict between the chosen companies and the independents illustrates some of the interrelations of competition and power. It is a conflict between two different types of competition — that among manufacturers for the favors of consumers and that among finance companies for the favors of dealers. It is also a conflict of vertical power between manufacturers and dealers over the size of the retail margin. In this case competition among manufacturers led to lower retail prices, but competition among finance companies led to higher retail prices. Consequently, the restraining of competition among finance companies by manufacturers has lowered prices.

Finally, manufacturers use their power to promote the sale of a maximum number of cars. Here the motivation is obvious, and its strength enhanced by the fact that average costs in automobile manufacturing decrease with unusual rapidity. A high proportion of total cost is irretrievably committed in plant and in specialized tools and dies. The greater the volume of cars over which these fixed costs can be spread, the lower will be the average costs per car. In addition, given models are seasonal commodities and their sale must be executed within short periods of time, if their costs are to be recovered. Consequently, under

---

[32] *Ibid.*, pp. 932–933.

[33] In 1938, on twelve-month loans, independent finance companies allowed dealers to retain financial charges amounting to 1.65 per cent of the credit granted. On eighteen-month loans the allowance was 1.85 per cent, and on twenty-four-month notes 2.52 per cent. *Ibid.*, p. 959. Some independent finance companies enabled dealers to secure this additional pack by providing them with two or more rate charts based on different rates of charge. *Ibid.*, p. 1076.

great pressure to maintain or expand their volume, and commanding great vertical power, manufacturers are constantly tempted to exploit it to promote sales. Objectives are expressed in quotas assigned to individual dealers. Failure to achieve a quota endangers a dealer's franchise, and an estimated quota is included in dealer contracts. A quota is usually based upon a given "per cent of price class." All makes of cars are divided into price classes — Chevrolet, Ford, and Plymouth cars, for example, comprising one class. Each manufacturer sets himself the goal of maintaining or bettering his percentage of a given price class. As the year progresses, tabulations of new-car registrations are broken down by territorial subdivisions, and quotas of dealers within these subdivisions are set accordingly.[34] If a dealer made 35 per cent of the sales of a price class within his district one year, he is expected to maintain or better this percentage in the next year. This percentage is usually expressed as a number of cars. The FTC's investigation shows that these quotas occasioned more frequent use of manufacturer power than did the other two general purposes discussed above. Once more, some examples will illustrate the scope and nature of this use of power.

Your January sales quota as follows: Cars ——, trucks ——, total ——. This is not just a sales quota but a definite sales assignment which we expect you to accomplish. Prorate quotas among dealers, then crowd all dealers hard to do better merchandising job. . .[35]

There has never been a year since 1925 that the factory didn't try to make us take cars and trucks that we did not want . . . there were frequent occasions when we were threatened with cancellation of contract . . . the last cancellation threat was in January of this year when . . . a truck representative insisted we surrender our contract because we did not give him a truck order, he swore and used abusive language . . . until the writer becoming very upset had to leave, this developed into a severe attack of stomach ailment which I had

[34] *Ibid.*, pp. 176–180.
[35] Wire from Ford Motor Co. to Ford branches. *Ibid.*, p. 182.

become subject to through worry caused by arguments and demands made upon us every time a factory representative called. It would make a book writing about all those occasions. . .[36]

With the Chrysler-Plymouth line this pressure was used this summer to dispose of Chrysler Imperials and Royals. The factory men stated we would have to help them dispose of these cars or they would look for another Chrysler dealer for this town. . .[37]

. . . Ford forced us under threats of cancellation to stock 22 new cars. . . Coercion has been the practice . . . rather than the exception. . . I formerly worked for the Ford Motor Co. . . and have been a roadman. I have been both a "coercer" and a "coercee." [38]

. . . I ordered only what I wanted regardless of the attitude of the representative, and was canceled.[39]

Almost every year . . . we have been forced to accept too many cars. . . In 1934 we were canceled out because we wouldn't accept what the factory wanted to give us. We gained reinstatement only by accepting the cars.[40]

We were obliged to have three, four and five warehouses on the outside to carry this unbalanced, excessive inventory which was forced upon us, a great many times with threats of "or else — if you don't sell them, some one else will," and at times through threats of cancellation. We were sometimes so crowded that in addition to the warehouses, our showroom was full to the doors with new cars. . .[41]

Manufacturers' power is perhaps best measured by a case in which it was used to the utmost. The Ford Motor Company once used its power to refinance its manufacturing plant. In early 1921 Ford was hard pressed to meet obligations of about $58,000,000, incurred as a result of the Ford family's purchase of minority interests in the Company. These obligations all came due on or before April 18, 1921, but in the winter of 1920–21 a business recession had retarded car sales, lowered

[36] Statement of a Dodge-Plymouth dealer. *Ibid.*, pp. 194–195.
[37] Statement of a Chrysler-Plymouth dealer. *Ibid.*, p. 195.
[38] Statement of a Ford dealer. *Ibid.*, p. 202.
[39] Statement of a former Pontiac dealer. *Ibid.*, p. 207.
[40] Statement of a Chevrolet-Cadillac-LaSalle dealer. *Loc. cit.*
[41] Statement of a former Chrysler-Plymouth distributor. *Ibid.*, p. 159.

car prices, but had not yet reduced the costs of materials and parts. Ford continued full production during late 1920 but held its purchases of parts and materials to a bare minimum, thereby transforming its stocks of parts and materials into finished cars. In late December the Company shut down its manufacturing plants and converted the finished cars into cash by shipping them to its dealers with sight drafts attached to the bills of lading. At the time of the shutdown dealers had already accumulated a surplus of almost 100,000 Model T's. Now they were forced to accept another 30,000. Thus the whole operation had shifted to Ford's 17,000 dealers the burden of meeting most of the Company's obligations.[42] Although an extreme case, this episode does demonstrate the power held by manufacturers.[43] Ford dealers were embittered, and the financial resources of many were severely taxed. Yet in the next few years Ford apparently had no difficulty in recruiting several thousand additional dealers.[44]

The pushing of cars on unwilling dealers has important consequences on retail competition. For, although manufacturers' list prices are, technically at least, customarily observed, and although cars made by different manufacturers tend to fall within certain price lines, there often is furious retail price competition. List prices lend a false air of precision to a selling process which involves vigorous bargaining over price. The sale of nine out of ten new cars involves a "trade-in." Precise valuation of used cars is difficult, and, in the absence of con-

[42] For detailed accounts of this episode, see *ibid.*, pp. 633–643; and E. D. Kennedy, *The Automobile Industry; the Coming of Age of Capitalism's Favorite Child* (New York: Reynal & Hitchcock; 1941), pp. 126–129.

[43] It is an extreme case but not the only one in which manufacturers have forced dealers to perform actions far removed from the retailing of cars. Ford dealers, for example, were once forced to buy Henry Ford a Cape Cod windmill. House Committee on Interstate and Foreign Commerce, Subcommittee on Motor-Vehicle Distribution Practices, *Hearings on H. J. Res. 389 Directing the Federal Trade Commission to Investigate Motor-Vehicle Distribution Practices*, 75th Cong., 2d and 3d Sess. (Washington: GPO; 1938), p. 10. (Hereafter cited as Crosser Committee Hearings.)

[44] Kennedy, p. 127.

trols, the allowance granted on a trade-in is determined by bargaining and may vary widely. This indeterminacy in trade-in allowances makes the real retail prices of new cars indefinite and subject to higgling. And since some consumers are torn between a new car and a late-model used car, the competition of used-car dealers intensifies downward pressure on the real prices of new cars. Price competition occurs even among dealers carrying the same line. Obviously the more a manufacturer presses his dealers to accept delivery, the greater will be the supply of new cars in local markets, lowering real prices by causing dealers to compete in trade-in allowances. This, the FTC's investigation indicates, is the principal complaint of the dealers. A few examples suffice to illustrate this complaint.

. . . factory representative would call and tell us what we had to take. I would ask him what we were going to do with them. He would laugh and say, "Run 'em in the lake." Then we would have to go out and trade wild and loose. The factory does not care what we sell, how we trade, as long as they get their check. The dealer that trades the longest . . . is the factory pet.[45]

. . . they would require the dealer to carry an oversupply of cars. During the clean-up season, the latter part of the year, they would force dealers to take more cars than they could sell at a profit, in order to clear their branches of all models, frankly stating that the dealer was not expected to make a full profit on all the cars that were sold. Oftentimes it was said in a way that implied if one did not do as requested they would find a dealer who would. In other words, they would threaten to cancel your franchise.[46]

I have sold many, many cars in the past on which we knew at the time that we were allowing entirely too much for the old car, in order to keep the manufacturer satisfied with our operation.[47]

In previous years cars have been shipped us without orders with the result that some must be sold at great discounts and extra-high allowances on used cars. . .[48]

[45] Statement of a DeSoto-Plymouth dealer. FTC, *Motor Vehicle Industry*, p. 200.
[46] Statement of a Ford-Lincoln-Zephyr dealer. *Ibid.*, p. 202.
[47] Statement of a Chevrolet dealer. *Ibid.*, p. 205.
[48] Statement of a Chevrolet dealer. *Ibid.*, p. 205.

Manufacturers were aware of these results. They promoted price competition, praising "volume-minded" dealers and threatening or canceling dealers who insisted upon full retail margins at the expense of volume — so-called "cherry-pickers."

We are in a market where fair-play tactics will not suffice. They could be injected and perhaps controlled . . . — but the public would then stop buying. . . We are faced with a market where "survival of the fittest" has the upper hand. . . I urge you to take aggressive action now. Accept the market as the laws of economics and politics have created it. Attack this market with "survival of the fittest" selling tactics and get for yourself and for Chevrolet that business upon which we are depending. . .[49]

This dealer has been ultraconservative . . . particularly with respect to insisting on making a net profit on his used-car operation. . . This dealer could afford to take a $50 loss on 6 to 10 additional new cars each month. . .[50]

Manufacturers frequently pressed dealers to grant overallowances on trade-ins.[51] When Ford shifted to the Model A and first encountered the problem of trade-ins to a substantial degree, it increased retail margins from $17\frac{1}{2}$ per cent to 22 per cent to enable its dealers to grant about $50 in overallowances on each new car sale.[52] Packard often granted late season bonuses on the sale of slow-moving models with the understanding that they would be applied as overallowances.[53]

Manufacturers' vertical power, then, created vigorous price competition. Nearly nine tenths of the dealers questioned by the FTC replied that they had to grant used-car allowances in excess of what they regarded to be fair values.[54] While it is second nature for dealers to complain that they are granting

[49] A letter from a Chevrolet regional sales manager to the dealers in his region. *Ibid.,* pp. 186–187.
[50] From the cancellation files of the Ford Motor Co., covering a dealer whose franchise was canceled. *Ibid.,* p. 189.
[51] For examples, see *ibid.,* pp. 213–249.
[52] *Ibid.,* p. 214.
[53] *Ibid.,* pp. 234–235.
[54] *Ibid.,* p. 241.

overallowances, an FTC study showed that, although dealers made an apparent average net profit of $97.85 on the sale of each new car in 1937, the resale of trade-ins resulted in a net loss of $102.11 per new car sold.[55] Thus the average sale of a new car involved a net loss of $4.26, and it was only a profit of $23.35 on related sales of parts, accessories, and service which produced a net profit of $19.09 on the whole transaction. Put another way, the dealer paid $752.34 for the average new car and sold it for $850.19. In making this sale he allowed $508.27 for cars which he could sell for only $406.16 It was the sale for $227.84 of parts, accessories, and services which cost him $204.49 that put him in the black.[56] Thus viewed, the sale of new cars was on a leader basis.

Since the dealer felt himself threatened and grievously wounded by vertical power and the rigors of competition, the attractiveness of group action both as a means of policing competition and of countering manufacturers' power was obvious. The successes and failures of dealers' efforts to organize, their weapons and goals, all throw some light on our political economy.[57]

Group attempts to control competition began in the early 1920's, but it was not until dealers had experienced a respite from competitive rigors under the NRA that they developed a

[55] *Ibid.*, p. 891. The average retail dealer had to sell 1.63 used cars as the result of each sale of a new car, because the resale of a used car often requires the acceptance of a second used car in partial payment.

[56] *Loc. cit.* The statistics on distributor-dealers, who sell both at retail and to subdealers or to associate dealers, were of the same order. The average new-car sale of distributor-dealers produced an apparent net profit of $51.74, but the subsequent loss on the sale of used cars produced an average net loss of $50.47, or a net profit of only $1.27 on each new car when overallowances are taken into account. The sale of related parts, accessories, and services yielded a net profit of $11.83, or a net profit of $13.10 on the whole transaction.

[57] In this chapter we proceed directly to an analysis of the political conflicts in this field, unlike our discussion of drugs and groceries, where consideration of the political conflicts was postponed for later treatment. The reason for this organization is that the political consequences of economic conflicts in the distribution of automobiles cannot be demonstrated through the examination of a single piece of legislation, as is the case with drugs and groceries.

strong taste for controls and learned how to secure them. Prior to the NRA extremely vigorous price competition marked the trade, whose Golden Rule was the David Harum saying, "Do unto the other feller the way he'd like to do it unto you — and do it fust." [58] Cutthroat competition in the early years of the Great Depression had caused so many bankruptcies and so demoralized the trade that dealers enthusiastically accepted the NRA. Their NRA code forbade sales below list price plus taxes, extra equipment, and transportation and handling costs, and prohibited many "unfair" trade practices, but its crux was its method of controlling trade-in allowances.[59] A code "Blue Book," published by the National Association of Automobile Dealers (NADA) bimonthly, listed used car "values" for given market areas. It was an unfair trade practice to grant allowances greater than the published values, which were computed by averaging the highest 80 per cent of prices received in sales of used cars in the preceding two months. So long as the code was observed, dealers enjoyed protection from the hazards of price competition. "Perhaps the nearest thing to Heaven that most automobile dealers will ever see was the NRA." [60] Accordingly, after the NRA had been declared unconstitutional, it was the NRA pattern of competition that dealers sought to revive, and their satisfaction with nonprice competition is indicated by the large number who attempted to avoid price competition through group action.[61] These attempts all centered on the problem of trade-in allowances, for if uniform allowances could be maintained, then observance of list prices would end price competition.

During the 1930's local groups developed two widely-used methods of controlling allowances. The first of these, the Michigan plan, set allowances based on the NADA's "Official Used

[58] "The Used Car," *Fortune*, June, 1938, p. 112.

[59] For a brief description of code provisions, see FTC, *Motor Vehicle Industry*, pp. 366–367.

[60] "The Used Car," *Fortune*, p. 38.

[61] For numerous examples, see FTC, *Motor Vehicle Industry*, pp. 369–400.

Car Guide." The value listed by the Guide was the top allowance which group members could grant and also tended to be
the minimum allowance. Uniformity in allowances was en-
forced by fines, which usually ran from $25 for the first offense
to $100 for the fourth, and by expulsion for the fifth. "Out-
laws," those who consistently exceeded Guide allowances, were
punished by retaliatory measures and boycotts. As the NADA
described it,

> All association members are pledged to report every deal in which
> the "outlaw" is concerned. They all center their attention on taking
> each deal away from him or in making each deal unprofitable for him,
> to the extent that the dealer who suffers a loss is reimbursed from
> association funds . . . every regular dealer is supposed to sever all
> relations with any bank, finance or investment company with which
> the "outlaw" does business.[62]

The second plan commonly used was the Hollywood plan,
whose key feature was a central bureau for the recording of
used-car appraisals. Before any dealer could appraise — i.e.,
bid on — any car offered him as a trade-in, he had to call the
bureau to see if any other dealer had registered a prior bid.
If the car was not listed, he could offer any sum he chose.
When the car had been previously listed within a thirty-day
period, the second dealer was variously limited in different
versions of the plan. In some, he could not exceed the prior bid
without notifying the first bidder and allowing him the opportunity to match or better the second bid. In others, the bidding
proceeded in $25 jumps; the second bidder either bid below
the first offer or bettered it by $25. This minimized higgling
and usually caused the first bid to stand. In yet other cases the
first dealer was virtually assured of the deal by requiring a
second dealer to bid at least $15 under the first bid and requir-
ing all subsequent dealers to bid at least $25 under the initial
bid.[63]

[62] An NADA bulletin, dated June 11, 1937, and mailed to all managers of state
and local associations. *Ibid.*, p. 370.
[63] *Ibid.*, pp. 370–383.

While there was much variation, the typical control plan combined the appraisal bureau of the Hollywood plan with the penalty provisions of the Michigan plan. Many plans were in operation, and they usually reduced overallowances by from $25 to $50 and minimized price competition.[64] Many bureaus handled large numbers of appraisals. A Los Angeles bureau, serving 85 Ford dealers, employed 17 persons and averaged 12,000 calls a month.[65]

Nationally, however, the success of these plans was limited. While the FTC found successful appraisal bureaus in many areas, it apparently found an equal number of cities in which they had failed.[66] And in perhaps a majority of areas bureaus were never established. The obstacles confronting dealers were many. Since there is much competition among different makes of cars, and since even a single manufacturer produces cars in several different price lines, to be fully effective such a plan must include an extraordinary majority of all dealers. Yet, although a bureau must have many dealers and must handle much traffic, in order to avoid antagonizing consumers as well as to avoid legal action, it must be kept secret.[67] Indeed, even its location was sometimes unknown by dealers, who knew only its post-office box and phone number and who identified themselves with symbols and code words.[68] The difficulty of imposing fines through a secret organization troubled some bureaus, and the cost involved caused the downfall of others. Yet another obstacle was the opposition of manufacturers. While some manufacturers on occasion did permit the organ-

[64] *Ibid.*, pp. 370, 372. The manager of one bureau stated that "the privilege of raising bids has never been abused by our dealers, as is proven by the fact that only 3 bids out of every 100 are raised." *Ibid.*, p. 384.

[65] *Ibid.*, p. 385.

[66] *Ibid.*, pp. 398–400.

[67] "The public resents a control plan of any type, and every effort should be made to keep the knowledge of its operation from the customer. When a prospect voices the opinion that the dealers are together on a plan, the best thing to do is deny all knowledge of such a plan." From the address of a bureau manager at an NADA convention, quoted in *ibid.*, p. 384.

[68] *Ibid.*, pp. 373, 376.

ization of bureaus performing limited services, most opposed all appraisal bureaus for fear of losing volume, sometimes implementing their opposition with threats of cancellation.[69] And no manufacturer could afford to risk public association of his name with a secret conspiracy to lower used-car allowances.[70] Other bureaus failed because their members could not resist the temptation to "chisel," which is not surprising in view of the trade's aggressively competitive tradition, the competition of used-car dealers, and the need to dispose of cars forced on dealers by manufacturers. Finally, the illegality of most plans was yet another obstacle. Some groups were prosecuted, and others disintegrated when dealers were unable to agree on whether to establish maximum allowances, which would clearly be illegal, or only to register bids, which would be less effective.

Dealers usually could not form sufficiently strong and cohesive organizations to overcome these obstacles. Nor were group efforts to improve vertical relationships any more successful. Manufacturers refused to discuss manufacturer-dealer relations with the NADA until adverse legislation confronted them in Wisconsin.[71] While the available evidence is sparse, it appears that this failure was partly due to difficulties similar to those which hampered the early labor movement — the diffi-

[60] E.g., see *ibid.*, pp. 317–318.

[70] E.g., see *ibid.*, pp. 377–378, for a letter from a Buick zone manager, addressed to all metropolitan (Philadelphia) dealers and marked "confidential": ". . . we received an anonymous prospect who said that he was informed that it would be unnecessary for him to try and secure a better price . . . inasmuch as used-car prices were controlled, and that the plan had the full backing of Buick Motor Co. He . . . inform[ed] us that he was fully acquainted with Federal and State laws regarding trade restraint. . . This is one of the many complaints that have come to us through 'loose tongues,' poor discretion and improper control of salesmen. In addition . . . two competitive companies are using the association's activities as a means of combating Buick competition. . . Therefore . . . you are hereby advised that the association is to disband, and its activities discontinued forthwith. The above decision has been arrived at reluctantly — but is final."

[71] Crosser Committee Hearing, pp. 105–106. And the president of the NADA complained that "year after year, the same appeals have been made to the manufacturers to revise their practices with dealers . . . but no real results have been obtained." *NADA Bulletin*, January 1940, p. 6.

culties of effective group organization among men who are at the economic mercy of powerful manufacturers favored by the legal rules.

Thus attempts at group action have had little success in the economic sphere and, as we shall see, but indifferent success in mobilizing the trade for consistent political action over any long period. This merits some explanation, for many factors making for successful group organization and action are present. Dealers are substantial merchants with annual sales many times that of a grocer or druggist.[72] In 1939 almost two fifths of them had an annual volume of over $100,000, while barely 1 per cent of independent druggists or grocers achieved this size. The connotations, in terms of the economic interests felt to be endangered and of the resources and abilities which can be mobilized, indicate the likelihood of effective group action. Cohesion would seem to be forced upon dealers by the rigors of intense competition and by the possession of common foes — the manufacturers.

Why, then, have they largely failed to form effective groups? Many factors play a part. The price of a car is such a large part of a consumer's budget that he shops around extensively and bargains vigorously.[73] The tradition of sharp price competition, in part the result of the difficulty of appraising used cars, is also relevant.[74] But a major cause, and one related more directly to my main strands of analysis, lies in dealers' relations with manufacturers, whose vertical power is both a spur and an obstacle to group formation and action by dealers. It is significant that the earliest successes of dealers' associations

[72] In 1939 the average dealer had sales of $143,000, as compared with $22,000 for the average independent druggist and $14,000 for the average independent grocer. *1939 Census of Business*, vol. I, part 1, p. 57; part 2, pp. 671–672.

[73] Yet the fact that so many dealers add packs or charge time payments above the competitive level indicates that this attentiveness to price does not extend to all elements of the purchase.

[74] Freedom of entry, too, contributes to the sharpness of price competition, but this factor is the direct result of a more basic one — manufacturers' vertical power.

were political rather than economic, for dealers and manufacturers at first shared common political goals, while their economic goals conflicted. Manufacturers usually opposed attempts to limit retail price competition, and their constant forcing of cars on dealers made it difficult for dealers to limit competition and still dispose of their stock.

It is hardly surprising that dealers turned to political weapons, for dealers' associations had been active politically as early as World War I, and associations had existed at local, state, and national levels since 1917. In that year the NADA had been founded by representatives of state and local associations who had assembled in Washington to lobby against a bill to tax automobiles. A few months later the NADA protested, and caused the revocation of, a War Industries Board order declaring the automotive industry nonessential and directing it to shift exclusively to war contracts.[75] In the early 1920's the NADA was active in legislation of interest to the whole trade, such as highway appropriations, motor vehicle theft laws, and petroleum tariffs.[76] In addition, many state and local associations were quite active in 1935 and 1936, when some state legislatures considered taxes affecting automobile sales.

What is significant about these activities is that the goals of dealers and manufacturers coincided. There is no evidence that manufacturers actually participated in the formation of the NADA, but most of them did not oppose it or its early activities.[77] That much coöperation in the pursuit of common goals occurred is shown by evidence that manufacturers frequently induced their dealers and dealers' associations to lobby for or against proposed state legislation much in the manner that a ward boss rounds up his vassals and shepherds them to the

[75] Christopher G. Sinsabaugh, *Who, Me? Forty Years of Automobile History* (Detroit: Arnold Powers, Inc.; 1940), pp. 226–227.

[76] See 1922 Convention address of the past president of the NADA. FTC, *Motor Vehicle Industry*, pp. 340–341.

[77] However, Ford, for most of its history a maverick among manufacturers, for example refusing to join the manufacturers' trade association, prohibited its dealers from joining retail trade association until the mid-1930's. *Ibid.*, p. 315.

polls. Their vertical power enabled them to control the political activities of many of their dealers and of some state and local associations. In other words, manufacturers used economic power to generate political power. A few examples will illustrate this use of power.

. . . I am inclined to think that house bill No. 318 . . . will be found dead at adjournment. . . The swift, aggressive and effective moves which the distributors, zone manager, and branch managers of the members of the Automobile Manufacturers' Association and of the Ford Motor Car Co. . . . have made with their dealers throughout the State generally, have been well nigh 100 percent thorough and correct. Without question, if all of the component elements of the motor vehicle industry . . . will predetermine . . . the problems which they must cope with in State legislation; find the correct answer for these problems . . . coach their distributors, zone managers, and branch managers thereon, and through them win the support of State and local dealer associations, powerful media can be built up in any State for protecting the automobile industry. . .[78]

At a meeting of the local association . . . one of the dealers present asked another member if he had received a letter from their factory urging affiliation with the State association. He had today received a very strong letter from the —— organization insisting on his taking his stand with the State association in its [legislative] efforts.[79]

Thus until the mid-1930's manufacturers had prevented dealers from organizing effectively to control competition or to change manufacturer–dealer relations but had encouraged them to organize for the pursuit of political goals. But manufacturers had sown the wind and would soon almost reap the whirlwind, for this political weapon could be turned against them.

If it was the manufacturers who taught dealers the art of political self-defense, it was General Hugh Johnson who offered them their first bout and their first major prize. Dealers quickly

[78] From report of manager of the legislative department of the Automobile Manufacturers' Association, quoted in *ibid.*, p. 67.

[79] From a letter of the secretary of a state association to a vice president of General Motors reporting on the success of the association in defeating a tax measure. *Ibid.*, p. 316.

took advantage of the political means offered them to gain relief from their economic woes. The depression, combined with intensified manufacturer pressure to accept cars, had produced cutthroat competition. Dealers' pressure for a code was so great, and their organization apparently so effective, that theirs was the first retail code adopted. The code had a twofold effect on dealer organization; dealers had to organize to obtain the code and had to maintain their organization to administer and enforce it. The NRA period was also the first time dealers and manufacturers had opposed each other politically. While dealers loved the NRA, manufacturers loathed it. The conflict, however, was not direct, for manufacturers' opposition was centered primarily on the NRA's labor provisions and not on the retail code.[80]

Immediately after the death of the NRA on May 27, 1935, dealers demanded a resurrection of the code and its Blue Book. President and Congress were "besieged by requests from motor-vehicle dealers and their trade organizations to put into effect a substitute plan." [81] The President passed the buck to the FTC, directing it to hold a trade practice conference. The NADA held preliminary meetings with the Commission, but it soon became obvious that under existing antitrust statutes the dealers could not here achieve their objectives, for they wished to fix or maintain prices, which was clearly illegal. On November 1, 1935, the FTC announced its disapproval of four out of the six rules proposed by the NADA because the rules "embodied an illegal price-fixing arrangement and would tend to unreasonably restrain trade in violation of Federal antitrust Laws, including the Federal Trade Commission Act." [82] After

[80] The almost daily verbal tilts between Hugh Johnson and Henry Ford will be remembered. For a brief account of manufacturers' opposition, see Kennedy, pp. 248–254.

[81] FTC, *Motor Vehicle Industry*, p. 367.

[82] *Ibid.*, p. 415. One of the proposed rules provided for resale price maintenance and another for the fixing of used-car allowances. The combined effect of these two rules, of course, would be to eliminate price competition.

this rebuff the dealers abandoned efforts to secure their goals by this method.

As we have seen, many dealers next turned to direct control of used-car allowances but met with only limited success. And, as we have also seen, direct dealings with manufacturers failed to ease the pressure on them to accept new cars. At this stage manufacturers gave dealers a final lesson in political tactics, inducing them to organize opposition to a wave of proposed state taxes which in 1935 and 1936 threatened to depress automobile sales. Thereupon the dealers applied this political weapon to their own uses in the last half of the decade and by 1944 had secured the passage of legislation regulating automobile sales in twenty-five states.[83] While clearly they wished to limit or end price competition, because of the necessity of broadening their particularistic programs to win outside support, all that they could win from most legislatures were dealer licensing to insure financial responsibility and the prohibition of such practices as turning back speedometers or adding packs to finance charges. These measures afforded the consumer some protection but limited price competition only indirectly.

In a few states dealers were more successful. By 1939 four states had passed laws whose major purpose was to protect dealers from competition.[84] These states license new- and used-car dealers, and a license may be revoked for "unfair trade practices." While many of the practices designated as unfair injure consumers, others harm only uncompetitive dealers. In Nebraska, for example, the "habitual" granting of "excessive" trade-in allowances is cause for denial, suspension, or revocation of a license. In Wisconsin dealers must justify above-average allowances to the Banking Commission, otherwise that agency may question whether they are "solvent" enough to

[83] *Business Week*, July 8, 1944, p. 90.

[84] Wisconsin, Ohio, Nebraska, and Iowa. Pennsylvania passed similar legislation, but the act had been held unconstitutional by a state court. FTC, *Motor Vehicle Industry*, p. 400. For summaries of these acts, see pp. 400–406.

merit a continuation of their licenses. Dealers have been frank in evaluating these laws.

The finest tribute to the banking commission's "solvency" plan is the fact that overallowances have been reduced from $25 to $75 over a year ago . . . this . . . means that Wisconsin, which will sell 50,000 new cars this year, will save $50 per car . . . which they otherwise would have passed on to new car purchasers. . . Overcrowding . . . is rapidly being eliminated . . . there are 500 less dealers in Wisconsin than a year ago and . . . replacement of such dealers is, in the vast majority of cases, being dispensed with. . . In addition, 110 applications were denied outright and 150 prospective dealers discouraged from entering business. In all, 760 competitors were eliminated.[85]

In addition, the laws of three states limited the power of manufacturers. Wisconsin forbids coercion of a dealer to accept unordered cars or parts and accessories, and three states prevent a manufacturer from forcing acceptance of a favored finance company. These legislative successes were gained over manufacturers' vigorous opposition, expressed both directly to legislators and through attempts to persuade dealers to cease their support.[86] This "persuasion" was exercised by the same factory representatives who "persuaded" dealers to accept overstocks of cars, parts, and accessories.

State regulation did not satisfy dealers, so they turned once again to the federal government. Not only were state and local associations too unorganized and weak to secure strong legislation in most states, but also even the strongest of state regulatory schemes could not fully protect dealers from manufacturers' power because of its interstate character.[87] It was the

[85] From an article by Louis Milan, Secretary of the Wisconsin Association, "Semi-Annual Report to Members, Wisconsin Automobile Trades Association," *Northern Automotive Journal*, July 1938, and quoted in FTC, *Motor Vehicle Industry*, pp. 405–406.

[86] *Ibid.*, pp. 67–70, 406–407. Since 1939 Rhode Island has enacted a law allowing contract cancellations to be appealed to, and reversed by, a state board. A. A. Berle, Jr., *20th Century Capitalist Revolution* (N. Y.: Harcourt, Brace and Co.; 1954), p. 81.

[87] The Wisconsin legislature's resolution which led to the Withrow Resolution noted that "some of this automobile manufacturer–automobile dealer relation-

Wisconsin dealers who enjoyed the fullest state protection, and yet it was they who led in pressing for federal action. The first stage in their campaign for federal aid was the Withrow Resolution, which directed the FTC "to investigate the policies employed by manufacturers in distributing motor vehicles, accessories, and parts, and the policies of dealers in selling motor vehicles at retail, as these policies affect the public interest." [88] This resolution was first introduced in the House by Representative Gardiner R. Withrow, of Wisconsin, and then in the Senate by Senator Sherman Minton, of Indiana, in response to resolutions of the legislatures of those two states. Withrow's speech on the House floor supporting his resolution and the committee hearings on it make it clear that the NADA was the major force behind the resolution, perhaps aided by independent finance companies.[89] Wisconsin was the obvious starting point, for it was here that the NADA was strongest.[90] While the resolution directed the FTC to investigate both manufacturer–dealer relations and dealers' retail policies, the NADA wished primarily to attack manufacturers' power and to investigate dealers only in order to show that unfair and deceptive retail trade practices resulted from manufacturers' abuse of their power.[91]

---

ship, because of its interstate character, is beyond the direct control of . . . the State of Wisconsin. . . ." *Cong. Record*, vol. 81, part 5, p. 5744. See also testimony of H. H. Roberts, attorney for the NADA, Crosser Committee Hearings, pp. 74, 78.

[88] Public Resolution No. 87, 75th Cong.

[89] *Cong. Record*, vol. 81, part 5, pp. 5744–5747.

[90] In 1938 slightly more than one fourth of the Association's members came from this single state, 85 per cent of its new-car dealers being members of the NADA, as compared with a national average of only 14 per cent. Membership totals for 1938 from FTC, *Motor Vehicle Industry*, p. 337, and 1939 new-car dealer statistics from *1939 Census of Business*, vol. I, part 1, pp. 58, 189, 323.

[91] The Wisconsin Resolution declared that "Whereas . . . automobile factory–automobile dealer relations [are] responsible for many of the existing unethical cutthroat competitive practices so harmful to the consuming public. . ." (*Cong. Record*, vol. 81, part 5, p. 5744). And A. N. Benson, NADA general manager, testified that "There is in existence a sales arrangement . . . commonly known as a contract, but which is more generally considered to be a franchise or right to sell. Probably all of the difficulties in the retail branch of the auto-

Only dealers and manufacturers appeared before the House subcommittee which held hearings on the resolution. NADA spokesmen contributed most of the testimony and exhibits, and manufacturers found such an unsympathetic audience [92] that their opposition was weakly stated, most of their time being devoted to a rebuttal of charges that they had abused their power. The dealers, on the other hand, found a receptive and sympathetic audience.[93] Representative Withrow had predicted that the hearings would produce "the most pitiful tales of coercion, of high-pressuring on the part of the automobile manufacturers," [94] and the testimony of NADA officials and letters from dealers lived up to this advance billing. Alleging that, because of manufacturers' forcing of cars, annual mortality rates were about 25 per cent,[95] their complaints were similar to those quoted earlier in this chapter, although their language gained in color and vigor by not having been sifted through the FTC's staff.

Some large manufacturers keep their dealers practically insolvent living up to their demands for pushing sales, and the conditions are on the verge of peonage instead of simple coercion.[96]

If you cannot make a living selling the cars they say you can sell they just get another "sucker" and he stays in for a year or less and goes out. . . I do not believe that Al Capone is any worse than the factories . . . and yet they put Capone in jail. I have over $25,000 invested in a business to make a scant living, and as we say in the

---

mobile industry stem from this arrangement. . ." (Crosser Committee Hearings, pp. 6–7).

[92] See, for example, the chilly reception accorded the remarks of Alvan Macauley, President of the Automobile Manufacturers' Association. Crosser Committee Hearings, pp. 41–46.

[93] Dealer support was not unanimous. Communications from some dealers and from one state dealers' association opposed the resolution. It appears, however, that in this one association, the Michigan Automotive Trade Association, whose officials opposed the resolution, the bulk of the membership may have actually supported it. *Ibid.*, pp. 63, 80.

[94] *Ibid.*, p. 3.

[95] *Ibid.*, pp. 3, 10.

[96] Letter from a Ford dealer. *Ibid.*, p. 82.

West, "I just have a bear by the tail." If I let go I get it now, and if I hang on it will just be a slow process of weakening. . .[97]

Since there was no floor debate, the hearing is virtually the whole legislative history of the resolution. Introduced by Representative Withrow on June 1, 1937 and having been the subject of House hearings in December, 1937, and January, 1938, it was reintroduced on February 10, 1938, passed by both Houses in short order, and signed by the President on April 13, 1938.

The NADA had been successful in the first stage of its campaign. But, if its ultimate purpose in securing an investigation was legislation to redress the balance between manufacturer and dealer, it was doomed to disappointment. The FTC conducted a fairly thorough and extensive investigation, submitting a 1077-page report to Congress on June 5, 1939.[98] This report described the operations and history of the manufacturers, manufacturer–dealer relations, competition, and trade practices. Its conclusions and recommendations disappointed the dealers, who had hoped that the Commission would find that manufacturer–dealer relations were marked by an inequitable manufacturer dominance which was responsible for whatever unfair retail trade practices existed. The FTC did find that the manufacturers possessed great vertical power — enough, in fact, to enable them to impose "unfair and inequitable conditions of trade" on dealers — [99] but it also found that

[97] Letter from a dealer in California. *Ibid.*, p. 83.

[98] FTC, *Motor Vehicle Industry*.

[99] "The Commission finds that motor-vehicle manufacturers . . . by reason of their great power . . . have been, and still are, imposing on their respective dealers unfair and inequitable conditions of trade, by requiring such dealers to accept, and operate under, agreements that inadequately define the rights and obligations of the parties and are, moreover, objectionable in respect to defect of mutuality; that some dealers, in fact report that they have been subjected to rigid inspections of premises and accounts, and to arbitrary requirements by their respective . . . manufacturers to accept for resale quantities of motor vehicles or other goods, deemed excessive by the dealer, or to make investments in operating plants or equipment without adequate guaranty as to term of agreement or even supply of merchandise; and that adequate provisions are

this power was used in furtherance of vigorous competition, and that, despite their great size and power, manufacturers were innocent of price-fixing or other monopolistic restraints commonly associated with great size and power. Their competition, although among but few firms, had been creative and socially desirable.

Active competition among automobile manufacturers, although some of them have made very large profits, gave to the public improved products, often at substantially reduced prices. . . Such competition has been the basis for the remarkable growth of the industry. *Consumer benefits from competition in the automobile-manufacturing industry have probably been more substantial than in any other large industry studied by the Commission.*[100]

Probably as a result of this finding that great size was not incompatible with effective competition, the Commission recommended only moderate limits on the vertical power which was a concomitant of this size.

It is recommended that present unfair practices be abated to the end that dealers have (a) less restriction upon the management of their own enterprises; (b) quota requirements and shipments of cars based upon mutual agreement; (c) equitable liquidation in the event of contract termination by the manufacturer; (d) contracts definite as to the mutual rights and obligations of the manufacturers and the dealers, including specific provision that the contract will be continued for a definite term unless terminated by breach of reasonable conditions recited therein.[101]

Not only did the FTC disappoint the dealers by heaping such praise and only mild condemnation on the manufacturers, it also attacked the attackers. While it found that "the retail motor vehicle trade is competitive in the sense that the individual dealer generally pushes actively the sale . . . of motor vehicles . . . and that the prices thereof . . . though quite

---

not included for an equitable method of liquidation of such investment. . ." *Ibid.*, pp. 1075–1076.

[100] *Ibid.*, p. 1074. (My italics.)

[101] *Ibid.*, p. 1076.

generally adhered to in appearance, are frequently cut by allowances for used cars," [102] it also found that dealers had often seriously limited competition.

> The Commission finds that local associations of motor-vehicle dealers . . . have engaged in the following practices to fix or maintain prices: (1) Fixing minimum prices on new cars, often by means of uniform maximum discounts from the manufacturer resale prices in transactions where no trade-ins are involved; (2) establishing maximum purchase prices, or allowances, for used cars taken in trade; (3) regulating bidding on used cars taken in trade by means of uniform price increases on all bids subsequent to the original bids to be less than the original bid; and (4) adopting published used-car price guides as a basis for maximum allowances for used cars. . . The Commission found that many local associations operate used-car valuation or appraisal bureaus that are essentially combinations of dealers . . . to restrict competition in used-car trading.[103]

Furthermore, the FTC specifically attacked many retail practices but did not directly attribute them to problems of manufacturer dominance. It condemned, for example, the padding of new-car prices, the packing of finance charges, the sale of driven cars as new cars, and called for itemized invoices. It then turned, in a final act of either administrative integrity or political naïveté, on the other group which had probably pressed for this investigation — the independent finance companies. While it attacked General Motors for deceptive advertising of its so-called six per cent plan (actually involving a charge of about 11 per cent), it admitted that "this plan constituted a substantial reduction from the rates of finance charge and interest that were in general use just previously." [104] But it severely criticized the independent finance companies.

> . . . in the methods employed by some of the companies engaged in financing the purchase of a new motor vehicle, serious abuses have developed, not only in permitting dealers to impose exorbitant

[102] *Ibid.*, p. 1074.
[103] *Ibid.*, pp. 1074–1075.
[104] *Ibid.*, p. 1076.

charges but also in serious deception, or even direct defraudation, of the purchaser. . . The more serious deceptions have been engaged in generally by the dealer, often in connivance with a finance company. The practices here referred to relate to the so-called "packs" (padding), which are additions made, for no extra service, by the dealer to the regular finance charges provided in the finance-company's minimum-rate chart; and certain finance companies provided their dealers with the instrumentalities for such deceptions by furnishing them with two or more rate charts based on different rates of charge.[105]

Thus the dealers had badly misgauged the results of an investigation. The FTC did find abuse of vertical power, but it found more to criticize in the activities of dealers. If it was the dealers' expectation that the investigation would lead to legislation limiting manufacturers' power and retail competition — and testimony before the Crosser Committee indicates that it was — then their campaign was a total failure. No legislation resulted. The Commission's value assumptions identified the public interest primarily with the consumer's interest and the absence of excessive deception, fraud, and power. Analysis and recommendations proceeding from these assumptions naturally differed from those of the dealers, who operated from assumptions which postulated their economic interests as basic goals.

A more fundamental reason for the dealers' failure to gain federal legislation was their inability after the NRA to achieve unity either in organization or in purpose. The NADA has never enrolled more than a small proportion of all dealers. Even in 1938, shortly after it had secured passage of the Withrow Resolution, its membership was only 4518 or only one seventh of all new-car dealers.[106] On a programmatic level the NADA has been even less successful in creating unity and

---

[105] Loc. cit.

[106] Ibid., p. 337. In 1939 there were 31,571 new-car dealers. 1939 Census of Business, vol. I, part 1, p. 58. Even this fraction overstates their organizational success, for there were also 6980 used-car dealers, 1170 motor vehicles and farm implement dealers, and 928 dealers who sold new cars at both wholesale and retail — all of whom were eligible for membership.

cohesion. At the height of its campaign for federal legislation in 1940 the NADA complained of an "apathy . . . [which] reveals how difficult it is to secure majority action on any program designed to change conditions within the industry." [107] Indeed, that the immediate goal of the NADA was investigation rather than legislation indicates its inability to agree on a program. Its spokesmen at several points in the Congressional hearings revealed their uncertainties about corrective measures. Their major emphasis was on the need to restrict manufacturers' power,[108] but they were eloquently silent about methods. A theme which recurred frequently throughout their testimony was a desire for milder, more regulated competition on the model of the NRA codes. A dealer's letter stated that

I sincerely hope our legislators will find means to outlaw the doctrine of war-like, unregulated, ruthless competition and to make lawful a profit system which rests on regulated sportsmanlike, fair competition. This tyranny of rugged individualism must yield to lawful, democratic methods in business. Regulation may cramp the style and initiative of the present school of business on its way to monopoly, but I hope for rules in the game. . .[109]

There was confusion, however, over the extent to which competition should be limited. Some proposals clearly contemplated governmental price regulation, and uniform prices had been the purpose of some state legislation. Yet the NADA stated its opposition to federal approval of price fixing only one month after its official publication had seemed to call for federal regulation.[110] Licensing dealers with certificates of convenience and

[107] *NADA Bulletin*, April 1940, p. 2.

[108] E.g., the statement of NADA Attorney Roberts in Crosser Committee Hearings, p. 76: "I would have the Federal law provide against coercion of dealers by manufacturers; and provide against unfair contracts; provide against overloading in finance charges and against forcing dealers to do the things they do not want to do, forcing them to take cars that they do not want to take and against being forced to buy parts and supplies of the manufacturer when they do not want them, cannot use them."

[109] Letter from a Connecticut dealer. *Ibid.*, p. 99.

[110] "We do not, as to [sic] a national body, approve of anything that attempts to fix price. This is what the States are doing." Statement of NADA Attorney Roberts, *ibid.*, p. 76. But the *NADA Bulletin* (November 1937, p. 16)

necessity was suggested by two spokesmen, who also seemed to advocate public utility regulation.[111] Territorial monopolies were also suggested.[112] In short, the dealers had failed to agree on a program.

This weakness in organization and program was further demonstrated in the next year. Representative Wright Patman of Texas, who in the late 1930's had championed small distributors against large corporations, promised the NADA to introduce and push a bill which the dealers hoped would be the Motor Vehicle Act of 1940, but the dealers were unable to agree on the bill's content. At a national convention in January, 1940, a proposed bill was presented and debated. It called for FTC regulation of dealer contracts and sharply limited manufacturers' cancellation powers. Dealers present were badly split on the bill, many fearing that regulation of manufacturers would lead to regulation of dealers.[113] Before having it dropped into the Congressional hopper, the Association submitted it to a referendum in which all dealers were asked to participate. Only about one fourth of the dealers voted on the proposal — and rejected it decisively.[114]

An important reason for this failure lay in dealers' operative ideals which have inhibited their political efforts. Although their horizontal and vertical relations seem to force on them a

had commented that ". . . we have seen the erection of many Federal Commissions to supervise and control industries that have proved incapable of self-regulation. Witness the Guffey Coal Commission, the Securities Exchange Commission. . . Will there have to be an Automobile Commission created by the Congress to regulate this industry and compel the adoption of policies more in harmony with the times?"

[111] See testimony of NADA Attorney Roberts and Representative Withrow, Crosser Committee Hearings, pp. 117–118, 131.

[112] "The present arrangement permits the automobile dealer to sell a car any place in America, but the dealers believe that if they were assigned a definite territory in which they could sell in [sic] and if another dealer could not come in that territory to sell that that would solve a great many of the difficulties that now exist in the business." Testimony of A. N. Benson, NADA general manager, ibid., p. 20.

[113] NADA Bulletin, February 1940, pp. 1–3, 12–17.

[114] Ibid., April 1940, p. 2.

common recognition of the possibility of improving their position by political means, dealers have been reluctant to press for legislation. Even in late 1938 a great majority preferred an industry conference to legislative action as a means of changing manufacturer–dealer relations.[115] This same preference for non-political means has often, but not always, been shared by NADA officials.

Although the FTC's investigation led to no legislation, the public attention it focused had considerable effect on factory–dealer relations. Repeatedly, indeed almost invariably, the FTC's replies from dealers showed that their relations with manufacturers had improved greatly during 1938. Outright threats of cancellation virtually disappeared, and less direct pressures, too, lessened substantially. In an attempt to protect dealers from excessive pressures by factory representatives who were more zealous in pushing cars on dealers than their home offices wished them to be, General Motors established a dealer relations board to review complaints by canceled or otherwise aggrieved dealers.[116] Most manufacturer–dealer contracts were substantially revised in 1938 and 1939 to improve in a number of minor ways the position of the retailers. The combined effect of these changes was to limit the possibility of abusing manufacturers' vertical power. The notice required for cancellation was extended from 10 or 15 days to 60 or 90 days; provisions were made for the repurchase of a canceled dealer's cars, accessories, parts, and tools and for meeting some of his rental commitments; and greater territorial protection was granted.[117] In short, the dealers had utilized the publicizing powers of Congress and the FTC.

The fact that publicity was sufficient to cause manufacturers to alter their dealer policies should not lead us to exaggerate

[115] When asked which procedures should be employed in bringing about these changes, 79.7 per cent designated the conference table and only 31.9 per cent state or federal legislation. *Ibid.*, October 1938, p. 12.

[116] FTC, *Motor Vehicle Industry*, p. 176.

[117] *Ibid.*, pp. 118–120, 124–128.

the force of this weapon. Four days of hearings before a small Congressional subcommittee are quickly forgotten, and, despite the hope of the FTC's creators that it would master the use of "pitiless publicity," its reports have never been bestsellers. Then the ability of such a puny force to reverse manufacturers' policies indicates the nature of their power. Although great size gives them power, it also makes them sensitive to public opinion, especially since their products are sold to household consumers. The same size that generates power makes publicity a more effective regulatory instrument. In addition, the success of this small dose of publicity — as well as the fact that such minor contract changes signified a major reduction in abuse of manufacturers' power — impresses upon us once again the great truth that power is a two-sided relationship involving consent as well as constraint. Evidently manufacturers' scales of judgment were already almost evenly balanced between a desire to maintain or increase sales by forcing cars on dealers and a desire not to push dealers too hard lest they shift to other manufacturers, retire, or go bankrupt. Faced with an abundant supply of existing or would-be dealers, a manufacturer wishes to push his dealers hard enough to eliminate the less fit and to keep them lean and hungry enough to compete vigorously, but he does not want to convert their hunger into rapacity or starvation. While he possesses great power over his dealers, he is also dependent on them and cannot afford to lose large numbers of them. Bad publicity, then, was sufficient to alter the balance between these two opposing tendencies, or to cause manufacturers to increase their valuation of dealer good will.[118]

---

[118] Manufacturers had been aware for some time of the dangers of abusing their vertical power. See, for example, the statement of Alfred G. Sloan, then president of General Motors, on July 29, 1925 (as quoted in *ibid.*, p. 174): "I know of instances where General Motors dealers have just before the close of the season been forced to take quantities of cars that they couldn't possibly sell except at a loss. . . The time has passed when we can look upon our own profit and loss as a measure of our success. We must consider the dealer, because whenever he must incur such a loss it is a debit against our good-will account, which is the most valuable asset we have. Contrary to what some of

The two-sidedness of the power relationship is also shown in the answers the FTC received from dealers. The latter, especially when enjoying some degree of territorial monopoly, tend to exaggerate a power which forces them to pursue a net profit the hard way — thin margins on many sales rather than fatter margins on fewer and easier sales. Yet, although protected by anonymity, many dealers admitted that they had been able to resist manufacturer pressures, some said that they had been subjected to no pressure, and a few said that they had been forced by manufacturers to expand their stock or plant but had found the expansion profitable. Indeed, one of the surprising features of the FTC's report is that, despite the many examples of pressure described by dealers, less than half said that they had ever been overstocked with new cars.[119] In 1939, although contracts had been changed in only minor ways, manufacturers' power was so much more gently used that very few dealers reported that they had had to take overstocks.[120]

That vertical power is limited by its very nature as a two-sided relationship, however, does not guarantee that its exercise is in the public interest. Even limited power may be abused. This was not generally true in automobile distribution, although there were many specific examples of abuse. In terms of the two groups directly concerned, there are two criteria of the public interest. While there is no public interest in protecting any one dealer or group of dealers, there is an interest in

us may have assumed in the past, it is not a smart thing for us to overload the dealer at the expense of his profit."

[119] Ford evidently had been the most aggressive of the manufacturers. Fifty-two per cent of the Ford dealers reporting to the Commission said that they had been overstocked before 1938. Only 28 per cent of the General Motors dealers and 23 per cent of the Chrysler dealers made the same complaint. *Ibid.*, p. 194. Since a dealership in the lines of one of these three major producers is usually more valuable than one with a lesser manufacturer, and so engenders more power, it is unlikely that other dealers were overstocked to even this degree.

[120] Six per cent of all reporting General Motors dealers, only 2 per cent of Chrysler dealers, and less than 1 per cent of Ford dealers so reported. *Ibid.*, p. 194.

some stability in the channels of trade. Excessive stability hampers economic progress, but excessive instability severely strains the social fabric.[121] Mobility, turnover, and change are desirable, but their benefits do not extend to their extreme forms. Furthermore, in a trade where entry involves substantial investment, excessive turnover will not contribute to efficiency even in the narrowest of senses. Judged on this criterion, manufacturers' power has not produced results which indicate consistent abuse. Although dealers claimed that their mortality rates averaged between 17 per cent and 25 per cent,[122] their evidence was unconvincing. General Motors, on the other hand, showed that the turnover rate among its dealers averaged 11 per cent annually for the years 1933–1937. This is not a low rate, but it is not unusually high for a period of financial stress in which, for example, several automobile manufacturers went bankrupt. Moreover, it includes all dealer changes, many of which resulted from causes other than business failure or contract cancellation.[123]

The second criterion of the public interest can be roughly applied by examining profit ratios. If manufacturers' power had been abused during the nineteen-thirties, it would have unduly depressed returns on retailers' investments and unduly raised them on manufacturers' investments. But the FTC found that in the period 1935–1937 dealers averaged a net rate of return of from 12 per cent to 15 per cent on their invest-

[121] Cf. Elton Mayo. Also one can agree with Polanyi's argument that an excessively free market so rends all the social ties as to produce demands for the imposition of monolithic social unity, without accepting his overstatement of this theme. Karl Polanyi, *Origins of Our Time: The Great Transformation* (London: Victor Gollancz; 1945).

[122] Crosser Committee Hearings, p. 10.

[123] General Motors listed eleven causes of changes in dealerships but did not specify the proportion of changes attributable to each cause. The causes listed were: death of dealer, change in firm name, disagreement among partners or stockholders of a dealership, change in location of dealership, move to take on a larger dealership in same city or another city, voluntary withdrawal to take a franchise with another manufacturer, voluntary retirement, business failure, and cancellation. *Ibid.*, p. 167.

ment.[124] While these averages are computed from individual dealers whose rates of return cover a broad range — about one fifth of them showing a loss — they do not suggest general exploitation. It is difficult to compare these returns with those of manufacturers because the latter vary extremely. In 1935, for example, while Chrysler made a staggering profit of 45.93 per cent on its motor vehicle investment, Ford made only 2.20 per cent, and Nash showed a loss of 15.65 per cent.[125]

While variation in manufacturing profits was so wide that no typical relationship can be demonstrated, the average rate of return on the domestic motor vehicle manufacturing investment of the three major and four minor manufacturers in the same period was almost twice as great as that on dealers' investments. It was 20.39 per cent in 1935, 28.82 per cent in 1936, and 19.92 per cent in 1937.[126] This is a high return but perhaps not excessive compensation for the risks involved — a rate of return computed for the whole industry should take into account the several dozen companies which failed in the two previous decades — and for the great gains in productivity achieved. The manufacturing end of the distributive chain was, in general, the more profitable, but dealers enjoyed a profit that was adequate and above the average for retailers.

Thus manufacturers' power was limited and had not been generally abused. But the very existence of power and the problems raised by its existence lie at the core of the interrelationships of politics and economics and deserve some discussion. It is because there is a mixture of the political and the

[124] On their total investment in the retail motor vehicle business (including borrowed capital), over 300 dealers in 45 states showed an average rate of return of 9.49 per cent in 1935, 14.74 per cent in 1936, and 12.64 per cent in 1937. When the return is computed only on their own investment, rates are higher, amounting to 10.75 per cent, 19.27 per cent, and 16.44 per cent. The average rates of return of distributors (selling at both retail and wholesale) were of about the same order. *Ibid.*, p. 827.

[125] *Ibid.*, pp. 567, 671, 703.

[126] *Ibid.*, pp. 491, 493, 567, 672, 680, 703, 753, 809, 827. The four minor companies included are Nash, Hudson, Packard, and Studebaker.

economic that there is confusion about the criteria for public policy. Were real markets like those postulated by classical economic theory, then power would play no part. Our criteria would be purely economic, except for the standard of "fairness," which still serves as a general criterion for regulatory policy. This standard, fairly simple in principle and hoary with age, attacks fraud, deception, and predatory practices with the dual purpose of protecting people from acts which are considered immoral on noneconomic grounds and of facilitating economic processes by enabling all participants to rely on the observance of certain standards of conduct by all other participants. The application of this standard to marginal practices is often uncertain, and its precise definition may change, but its general nature is clear.[127] Manufacturers, while not guiltless, score higher than dealers by this standard. They have done some deceptive advertising and until 1938 possibly practised some deception in the wording of contracts; but dealers sinned more, padding prices, packing finance charges, selling driven cars as new cars, altering speedometers, and rigging bids on used cars. Consequently, if regulation of trade practices is required — and it probably is — it is dealers' practices that most need regulation.

It is the other criteria that are troublesome. The general policy, of course, is to promote competition and attack monopoly. The problem is to establish standards of competition. Dean Edward S. Mason has shown that the Supreme Court in its recent interpretations of the Sherman Act appears to be using two different criteria — the market structure and business performance tests.[128] One identifies competition with the results of market operations or with the performance of business firms.

[127] The leading works are Watkins; John Perry Miller, *Unfair Competition; A Study in the Criteria for the Control of Trade Practices* (Cambridge, Mass.: Harvard University Press; 1941); and Milton Handler, "Unfair Competition," *Readings in the Social Control of Industry* (Philadelphia: Blakiston; 1942), pp. 76–180.

[128] "Current Status of the Monopoly Problem in the United States," *Harvard Law Review*, June 1949, pp. 1265–1285.

It equates competition with those results and that performance which were believed to characterize the perfect market of classical theory.[129] The other — the market structure test — identifies competition with those market situations which set "severe limits to the power or control exercised by the individual firm." It requires, "principally, a fairly large number of sellers and buyers, no one of whom occupies a large share of the market, the absence of collusion among either group, and the possibility of market entry by new firms." [130] Mason then points out that these two criteria often conflict.[131] A market situation may be acceptable under one standard but unacceptable under the other. While these two standards cannot be completely reconciled, neither can be completely ignored; they "must be used to complement rather than to exclude each other." [132]

Their joint use raises some problems which must be solved before they can be applied to automobile distribution. The performance test can be readily applied. By this standard automobile manufacturers scored higher marks than any other large industry studied by the FTC.[133] Their performance has been highly competitive, leading to great increases in productivity, with most of the resultant benefits being passed on to the consumer in the form of improved product and, until recently,

[129] Mason includes as examples of desirable behavior which would indicate satisfactory performance the following: "an unremitting pressure for product and process improvement, downward adjustment of prices concomitant with substantial reductions in costs, concentration of production in units of the most efficient size, neither larger nor smaller than those required for low-cost operation, and efficient adjustment of capacity to output, and the avoidance of a waste of resources in selling activities." *Ibid.*, p. 1268.

[130] *Ibid.*, pp. 1266, 1268.

[131] E.g., Mason cites the National Lead Case (*U.S. v. National Lead Co.*, 332 U. S. 319 [1946]) as one in which the Court found monopoly, or oligopoly, in terms of the market structure test, but refused to split the industry's two major companies because it felt that, in terms of the business performance test, the industry had been highly competitive. *Ibid.*, p. 1276.

[132] *Ibid.*, p. 1280.

[133] "Consumer benefits from competition in the automobile-manufacturing industry have probably been more substantial than in any other large industry studied by the Commission." FTC, *Motor Vehicle Industry*, p. 1074.

lower prices.[134] The dealers do not score as high. Were it not for manufacturers' pressure and the fear of antitrust prosecution, dealers would wage much less vigorous competition, emphasizing factors other than price and retaining a larger margin. The postwar shortage of cars showed how dealers operate in less competitive markets, increasing real retail margins by making used-car *under*-allowances, demanding under-the-table payments, and attaching unordered, high-margin parts and accessories.

It is the market structure test which is the stumbling block. It is difficult to apply the business performance test to concrete situations; the formulation and application of precise standards of acceptable performance are difficult tasks. But it is the market structure test which betrays the greatest analytical confusion. Even Mason's penetrating and provocative analysis does not completely avoid this confusion, which arises from the inclusion of diverse and unrelated factors. In addition to ease of entry, this test requires a market to have a fairly large number of buyers and sellers, no one of whom commands a large share of the market, and an absence of collusion. But there is no necessary correlation between size and/or number and collusion. Manufacturers, although so few in number and so great in size as to violate the first part of this test, were guilty of no collusion and engaged in little significant joint action. Yet metropolitan dealers were great enough in number and small enough in relative size to meet the first part of this test, while they often engaged in collusive joint action and so violated the second part of this test. There is conflict within this standard as well as between the two tests. The solution lies in the fact that it is power which differentiates actual markets from those posited by classical economic theory. Power over market participants, or control of market operations, can result either

[134] The FTC demonstrated this in a number of ways: e.g., demonstrating steady decreases in prices per pound of automobile and in prices per maximum brake horsepower, and describing many product improvements which had accompanied overall price decreases. *Ibid.*, pp. 892–919.

from a situation in which a single participant is sufficiently large in relative size or from a situation in which many small buyers or sellers collusively act together. Power, then, is the essence of the market structure test.[135]

Now much of the difficulty of reconciling the two standards disappears. The business performance standard is a purely economic one. "From the point of view of economic policy, competition is supposedly desirable, not as an end in itself, but for the results that are expected to follow from it." [136] But, power may be feared *per se*, or it may be evaluated by its consequences, or by its intent.[137] It may be opposed on economic grounds on the argument that each injection of power into a market is by definition anticompetitive since competition is visualized in terms of the classical ideal. This is the major economic argument for a structural standard, although it is often really based on other than economic reasons. Power may also be attacked for political and social reasons. As we shall see in dealing with chain taxes and the Robinson-Patman Act, many who define competition in terms of the market structure test and who equate competition with the continued existence of small firms do so for social rather than economic reasons. Because of a failure to realize that market power can result from the collusion of many competitors as well as from size

[135] Under this interpretation it is necessary to alter Mason's definition but slightly. His, it will be remembered, held that ". . . competition is . . . a type of market organization setting severe limits to the power or control exercised by the individual firm." (Mason, p. 1266) I suggest that workable competition, in terms of market structure, exists when there are severe limits on the power or control exercised by a firm or a group of firms.

[136] Mason, pp. 1266–1267.

[137] By its *intent*, as well as by its consequences, because I agree with Kahn's criticism of Mason's analysis. (Alfred E. Kahn, "Standards for Antitrust Policy," *Harvard Law Review*, November 1953.) Kahn shows that in view of the difficulties of establishing clear criteria of acceptable performance and because "a progressive and efficient company may . . . violate the law in ways which contribute little or not at all to its good performance," while "market power and economic consequences must be considered," the "relevant consequences . . . are . . . the mutual suppression of rivalry or the unfair exclusion or threatened exclusion of competitors." Kahn, pp. 42, 54.

or from fewness in number, the market test is often turned into a simple attack on bigness.

This fear of power is part of an honorable tradition. It is the same fear of concentrated power and desire for individual independence which motivated the framers of the Constitution and the authors of the Bill of Rights to restrain governmental powers and guarantee certain specific liberties. It is part of a social philosophy and structure which tolerates greater individualism and social mobility than do most. And it is in part a product of an environment which permitted much individual initiative in economic matters. But today, especially in economic relationships, power plays an increasingly important role. Where once the family was often largely self-sufficient, now we are dependent on others. A coal strike in Pennsylvania and West Virginia can close schools in New England and automobile plants in Detroit. A North Dakota wheat grower's income may depend on what traders do in Chicago or what Congressmen and statisticians do in Washington. With these interrelations also arises organization. And this organization, in turn, whether it be the control of many different economic activities by a single corporation or the political and/or economic organization of smaller economic units sharing common goals, breeds power. The problem of public policy is to limit power and to evaluate its consequences. It may well be that some organizations — corporations or labor unions, for example — have gained such size and so much power that the base for this power, the organization itself, should be split up, regardless of how the power has actually been used. The argument would be that its very existence endangers other groups and challenges the authority of the government. In such a case, the criterion of size might well conflict with that of business performance, but this problem is beyond the scope of our study.

If power is inevitable, reconciling Mason's two standards is much easier. When economic values are considered, the structural test is secondary. It is the results which are valued as ends, and structure is only a means of effectuating these ends. Or, if we accept Kahn's analysis, then only that power is attacked which is used in attempts to suppress competition by collusion or exclusion.[138] Not all exercises of power are acceptable, and certain forms of power — such as collusive agreements on price — may usually have undesirable results, but market power is not inherently undesirable. Even agreements literally restraining trade may be acceptable: e.g., an agreement by competing stores on common hours of business. Thus an economic rule of reason is applied to market power. Power is examined in light of its consequences and intent, and structural tests are used only in terms of the probable or proven consequences of certain forms of power.

Applying these criteria, manufacturers pass the performance test with high grades. Dealers' performance is harder to assess because their function is the rendering of services. In general, their low net profit per car during the 1930's indicates that their charges for these services were reasonable, due to retail competition and to manufacturers' power used in pursuance of competition among manufacturers. There is an interesting relation between manufacturers' vertical power and retailers' performance. A weak use of power leads to a relaxing of competition, increases in real retail margins, and hence a lowering of business performance. An excessive use of power, on the other hand, causes dealers to resort either to deceptive and fraudulent practices or to secret conspiracies to avoid competition, thus also lowering performance.

Thus competition is economically acceptable when it is "effective": i.e., produces results that are economically valued. But for behavior and performance to be competitive there must be opportunities for meaningful choice. Size and fewness in number are not attacked unless they interfere with this choice. The same is true of agreements. This coincides well with the

---

[138] "Mere unexercised power to exclude . . . [and] mere power to influence price . . . should remain free from condemnation." Kahn, p. 54.

standards dictated by social and political values. Since power cannot be avoided in an interdependent and integrated community, then the obvious answer is to check and restrain this power. But this corresponds closely to what effective competition does. Just as a perfectly competitive market would eradicate all power, so an effectively competitive market limits and checks power. It approximates an economic translation of the political theory that individual liberties can be preserved through a separation of power in which the power of one agency checks and balances that of other agencies. Effective horizontal or intertype competition checks the power of individual firms, and, with meaningful freedom of choice, vertical power may check other vertical power. In short, there is high correlation between the economic and the political criteria.

The automobile trade illustrates this correlation. While the Big Three, especially General Motors, may be larger than necessary to achieve economies of scale in production, management, and marketing, nevertheless it takes great size to manufacture and market most efficiently a product as complicated and expensive as an automobile. The postwar experience of Kaiser-Frazer shows that profitable operations require great size. Power necessarily accompanies this size, and were the vertical power of manufacturers less, as it was in the years immediately after World War II, then greater power would be exercised by retailers. Manufacturers' power is limited by their competition for dealers. Horizontal competition among manufacturers adds to the vertical power of dealers, just as competition among dealers for a franchise increases the power of manufacturers. Consequently, so long as the conditions do approximate those of a market and there is some real freedom of choice among dealers, manufacturers' power is limited. Of course, much of a dealer's freedom of action disappeared in the thirties, when opportunities for alternative employment of services and capital were radically diminished. This added to a manufacturer's power, but the cause, and proper object of criticism and correction, was the general economic distress of the times, not the power thereby produced.

Yet, as we have seen, this power can be abused. Once a dealer has committed his capital and has built up good will associating his firm's name with that of his manufacturer, he is not a free agent and cannot freely shift his services and capital. The relationship is no longer one of the market, and abuse of power can occur and did occur under the contracts made before 1938. But even then manufacturers' power was subject to many restraints. A general policy of pushing his power to extremes will decimate a manufacturer's sales force and tends, as developments in the 1930's showed, to cause the organization of counterpower. It led the dealers to try to organize, although in the main unsuccessfully, controls over retail competition. It also caused them to organize politically. These attempts had only moderate success but were sufficient, in combination with other factors, to reverse manufacturers' policies.

Our final conclusions have to do with other aspects of the interrelations of economics and politics, which we have seen to be most intimate and intricate. Indeed, the dividing line is often hard to draw. We have found power and organization throughout this field. Power and organization are the subject matter of politics, and yet we have found them in an economic background and directing economic functions. In other words, to the extent that the conditions of a market are lacking, a private government regulates economic operations. This is obviously true within a giant corporation; it is also private government of retail competition that some dealer groups tried to create — one patterned after the semiprivate government begun under the NRA. It was also somewhat true of relations between dealers and manufacturers during most of the 1930's. Dealers were often subjected to thorough regulation in virtually all of their business activities, including even their accounting methods.

Big business is making an awful holler about Government interference but car manufacturers are not alone interfering with our
business, they are running it. . . No . . . present dictatorship has
a thing on the way they enforce the rules on their dealers. . .[139]

Here is a regimented industry opposing government control but
having a government of its own with a set of laws and corresponding
penalties which approximate the laws of a commonwealth.[140]

To some extent the question is not whether there should be
regulation, whether power should be employed, but rather
whether the regulation should be public or private and what
purposes the power should serve.

When it comes to generalizations about the transference of
economic conflicts into politics — the central concern of this
study — it is clear that the prevailing method of analysis, the
Bentley group hypothesis, which describes governmental action
as the result of a process of struggle and compromise among
groups, initiated by the attempts of some groups to secure
political redress of their economic grievances, must be used
with care and judgment. The group concept is only an analytical tool and must not be confused with reality itself. It helps
to explain the actual situation, but it is not an exhaustive explanation or description. It is invaluable in the analysis of
political processes, but it is not a substitute for analysis. The
basic process at work here has perhaps been one in which dealers, economically aggrieved and unable to improve their position by economic means, organized to seek governmental assistance, but such a simple description so distorts the full interactions of the political and the economic as to give a false picture. Group analysis must include an examination of the extent
to which potential groups become operative groups, degrees of
group cohesion, and — of special concern here — the ways in
which the political strengths and weaknesses of economic
groups are conditioned by the circumstances of their economic

[139] A dealer's letter quoted in FTC, *Motor Vehicle Industry*, p. 174.
[140] Editorial in the *NADA Bulletin*, December 1939, p. 6.

positions. Group conflicts occur within, and are shaped by, both their political and their economic environments.

Dealers' grievances existed because manufacturers were favored by the existing framework of law. Both the rise of large corporations and the interpretation of contracts resulted from a public policy primarily stated by the courts. Another general policy — disapproval of price fixing and other restraints of trade — limited dealers' attempts to end their grievances by joint economic actions. Thus even the initial economic problems were vitally affected — almost defined — by governmental actions made in pursuance of general policies. Yet the groups affected had virtually no part in the formation of these policies; a simple group analysis, accordingly, explains nothing about them. Even when dealers turned to politics, their first major use of political weapons was not on their own initiative, rather they were cordially invited to do so by the NRA. Experience under the NRA explains much of the remaining political-economic history of the trade, but the trade, its problems, and its politics, do not explain the NRA.

Thus far political aspects of our political economy seem to be more basic, since general governmental policies define dealers' economic conditions and confine their political reactions, but in just as many respects economic aspects appear to be more causative. When dealers did win some aid from federal and state governments, it was not a simple and automatic use of political strength. Problems of organization constantly plagued the dealers. The NADA never organized more than a small proportion of dealers, nor was it successful in producing programmatic agreement. This weakness in part reflects the economic power of the manufacturers, who prevented some dealers from joining associations, "persuaded" others not to seek certain political objectives, and placed wholesale distributors and manufacturer-controlled dealers in strategic offices in at least several state and local associations.[141]

[141] FTC, *Motor Vehicle Industry*, p. 1067.

A more important cause of weakness was diversity among dealers. Twelve per cent of all new-car dealers in 1939 had annual sales of over $300,000, and 30 per cent had sales of over $100,000, while 39 per cent had sales of less than $50,000.[142] The problems and the attitudes of a dealer with an annual volume of a third of a million dollars may differ considerably from those of a dealer who makes sales of less than fifty thousand dollars. There are equally important differences between a metropolitan dealer who competes with other dealers carrying the same lines and a dealer who enjoys a territorial monopoly. Equally great differences exist between a Cadillac dealer and a Ford dealer, between a dealer who stresses volume and high turnover and a dealer who stresses service, and among Ford, Plymouth, and Chevrolet dealers who compete with each other but whose relations with manufacturers differ. The economic environment not only provides the bases for political conflict, it also conditions the outcome. It poses the problem and influences the political solutions.

This holds true in more striking respects. We have already seen that the dependence of manufacturers on dealer and consumer good will enabled the slight force of Congressional and FTC publicity to reverse their policies. A more important example occurred in the postwar period, when for a few years economic changes reversed the balance of power. Wartime cessation of production caused many dealers to cancel their franchises and dammed up consumer demand for new cars at the same time that high levels of national income enabled many consumers to enter the new-car market for the first time. After the war a dealer could easily sell all the cars of any standard make he could receive, while a manufacturer could tap this rich market only through dealers. The power structure had temporarily been drastically altered. A dealer could weigh the offers of several manufacturers, while manufacturers competed vigorously for strong dealers. These changes were speedily re-

[142] *1939 Census of Business*, vol. I, part 2, pp. 671–672, 679–680.

flected in franchise contracts. Late in the war manufacturers, one after another, announced contract changes far more important than those which occurred in the late 1930's.[143] General Motors extended the franchise period to two years and denied itself power to cancel without cause. Manufacturers increased retail margins and granted more exclusive territorial franchises. Had the dealers gained national legislation regulating contracts, it is doubtful that the regulation would have produced changes as beneficial as these. Limited state regulation has had, and limited federal regulation probably would have had, almost no lasting effects. The industry, and the national economy it reflects, has been too dynamic to be controlled by these weak restraints. (This dynamism, of course, is in part the consequence of other, more general governmental actions and policies.) Power relations between dealers and manufacturers change with every shift in the industry's competitive structure. Indeed, recent intensification of competition between manufacturers — especially between Ford and Chevrolet — has caused dealers once again to wail that manufacturers, with "unbridled license and totalitarian methods," are abusing their power and to complain of their cancellation privileges.[144]

Furthermore, a significant relationship between group political actions and the level of national income is demonstrated. The lower the national income and the greater the economic distress, the more intense is political pressure for particularistic legislation. Yet at the same time the need increases for more general remedial governmental actions. If general programs can ease the economic distress, then, in so doing, they ease particularistic pressures. In terms of general trade regulation, the thesis that more vigorous antitrust enforcement would limit cyclical downturns has reversed the proper chain of causation. If the principles behind recent antitrust enforcement and inter-

[143] For examples of these contract changes, see *Business Week*: July 15, 1944, pp. 103–104; August 19, 1944, p. 90; September 23, 1944, p. 94.

[144] See the remarks of the NADA's executive vice president at the 1955 convention. *New York Times*, Feb. 3, 1955, p. 15.

pretation are to be effectuated, then the avoidance of economic distress is the first order of business.

Yet another factor which must be taken into account by group analysis, which tends to ascribe a passive role to governmental agencies, is to be found in the relatively independent role played by the FTC. Of course, its independence and its influence were enhanced by the inability of the NADA to mobilize dealers behind a concrete program. Nevertheless, the FTC disappointed the backers of the Withrow Resolution by praising the manufacturers with faint damns, and it extended the focus of its investigation to spotlight some unsavory and many undesirable practices of dealers. It did far more than passively play host to competing groups and provide an arena for conflict and compromise; it applied standards of what it conceived to be the public interest, and it framed the problems in terms of those standards. It had an impact of its own on this political struggle. Had any legislation resulted, the effect of the FTC's participation would have been to make its terms less particularistic. This is but a special case of the process which has been called the democratization of politics, or the process by which groups, in attempts to secure wider support for their programs, broaden them and make them less particularistic.[145] Much of this broadening process is only verbal, but much of it is real. This, as we have seen, was true of most of the state laws which dealers secured.

In summation, then, the Bentley hypothesis provides a useful starting point for an understanding of the process of policy formation, but it is a far cry from complete explanation.

[145] "The democratic process compels each social group to strive for mass support. Each group, therefore, must present its egoistic interests as universal. . . But the valuable side of this process must equally not be forgotten. The very need to appeal to social groups larger than the immediate interest group compels adjustment of various interests. Politics becomes democratic." Franz L. Neumann, "Approaches to the Study of Political Power," *Political Science Quarterly*, June 1950, p. 173.

## Chain-Store Taxation

The political repercussions of economic conflict in grocery and drug distribution in the 1930's greatly exceeded those in automobile distribution for two main reasons. First, grocers and druggists, unlike automobile dealers, recruited support from many other retailers because their enemy — the chains — had invaded many trades. Second, intertype competition encourages political grouping for all-out battle; no ties bind independent retailers to chains. Car dealers, on the other hand, were engaged in a struggle of vertical power. Because of the necessarily two-sided character of the power relationship, the struggle was a limited one, involving only the terms of an arrangement which was mutually advantageous. Total victory, however, was the ultimate goal of grocers and druggists and was the immediate purpose of some state legislation and of the proposed federal chain-store tax, but, significantly, the Robinson-Patman bill, designed to hamstring chains, was amended in the interest of producers who stood in a vertical relationship with chains and who, accordingly, desired to improve their position but not to cripple chains.

In the fifteen years after World War I chains had expanded so greatly as to revolutionize many marketing channels and to endanger hundreds of thousands of independent retailers and wholesalers. By 1929 chains made one fifth — 20.3 per cent —

of all retail sales. The early years of the Great Depression added to the economic distress of independents and intensified their fear and hatred of the chains, whose price appeal was sharpened by the slash in consumer income. While their rate of growth fell during this period, they increased their share of retail sales to 23.3 per cent by 1935, having reached a peak of 25.2 per cent in 1933.[1] Chain competition was especially felt by grocers because so many of them were marginal and because chains had been particularly successful in this trade, making 38.5 per cent of grocery sales in 1929.[2] This, and the fact that they are the largest single class of retailers,[3] made grocers the group primarily appealed to by the movement to tax chains,[4] although wholesalers and other retailers often played an important role.

As we have seen, retail and wholesale grocers first tried to focus group pressure on manufacturers who sold to chains or who gave them special concessions. But direct or indirect boycotts were unsuccessful. Independent merchants then tried to influence consumers by press, radio, mail, and personal contacts. By 1929 there were active groups fighting the "chain-store menace" in more than 400 cities and towns.[5] While probably wholesalers, larger and better organized than their retail allies, played an important part in aiding and financing this movement,[6] nevertheless its widespread spontaneity and grassroots

[1] *1939 Census of Business*, vol. I, part 1, p. 10.

[2] *1929 Census of Business*, vol. I, part 1, p. 71.

[3] In 1939 the nation's 346,987 independent grocers and combination grocers were 21.1 per cent of all independent retailers. The 510,394 independent food merchants of all types were 31.0 per cent. *1939 Census of Business,* vol. I, part 2, pp. 671–672.

[4] This generalization is subject to some exceptions. E.g., a West Virginia chain-store tax was primarily aimed at, or had its major effect on, chains of filling stations owned and operated by refiners. An oil company produced evidence which showed that this statute secured 84.5 per cent of the revenue it yielded from filling station chains, although they did only 4.6 per cent of the total business done by chains. *Fox v. Standard Oil of New Jersey*, 294 U.S. 87 (1935) at 95.

[5] Beckman and Nolen, p. 247.

[6] This inference is based on the fact that it can be demonstrated that the

origins are striking, although not surprising, since chain-store gains directly hurt well over a million retailers. What is surprising is that a circumstance in which so many people shared a common grievance produced so little in the way of organization and lasting legislative results.

This campaign to influence the public had little effect on chain sales, so independents sought to invoke governmental aid. At first they tried to forbid further chain expansion by statute. Maryland, for example, in 1927 forbade chains to add more units within that state, but this act and similar laws in a few other states were speedily declared unconstitutional by state courts.[7] Its probable unconstitutionality and the difficulty of passing such direct legislation dictated the use of another method. There was some precedent for their next choice. In the late nineteenth century similar agitation had produced bills levying discriminatory taxes on department stores. Not only did special taxation of chains permit the particularistic purposes of the independents to be obscured behind the façade of a revenue bill at a time when state legislators were casting about desperately for new sources of revenue, it also commanded broader support. The reliance of cities and towns and of many states on property taxes does give chains some advantage over independent stores;[8] accordingly, some discriminatory taxes can be justified.

---

wholesalers were the prime movers in the initiation of boycotts and of the movement which led to the Robinson-Patman Act. Consequently, it is likely that they were influential in the battle for the consumer's good will and for state legislation.

[7] "Chain Stores — Their Economic Significance," an article appearing in *Index*, a publication of the New York Trust Company, and reprinted in Daniel Bloomfield (ed.), *Chain Stores and Legislation* (New York: H. W. Wilson; 1939), pp. 74–75.

[8] A leading tax authority lists five advantages which may be enjoyed by a chain in paying property taxes. First, it usually operates with a higher rate of turnover so that a tax levied on its stock on hand on any one date amounts to a lower proportion of its total annual sales or total annual investment than does a similar tax imposed on an independent. Second, it is difficult for a local assessor to secure accurate information from a chain store whose full records may be stored in another state. Third, a considerable portion of the chain's in-

Consequently, it was to chain taxes that grocers and other independent merchants devoted most of their political effort. The movement began in 1923, when Missouri considered such a measure. It slowly gathered momentum for a few years. In 1927 thirteen bills were introduced in state legislatures, and four were passed. Then, as the depression intensified the distress of independents and increased the need for new sources of revenue, the movement swelled and quickened. When, after a period in which state courts had declared many similar acts unconstitutional, the Supreme Court in 1931 first passed on such a measure and held it to be constitutional,[9] the movement became a flood tide. "Wherever a little band of lawmakers are gathered together in the sacred name of legislation," said one observer, "you may be sure that they are . . . thinking up things they can do to the chain stores."[10] In 1931 a total of 175 tax bills were introduced, although only three were passed. In 1933 the movement reached its peak with the introduction of 225 bills and the passage of 13.[11] The movement then slowed down and ebbed. By 1939 twenty-seven states had passed chain taxes, although some had lapsed, been repealed, or been invalidated by the courts.

At first glance, this twelve-year period appears to offer convincing evidence of effective retailer organizaton. The appear-

---

vestment may be in intangible property, such as "organizational value." Fourth, assessors frequently assess stocks of goods on a cost basis. Since a chain pays lower purchasing prices, the independent is often taxed on his disadvantage in purchasing prices. Fifth, differences in assessment dates among municipalities or states may enable a chain to shift much of their stock so as to avoid the payment of some taxes. Harold M. Groves, *Financing Government* (New York: Henry Holt; 1945), pp. 113–114. The far more common argument — that chains usually rent their quarters and so avoid property taxes — is unsound. This burden is shifted to them by their landlords, and the option of doing business in rented quarters is also open to independents.

[9] *State Board of Commissioners v. Jackson*, 283 U.S. 527.

[10] John T. Flynn, quoted in Charles F. Phillips, "State Discriminatory Chain Store Taxation," *Harvard Business Review*, Spring 1936, p. 354.

[11] Statistics on number of bills introduced and passed from Beckman and Nolen, p. 250, and Godfrey M. Lebhar, *Chain Stores in America: 1859–1950* (New York: Chain Store Publishing Corp.; 1952), p. 129.

ance is deceiving. While some retailers did lobby, and while some wholesalers were relatively well organized, the general tone is one of a relatively disorganized movement. This was not the carefully organized campaign of a cohesive national association, agreeing on a program and then focusing pressure and propaganda on legislators and other important people. Instead, it was a situation in which legislators, aware of need for increased revenue, retailer fear of chains, general suspicion of "foreign" (out-of-state) corporations, and general disenchantment in the early 1930's with large-scale business organization, introduced chain taxes on their own initiative. Legislators capitalized on, and further developed, existing but largely unorganized opinions, eliciting support from independent merchants and donning the robes of champions of small business. The political raw material was readily available, but it was legislators, not organized groups, who predominated in mining it and exploiting it. The fact that 225 bills were introduced in a single year indicates organizational weakness, not strength. That as many as a dozen bills were introduced in a single state during one session strongly suggests that legislators were competing to elicit and harness a popular but unorganized sentiment. An organized group would focus support on a single bill, as druggists did in their campaign for state fair trade acts. And taxes vary so extremely from state to state as to show that no national group was able to coördinate the activities of its state and local units, although the NARD did facilitate communication among its state units.[12]

Furthermore, chain taxes first arose and were the most prevalent and the harshest in Southern and Western states, where there is latent fear of, and animosity toward, "foreign" corporations dominated by Northern and Eastern financial interests — "Wall Street." These are emotions which are difficult to institutionalize and in the absence of manipulation tend to lie dormant. This lack of organization and of spontaneity accords,

[12] E.g., see *NARD Journal*, Feb. 21, 1935, p. 202; and July 16, 1936, p. 933.

of course, with Chapter III's generalizations about the difficulties of organizing retail grocers.

That this was a process in which latent and unorganized opinion and prejudice was manipulated and appealed to is also indicated by a number of antichain organizations which were formed with a primary goal of enriching their promoters. One of these was the "Merchants' Minute Men," organized by W. K. ("Old Man") Henderson, who used his radio station KWKH and his "Hello World Broadcasting Corporation" to appeal to independent merchants for $12 membership fees and to offer to the general public a chance to contribute to the antichain cause by buying his coffee at $1 a pound, although the prevailing retail price was less than half that price.[13] Other organizations, designed to profit their promoters in more orthodox ways, also preyed on retailers.[14] In 1930 the NARG warned its members that "there are . . . literally thousands of individuals interesting themselves in anti-chain store campaigns purely for the money they can make out of it for themselves. . . Retail grocers . . . should be warned against parting with their money . . . these organizations are set up to make money for the promoters."[15]

Thus the failure of a group to mobilize its potential strength and to coördinate the actions of its members meant that policy was not determined by the goals and strengths of organized groups. Just as automobile dealers' lack of organizational cohe-

[13] Lebhar, p. 157.

[14] A "National Antichain Store League" solicited membership dues and contributions from retail associations and "sucker lists." Individual memberships were sold to retailers for $10, of which the solicitor retained $4 and the state manager $1.50. On memberships secured directly by the state manager, he retained the full $5.50, and he also received a commission on sales of the League's journal. A want ad, seeking applicants for these jobs and appearing in the Washington *Evening Star* of February 10, 1935, indicates the nature of this organization. Under the heading "AGGRESSIVE FIELD REPRESENTA-TIVES," the advertisement began: "Unusual opportunity offering earnings and advancement, limited only by initiative, energy, and ability." Patman Committee Hearings, vol. I, pp. 191–215. For other examples see Lebhar, pp. 158–159, 236.

[15] A bulletin, dated February 14, 1930, and quoted in Lebhar, p. 158.

sion and programmatic agreement gave the FTC great discretion in its policy recommendations, so the organizational and programmatic weaknesses of grocers gave state legislators freedom in forming policy. This policy was more than an automatic result and simple reflection of group pressures. It is perhaps as true to say that policy created a balance of groups as it is to say that the balance among groups produced policy.

Most chain taxes were graduated license taxes, levying taxes on every store, or on every store in excess of a certain number owned by a single organization, with the size of the tax on each additional unit increasing with the number of units in the chain.[16] Except for the Louisiana law, only stores within a state were included in the computation. This type of tax was sustained by the Supreme Court by a narrow margin — 5 to 4 — in 1931,[17] and it was this type which was enacted by most of the states passing chain taxes. This single type, however, covers a broad range of variation. Some acts defined chains broadly, a few even including coöperative chains. Others applied more limited definitions, exempting, for example, filling stations. Effective tax rates varied greatly because of differences both

[16] Some states had passed graduated taxes on the gross sales of an organization, regardless of the number of units operated. In an attempt to ensure its constitutionality, the tax was applied to all stores, but it necessarily imposed special burdens on chains and department stores. In 1935 this kind of tax was held to be unconstitutional on the ground that a classification by volume of sales alone was unreasonable and arbitrary. *Stewart Dry Goods Co. v. Lewis*, 294 U.S. 550.

[17] The majority held that the distinction between chains and other retail stores was a reasonable one, in that the chain feature could be considered to give the firm an additional ability to pay. *State Board of Commissioners v. Jackson*, 283 U.S. 527. Also see: *Fox v. Standard Oil of New Jersey*, 294 U.S. 87 (1935), in which, again by a 5 to 4 decision, the Court held that it would not examine the amount or degree of the tax, if the classification on which it is based be reasonable; *Great Atlantic and Pacific Tea Co. v. Grosjean*, 301 U.S. 412 (1937), in which the Court approved a classification based upon the number of units owned by the chain throughout the nation, holding that the competitive advantages of a chain may be regarded to increase with the number of units, wherever located; and *Louis K. Liggett Co. v. Lee*, 288 U.S. 517 (1933), in which the Court, by a 6 to 3 vote, held that a classification based on whether the chain extended into more than one county was unreasonable. For a summary of these cases, see Groves, pp. 286–290.

in the tax base — the number of stores in tax brackets — and in the rate or amount of tax levied on each store in a bracket, as a comparison of the laws in 21 of the 24 states having such legislation in 1937 shows.[18] In Montana a chain paid the maximum tax on every unit in excess of four, but in North Carolina the top bracket began at 201 units and in Pennsylvania at 501. There was equally great variation in the tax levied on each store in the top bracket. In Wisconsin it was $100, but in Idaho and Pennsylvania it was $500, and Texas applied a tax of $750.[19] Such extreme variations indicate both the disorganized nature of the political campaign for the passage of these laws and the varying purposes of the legislative majorities which passed them. Some evidently resulted from a conviction that chains commanded an unfair advantage in their buying prices or from the belief that chains were not paying their fair share of taxes.[20] In these cases special taxes were regarded as an evening of the scales to ensure that independents were not discriminated against. But other taxes reflected a desire to shackle, or even eliminate, chains, and many statutes represent varying combinations of these two motives.

The haphazard results of the taxes are perhaps equally as indicative of the nature of the political movement which produced them. If each state passed a relatively mild law, such as that of Indiana, which imposed taxes ranging from $3 on the first store in a chain to $150 on every store over 20, the results would vary enormously from state to state and from chain to chain.[21] The F. W. Woolworth Co. would pay $3 on its one

---

[18] Three of the states had laws based on somewhat different principles. This data from Maurice W. Lee, *Anti-Chain-Store Tax Legislation* (Chicago: University of Chicago Press [reprint of Studies in Business Administration, vol. IX, no. 4]; 1939)', p. 9.

[19] Although no figures are really typical and averages have little significance, the average tax was levied after a chain had 1.28 units and began with a charge of $7.52. A chain with more than 91.24 units would pay a tax of $285.36 on each additional store.

[20] Wisconsin, for example, allowed a proportion of other state taxes paid by a chain to be deducted from its license taxes.

[21] This example and the resultant statistics are taken from Lee, pp. 40–48.

unit in Nevada and an average of $139 on each of its 225 stores in New York. Its total tax would be $178,674, or an average of $98 on each store. This tax would hardly have been noticed, for the average Woolworth store showed net profits of $14,748 in 1929 and $9,051 in 1932, the chain's best and worst financial years in the immediate time period. Thus Woolworth's tax bill would never have been more than 1.06 per cent of its net profits. The Kroger Grocery and Baking Company would not fare so well because it operates more units and because they are geographically concentrated. Its total bill in all of the eighteen states in which it operated would be $604,264, an average tax of $139 on each of its units. The tax penalizes geographic concentration, although there was no contention that this factor enabled a chain to avoid taxes or to receive undue allowances and discounts, or that this factor made a chain less socially desirable. A small chain concentrated in a single state — as many small chains are — would suffer more than a large chain which scattered its units well. Kroger, with total sales only about 80 per cent of Woolworth's and with profits only about one-seventh as great, would pay a total tax more than three times as great. Its tax bill would account for about 40 per cent of its net profit, as compared with 1 per cent for Woolworth, and would cause Kroger to close some marginal stores, for in 1932 its average net profit per store was only $347. Thus the tax would take no account of a chain's ability to pay, pressing hardest on chains with lowest net profits per store.

The nation-wide application of a tax such as Louisiana's would produce quite different effects. This measure taxed each unit within the state at a rate which increased with the total number of units in the system. A harsh measure designed to cripple chains, it heavily penalized any long chain, levying a tax of $10 on every unit within Louisiana of a system containing up to 10 units, with the rate rising on each bracket until any chain with over 500 units was taxed $550 on each store within the state. Had each state enacted such a tax, the effects would vary widely even among the longer systems.[22] In 1933 such a tax would have taken three fifths of A & P's net profits and half of its net profits in 1937. In 1935 it would have caused Safeway Stores to operate at a loss and would have taken three fifths of its profits in 1937. But many chains not in the grocery field would have fared much better. In 1937 such a tax would have taken only 10 per cent of Walgreen's net profits and only 3 to 4 per cent of the profits of Woolworth and J. C. Penney. These effects vary so because chains differ both in length and in average volume and profit per store. In 1937 chain grocery stores averaged an annual volume of sales of only about $60,000, while drug and auto supply chains averaged over $100,000 per unit, and variety chains about $250,000. Even chains of the same type vary considerably. A & P and Kroger stores made average sales of about $60,000 but Safeway units averaged over $100,000. And net profits also varied greatly. Shoe chain stores, for example, had an annual volume of only about $50,000 but enjoyed a net profit more than two-and-one-half times that of chain groceries. Although the Louisiana law was designed to penalize bigness, it measured size only by a chain's length. Yet any meaningful measurement should include volume, number of employees, amount of invested capital, and amount, and perhaps rate, of profit. Here, too, the effects of the tax but poorly reflect the purposes it was designed to promote. In summary, then, the haphazard results of chain taxes demonstrate the nature of the movement which produced them.

The chain tax movement weakened after 1935 for reasons which highlight some of the factors limiting the political success of economic groups. Improvements in general economic conditions both decreased the need for new sources of revenue

---

[22] 1933 and 1935 statistics in this paragraph from Lee, p. 50; 1937 figures from Willard L. Thorp, "Changing Distribution Channels," *American Economic Review*, vol. XXIX, no. 1, supplement, March 1939, p. 82.

and slackened competitive pressures on independents, lessening their political energy — another example of the general rule that depressed conditions increase particularistic pressures. Yet another reason lay in the very successes which independents had won. Political group warfare usually yields not total victory but a new group equilibrium. This is in accordance with the Bentley hypothesis, which holds that political struggle tends toward an equilibrium reflecting an underlying social and economic equilibrium. With every victory the independents lost strength. Even though experience showed that most taxes did no more than annoy chains, most states did not increase tax rates, in part because the Robinson-Patman Act satisfied those who had earlier supported chain taxes only as a crude method of compensating for the unfair buying advantages they thought chains enjoyed, and in part because the federal and state fair trade acts tended to satisfy druggists, lessening their enthusiasm for chain taxes.

In several respects, however, Bentley's explanation fails to do justice to the complexities of the equilibrium which does arise. Political equilibrium is more than a simple reflection of the relative political strength of the groups immediately concerned. It also registers the impacts of strands and crosscurrents of contemporary political, economic, and social beliefs. The Great Depression had profoundly shaken public confidence in the leadership of big businessmen, and in many sections the reaction was extreme. Economic misery and some of the revelations of Congressional investigating committees had made many quite skeptical of the value of large-scale economic organization itself. Now to rural areas and most small towns the chain store epitomized Big Business.[23] It was Wall Street. It was, they thought, the creature of the same few wealthy, bloated financiers who had caused the depression through their lust for the profits to be derived from great concentrations of

[23] Hence, again, the prevalence of chain-store taxes in the Southern and Western states.

economic resources.[24] "The general antagonism to big business created a most favorable background for such a[n antichain] crusade." [25]

Residents of Northern and Eastern industrial areas usually had more immediate targets on which to vent their spleen and express their frustrations. The distress of many could be attributed directly to the factory which had discharged them or reduced their pay, or to the financial promoter who had dissipated their investments. But in many rural areas and small towns the causes of reduced agricultural income or of the closing down of the small factory were remote and impersonal. For many of them the local chain store conveniently personified Big Business, which was responsible for their woes. It served as a symbol, as a scapegoat, in an inchoate class war. Nor is "class war" too strong a term. Today, in a period of prosperity when Big Business has been returned from purgatory and restored to grace, it is easy to forget the bitterness with which even — or perhaps especially — small businessmen assailed Big Business in the depths of the Great Depression. Listen, for example, to the official voice of your friendly neighborhood druggist:

, . . privilege-seeking few . . . [who] seek . . . the dictatorship of big money — a state of financial feudalism . . . privilege-seeking tycoons . . . would-be dictators.[26]

Today we look back with horror at slavery. . . Yet the youth of today may be meted out a comparable fate. . . The selfishness of

[24] One of the more significant vehicles of antichain propaganda in 1934 and 1935 was a motion picture, "Forward America," usually sponsored by local merchants, which advanced the thesis that the chains were responsible for the depression, relying on a distorted version of the FTC's investigation, and which paraded the notoriously extravagant and extravagantly notorious "Babs" Hutton, Woolworth heiress, before the camera as an example of where chain profits went and as implied demonstration of the allegedly giant profits earned by chains, in much the same manner that Jacobins must have cited Marie Antoinette. See Patman Committee Hearings, vol. I, pp. 278–288; vol. II, p. 133.

[25] Don Francisco, director of the chains' campaign against chain taxes in California. Quoted in Lebhar, p. 228.

[26] *NARD Journal,* April 2, 1936, p. 397.

those who would control the money power of the nation, if their greed is allowed to develop unchecked . . . would shame the Simon Legrees of the 'sixties . . . masses of Americans wholly at the mercy of the despotic power of a monopolistic class . . . mere existence for the working millions — luxuries and profits being reserved for the few.[27]

Newspapers . . . prate verbosely about the "freedom of the press;" . . . but, with an iron hand from which European dictators could take lessons, the . . . mouthpieces of Big Business . . . direct the people as to what thoughts they should ponder . . . and persecute with a deft finesse never approached by the Spanish Inquisitors those . . . who dare oppose their wishes. Thus, while mouthing maledictions upon dictatorships, they seek to saddle on the American people a dictatorship of greater magnitude than that which they condemn: the dictatorship of big money — a state of financial feudalism.[28]

Many chains had contributed to these antagonisms, as have so many large corporations, at least in their early stages, by excessive centralization and bureaucratization and by too narrow a view of efficiency. They had offended local sensitivities by failing to participate in local charity drives, honor local holidays, and use local services. Managers were often denied sufficient autonomy to be regarded as local merchants, and low chain wages epitomized the wage slavery believed to be the necessary result of large-scale organization. A result and a reflection of the depression, this popular feeling waned in the late 1930's as economic conditions gradually improved, and the end of the decade brought the chain tax movement to a halt.

Yet another reason for the shift in the balance of forces and the striking of a new political equilibrium lay in the actions of groups not directly concerned in the immediate struggle, for the outcome of the antichain campaign was determined by the ability of the principally concerned groups to recruit allies. The economic basis for the antichain crusade existed in the

[27] *Ibid.*, May 21, 1936, p. 681.
[28] *Ibid.*, April 2, 1936, p. 397.

1920's, yet independents won no substantial victories until the depression gained them powerful allies. The late 1930's saw the political balance change. Independents, as we have seen, suffered serious defections, while chains gained powerful allies. At first chains had fought alone; the battle tended to be one between chain money and independents' numbers. The result was usually a chain defeat; legislature after legislature enacted chain taxes, and a few later increased them. Nor was their legal defense much more successful; may acts were declared unconstitutional, but a majority were upheld. At first the chains, probably because of political inexperience, fought on narrow fronts; in the main they apparently contented themselves with hiring lawyers and agents to represent them in courts and legislatures.

In the next stage their campaign was broadened somewhat but was still weakened by a narrowness resulting now from oversophistication or cynicism. They increased substantially their expenditures for "representation" before state legislatures.[29] From the frequency with which chain spokesmen complained of "racketeering" bills and legislators in testimony before the Patman Committee, it appears that some of this money was used to hire legislators as well as lobbyists. Efforts were made to win allies, but the emphasis was on manipulating, coercing, and buying support. The struggle was still one of money against numbers. Manufacturers selling to chains were coerced into opposing antichain legislation;[30] when passage of a tax bill appeared certain, chains would try to add amend-

[29] E.g., in fiscal 1934 fourteen chains paid one attorney $175,000 to be used in combating state chain taxes. In this same year eleven of these fourteen firms spent $200,000 for general public relations work. Patman Committee Hearings, vol. II, p. 85.

[30] E.g., see letter of John A. Logan, executive vice president of Food & Grocery Chain Stores of America, Inc., regarding a Mr. John Brandt, head of a large Minnesota coöperative creamery organization — Land O'Lakes — at a time when that state was considering a chain tax: "It appears that considerable 'persuasion' may be necessary in order to induce Mr. Brandt to 'to go bat' for the chain stores in Minnesota, although it seems to be obvious that chains are among the very best customers of farmer cooperatives in that state." Patman

ments covering voluntary groups, coöperatives, and filling stations in order to force these groups into an alliance with them; [31] chain associations sent their members samples of letters they should induce their employees, customers, landlords, bankers, stockholders, and manufacturers to write to legislators; [32] and publicists were hired to issue chain propaganda under false colors.[33] These tactics were unsuccessful and boomeranged painfully when the Patman Committee uncovered them.[34]

Not until chains developed a technique of eliciting the support of allies did they succeed in reversing the legislative tide. This reversal occurred in late 1936, when by popular referendum California rejected a chain tax by a decisive margin. It was in this battle that grocery chains first won the willing support of other groups and that A & P for the first time fought politically, although it had been the principal target of many chain taxes. Using an advertising agency, A & P won much consumer support by stressing its low prices and efficiencies, but its appeal to agricultural groups had even greater success. Here advertising and public relations campaigns described the importance of chain purchases, but deeds proved more effective than words.

---

Committee Hearings, vol. I, p. 376. For further data on this instance, also see p. 350, and vol. II, pp. 55–58.

[31] E.g., see a wire from Logan to his agent in Texas: "If any chain-store tax is necessary I strongly urge advisability of including voluntary chains and all other agencies served through general warehouses on cooperative plan. Suggest including as many distributive outlets as possible to make force for repeal greater and equality of assessment more logical. Also include filling stations and all others who might assist in blocking passage or in repeal movement." *Ibid.*, vol. II, p. 38. For other examples, see vol. I, pp. 377, 414; vol. II, p. 37.

[32] *Ibid.*, vol. I, pp. 355–371.

[33] E.g., the Kroger Company hired a former Farm Bureau Federation official to turn out, for farm consumption, mimeographed material praising the chains and appearing to be issued by independent or governmental agencies. *Ibid.*, vol. I, pp. 46–58; vol. IV, pp. 45–58.

[34] A majority of the committee clearly believed that American Retail Federation, whose investigation was the ostensible purpose of the committee, was simply another attempt of the chains to manipulate small distributors into a support of chains' policies. The investigation, however, did not establish this.

Fortunately for the chains, 1936 was a bountiful year for Californian agriculture, producing several commodity gluts. Early in the year growers and canners were threatened by a peach surplus. The chains, especially A & P, moved in, bought up the surplus, and successfully promoted the sales of canned peaches. Later in the year they did the same thing with dried fruit.[35] Their public relations agents, of course, made the most of these deeds.[36] While the state rejected the tax by a 2 to 1 vote, chains won a 3 to 1 victory in agricultural areas.[37] Chains used this new tactic vigorously. The National Association of Food Chains promoted and publicized eight "Product-Consumer Campaigns" within the next year.[38] In the summer of 1936 chains pushed the sale of meat when a drought forced the slaughtering of large numbers of livestock. Another dramatic promotion occurred at the very moment when the Florida Senate was considering, and apparently about to pass, an extremely harsh bill which had already passed the House. At this moment Nature intervened, presenting the citrus growers with a crop 30 per cent greater than normal. A & P speedily moved in, shipped 1425 carloads, or three-and-a-half times its normal volume, in eight weeks and caused a 20 per cent increase in prices at the shipping point.[39] Citrus growers and canners voiced their appreciation to their senators, and the bill was defeated.[40] And in Maine the pressure of farmers caused the repeal of a chain tax.[41]

[35] "A & P goes to the Wars," *Fortune*, April 1938, p. 141; and H. E. Erdman, "Relation of Mass Buying to Mass Selling," *Journal of Marketing*, vol. II, no. 1, July, 1937, p. 17.

[36] And with some justification, for it is only a centralized, large organization which can effectively organize such massive promotions on short notice. "In each of these cases the independents were also called upon and made a fine response. . . However, the very setup of the chain store system makes the chains particularly responsive to sales stimulation in such situations." Erdman, p. 17.

[37] *Fortune*, April 1938, p. 141.

[38] Lebhar, pp. 303–307.

[39] *Fortune*, April 1938, p. 96.

[40] Godfrey M. Lebhar, "Chain Store Trends," in Bloomfield, p. 27.

[41] *Loc. cit.*

The next stage in this shift of the balance among groups is best demonstrated by the outcome of the Patman bill to levy a national tax on chains. Had this shift not occurred, it is probable that at least the House would have passed this bill. The House had recently shown that it shared the same general animosity toward the chains which had led a majority of states to tax them. In 1935 it had passed by unanimous consent and without referring to committee a resolution establishing a special committee to investigate the newly formed American Retail Federation.[42] This resolution, while primarily concerned with lobbying, expressed a violent antipathy toward large chains and department stores.[43] In 1936 the House had passed the Robinson-Patman bill, designed to hamstring chains, by a big margin and, as late as June 17, 1937, it accepted an appropriations bill amendment which applied to the District of Columbia the harsh provisions of the Louisiana chain tax, which had been devised to drive A & P out of that state.[44] The Senate rejected the amendment, but the House had shown that it wished to cripple or eliminate the large national chains in the District. Consequently, when Representative Patman introduced a federal chain tax on February 14, 1938,[45] its prospects

[42] H. Res. 203. See *Cong. Record*, vol. 79, part 6, pp. 6338–6340.

[43] "Whereas it is apparent that said American Retail Federation is organized for the purpose of increasing the profits of big business, through lobbying tactics, designed to prevent small businesses from securing competitive opportunities equal to those enjoyed by corporations representing vast aggregations of capital . . . the greatest aggregation of rich and powerful department stores and chain stores . . . ever brought together for the purpose of . . . nullifying the effects of the N.R.A., the A.A.A., the Sherman Act, the Clayton Act . . . and,

"Whereas it is inimical to the welfare of the citizens of the United States to permit the organization and functioning of such a superlobby. . ."

[44] *Cong. Record*, vol. 83, part 2, p. 5936. The target was corporate bigness, and the goal was opportunity for individual enterprise, as Representative Dies, who moved the amendment, made clear. "If we are to restore equality of opportunity and open the doors of equal chance . . . to ambition, energy, and thrift, we must fulfill the pledge we have made. . . Today every door of opportunity is being closed to the youth of the land. If a man undertakes to go into the grocery business there is hovering over him the shadow of the Great A & P." *Loc. cit.*

[45] H. R. 9464. *Ibid.*, vol. 83, part 2, p. 1921.

of passing the House seemed bright, even though it was designed to prevent a chain from operating in more than one state.

This bill will restrict chain-store business to its proper territory,
to each individual state.[46]

. . . it will restrain the greed of absentee owners, because the tax
will be so high that they will be unable to operate profitably in a
number of States. . . The largest food chain . . . might, for example, be restricted to 500 stores in one State.[47]

Section 1 levied a tax of $50 on each store in chains with
from 9 to 15 units, a tax of $100 per store on chains with from
16 to 25 units, and so on up to a maximum levy of $1000 per
store in chains with more than 500 units. This section heavily
burdened chains, but Section 2 imposed a death sentence on
chains extending into more than a few states. It required a
chain to multiply the tax applicable under Section 1 by the
number of states in which it operated.[48] Under this bill A & P
would pay a tax of $524,000,000, although its 1938 sales were
only $882,000,000.[49] Even a regional chain like First National
Stores, then operating in seven states, would have to curtail its
operations drastically. It would pay a tax of $7,361,000, al-
though it lost almost $1,000,000 on sales of $56,000,000 in
1938.[50]

For a while events seemed to confirm the expectation that
at least the House would pass the bill. When Patman first pre-

[46] Extension of remarks of Representative Patman, *ibid.*, vol. 83, part 9, p.
1062.
[47] From a radio address made on May 10, 1938, by Patman, *ibid.*, vol. 83,
part 10, p. 1955.
[48] In order to allow large chains some time in which to dispose of their
stores, the bill would levy only 50 per cent of the full tax in the first year, and
75 per cent in the second. In committee hearings on the bill in 1940 Patman
offered an amendment to postpone the application of Section 2 for seven years.
Subcommittee of the House Committee on Ways and Means, *Hearings on
H. R. 1, A Bill Providing for an Excise Tax on Retail Stores*, 76th Congress,
3d Session (Washington: GPO; 1940), p. 5. (Hereafter cited as McCormack
Committee Hearings.)
[49] *Ibid.*, p. 153.
[50] *Ibid.*, p. 154.

sented his bill, on February 14, 1938, it bore the names of 74 other Representatives as co-sponsors.[51] On January 24, 1939, he claimed that over 100 Representatives had pledged their support,[52] and by August 5 the number had grown to 150.[53] Despite this apparent success, the bill lay dormant in the Ways and Means Committee. By March 17, 1940, when the Committee finally began hearings, the balance of political forces had shifted so far that no such measure could be passed. The Committee never reported the bill out. Patman introduced it for a third time in the next Congress,[54] but the Committee held no hearings, and the proposal was dead.

Both Patman's forces and his campaign illustrate how potential group conflicts often produce only the raw material for political leaders to exploit rather than a political battle primarily precipitated and waged by organized groups. Group interactions produce the possibility of political conflict, but they often do not define or determine the partially autonomous political processes by which policy is enunciated. Just as state taxes resulted more from the initiative of political leaders who recognized an issue which could be exploited than from organized retailers, so Patman exercised considerable initiative and had major responsibility for the national campaign. While the record of behind-the-scenes pressures is scanty, the NARD apparently was the only major association which played an important role.[55] Consequently, Patman had to rely on appeals to unorganized or only partially organized groups. He made a nation-wide speaking tour, for he was appealing to the millions

[51] *Cong. Record*, vol. 83, part 9, pp. 598–599.
[52] *Ibid.*, vol. 84, part 1, p. 712.
[53] *Ibid.*, vol. 84, part 14, p. 4054.
[54] *Ibid.*, vol. 87, part 1, p. 11.
[55] There is some evidence that the drug wholesalers, especially McKesson & Robbins, were influential in initiating this campaign. This firm financed much of the nation-wide speaking tour which Patman made before he filed the bill. *Ibid.*, vol. 84, part 1, pp. 715, 721. It was at this time, however, that the firm was shaken by a financial scandal which seemed to render it politically impotent, despite its excellent political connections.

who feared corporate concentration, Wall Street, absentee ownership, and who deplored the personal although public life of
Miss Hutton, as well as to the hundreds of thousands of independent retailers. His task was not the simple one of insuring
that already organized groups communicate their desires to
Congressmen and apply pressure. Instead, it was to arouse
the latent fears and desires of largely unorganized groups and
to cause them to react politically. Again and again in his
speeches and radio addresses he included such pleas as "advise
your lawmakers how you stand on this important issue." [56] This
was a situation in which a leader sought to create and evoke
political power out of an economic situation, as Patman himself made clear in an unusually explicit statement.

> When I came to Congress . . . I very quickly realized how insig-
> nificant I was and how feeble and weak my efforts would be in this
> great lawmaking body. I . . . decided that although my influence in
> this body was very limited, I could appeal to a higher source, to . . .
> the people of the United States. I commenced a program to sell the
> people on my proposals, knowing that if I sold them that Congress
> would gladly carry out their will and wishes. Such campaigns caused
> the enactment of the bill to pay the veterans the remainder due on
> their adjusted-service certificates, the Robinson-Patman Act, and
> other proposals. I could have introduced all of these bills and made
> a speech each session . . . but nothing would have been accom-
> plished. . . It was my desire to actually accomplish something, and
> that is the reason I resorted to the method of speaking campaigns
> to sell the people.[57]

The hearings on his bill, granted primarily because of Patman's personal pressure,[58] reveal his tactics and the relative

[56] Radio address printed in *ibid.*, vol. 84, part 11, p. 668. For other examples,
see vol. 84, part 11, pp. 345–347, 441–442, 666–669.

[57] *Ibid.*, vol. 84, part 1, p. 727.

[58] Representative McCormack, chairman of the subcommittee which held
the hearings, said: "The activity and the interest of the N.A.R.D. was not
what caused a hearing on the bill. For the public record, this hearing . . . was
granted for you personally." (McCormack Committee Hearings, p. 143). On
February 28, 1940, Patman had introduced a resolution making his bill a special
order of business but then had this resolution tabled on March 4, apparently

failure of his campaign. Representatives of only three national retail associations testified,[59] and, with the possible exception of the NARD, it does not seem that this bill was major plank in their programs or that their members were aroused over the issue. Only one major wholesalers' group, the United States Wholesale Grocers' Association (USWGA), sent a representative.[60] And Patman had been able to cause the organization of but few *ad hoc* groups and to evoke the active support of but few state and local organizations, for spokesmen of only a few of either type of group appeared.[61] A few Representatives testified at the behest of constituents, but there is little other evidence that Patman had been able to evoke active, popular support either from those who feared corporate concentration and Wall Street domination, or from the great mass of small, unorganized retailers — the "Mama, Papa, and Rosy stores." Only one ostensibly nonoccupational organization, the Freedom of Opportunity Foundation, sent spokesmen. The flimsiness, and the parentage, of this body became apparent when its president and vice-president testified primarily in their capacities as, respectively, public relations counsel of the NARD and president of the Motor and Equipment Wholesalers' Association.[62] Moreover, Patman had but little support from other than distributors. While some manufacturers had supported the Robinson-Patman Act because it improved their vertical relations with chain buyers, few wished to cripple or kill chains. Only a few small manufacturers testified for the bill, and none of them sold to chains. In addition, a small farmers' association endorsed it. The weakness of his forces is indicated by the fact

---

after having secured a promise that hearings would be held, for these hearings were begun on March 27. (*Cong. Record*, vol. 86, part 2, pp. 2138, 2330.)

[59] The NARD, the NARG, and the National Retail Hardware Association. McCormack Committee Hearings, pp. 323 ff., 417 ff., 459 ff.

[60] *Ibid.*, pp. 357 ff.

[61] E.g., the Independent Business Men's Association of Iowa, the Iowa Pharmaceutical Association, and the United Independent Retail Grocers' and Food Dealers' Association (of New York City). *Ibid.*, pp. 325 ff., 329 ff., and 126 ff.

[62] *Ibid.*, pp. 188 ff., 432 ff.

that over a quarter of the testimony favoring the bill was that
of Patman himself.

The chains, however, had applied vigorously the tactics
learned earlier in California and had marshaled many allies.
They had cemented their ties with farmers. The Farm Bureau
Federation vigorously opposed the bill, and was seconded by
a dozen state farm bureau federations.[63] A score of other agricultural groups also opposed the bill. And chains had elicited
the support of several other important groups. Many food
manufacturers and processors rallied to their cause. Several
state and city chambers of commerce testified for them, and
the National Association of Real Estate Boards strongly condemned the bill.[64]

Of perhaps greater significance, in view of the bill's appeal
to those opposing Big Business, was chain success in gaining
the support of labor unions. As recently as 1937, the American
Federation of Labor had passed a resolution severely criticiz-
ing many chain operating and trade practices. A & P, however,
brought about an almost overnight change of attitude in much
the same manner that it had wooed the farmers. Under the
direction of Carl Byoir, its public relations counsel, it signed a
series of collective bargaining contracts with AFL unions in
1938 and 1939.[65] The worth of these contracts was demonstrated at these hearings when the bill was vigorously opposed
by the International Allied Printing Trades Association, the
International Retail Clerks' Protective Association, the Amalgamated Meat Cutters and Butcher Workmen — all AFL affiliates — and by numerous union locals and state federations of
labor.[66]

Chains also won over consumers and public opinion with a

[63] *Ibid.*, pp. 681 ff., 775 ff., 793 ff., 966 ff.

[64] *Ibid.*, p. 874.

[65] *Food Field Reporter*, September 19, 1938, pp. 1, 25, and November 14,
1938, pp. 1, 17.

[66] McCormack Committee Hearings, pp. 966 ff., 1060 ff., 1078 ff., 1105 ff.,
1345 ff., 1362 ff.

strong public relations and propaganda drive. A & P alone bought space in 1300 newspapers, and chain spokesmen, sometimes bearing deceptive labels, addressed thousands of women's clubs. The success of this campaign, too, is reflected in the hearings, for several women's associations attacked the bill as a threat to efficient and cheap methods of distribution.[67] *Fortune* polls registered the general shift in public opinion. Two years earlier slightly over one half of those interviewed favored a special tax to put chains on a price parity with independent stores, but in early 1939 only 37.3 per cent of those interviewed favored special taxation.[68] Final indication of the chains' great success in winning popular and group support is afforded by the fact that the Administration, in contrast to its attitude toward the Robinson-Patman bill, opposed this bill.[69] The Secretaries of Agriculture and Commerce both publicly attacked the bill.

This brief description demonstrates the need to apply the Bentley group analysis with care. While the economic environment does create problems which become political, and while it lays the bases of group conflict, or creates situations from which group organization and conflict among groups may arise, this does not mean that the formation of public policy in economic matters is necessarily or exclusively a process of conflict and compromise among groups which are economically defined and derived. Politics is both more and less than a simple reflection of economics; it reflects economic situations imperfectly, and it reflects many noneconomic forces. Economic circumstances provide obvious bases for grouping but do not ensure that members of a group will achieve group consciousness and organization, or that they will undertake political activities.

[67] The American Association of University Women, the American Home Economics Association, and the District of Columbia Federation of Women's Clubs were among those appearing. *Ibid.*, pp. 1114 ff., 1121 ff., 1127 ff.

[68] *Fortune*, February 1939, pp. 88–89.

[69] E.g., see letter from Department of Commerce, McCormack Committee Hearings, pp. 2255–2257.

Potentialities for group organization and action may lie dormant unless they are exploited by outside organizations or individuals. Retail druggists and drug and grocery wholesalers tended to operate in accordance with the group hypothesis, but the great majority of retail grocers never joined any association. Without the catalyst provided by state legislators, most retailers, especially grocers, would have remained politically impotent. State legislators sometimes succeeded in developing and harnessing these potentialities for group action; Patman did not. Thus, a group analysis of political processes must not be pushed too far: because group action is often a potential rather than a necessary consequence, there is a sizable autonomous area within which politicians and governmental agencies play an independent role.

In addition, group analysis omits important elements. We have seen, for example, that the antichain movement was indebted to feelings which did not result from a rational calculation of group interest and which were too pervasive to be expressed through economic groups. These were in large part repercussions of the Great Depression — an antipathy toward Big Business and a need to find a scapegoat — which found one expression in an attack on the chains. This feeling is not readily expressed through groups, but it, too, is a potential which may be shaped, manipulated, or harnessed by political leaders. Roosevelt, Huey Long, and Father Coughlin each made something different out of this potential. To some extent public policy is not determined by the existing balance among groups; instead, group balances form around the policies proposed or established by political leaders.

Furthermore, even within the terms of group analysis, the policy-making process can be more dynamic and creative than a simple and automatic aligning of immediately concerned groups on different sides of an issue. A broader, public interest often arises out of such a clash. The particularistic aspects of the clash and the resultant policy are not eradicated, but they do tend to be broadened. This process may be seen in the maneuvers of chains to win allies. At first they tried to manipulate or coerce allies into their camp, or they financed sham associations to give themselves the appearance of enjoying allies. Manipulation failing, they were forced to redefine their relations with other groups. They won the aid of labor by signing union contracts and improving pay and the conditions of work, and gained the aid of farmers by improving buying practices and aiding in the disposal of commodity gluts. Now, with some justification this may be regarded as the purchase of good will by concessions. Yet, even admitting this, the process of group alignment has been a dynamic one, changing the underlying economic bases of the conflict. An A & P which recognizes unions and assumes some responsibility for aiding distressed farmers is a changed organization.

The final stage in this process was the courting of consumers and public opinion. Here again, chain motives were based on self interest, and chain propaganda activities often involved manipulation and deception. Because of chains' great advertising expenditures, some newspapers presented a partial view of the controversy.[70] Nevertheless, a degree of objective public enlightenment and education did take place. Although measurement of rationality is most difficult, a severe federal chain tax clearly would have been an irrational act. There is a rational argument against business bigness *per se*,[71] but this argument was usually distorted in popular attacks on chains, and a tax based only on chain length imperfectly reflects this argument. Although a few chain buying practices are of questionable equity, they account for but a small share of the differences between chain and independent prices. Consequently, the argu-

[70] There was some explicit use of this power engendered by large advertising budgets. Patman revealed a case in which seven small newspapers all printed as their own the very same editorial attacking his bill. McCormack Committee Hearings, p. 1992.

[71] Justice Brandeis states such an argument in his dissent in the Florida chain-store tax case. *Louis K. Liggett Co. v. Lee*, 288 U. S. 517 (1933).

ment that chains should be taxed to increase their prices to a parity with those of their competitors rests on dubious grounds. Viewed in this light, the *Fortune* polls which registered a popular shift away from a support of chain taxes indicate that group struggle had enlightened and educated public opinion. Perhaps the best statement of this shift and of its finality came from one of the independents' spokesmen in his comments on the California referendum of 1936.

> The battle of the century, waged in California, is over. . . . The issue was clearly presented. The campaign was long and arduous. . . So the voter was possessed of the facts. . . . The chains in this campaign were enabled to present themselves as the champions of consumers, the barrier between low prices and the profit gougers. We hope consumers have a short memory. . . And so it may be in order to ask . . . whether the future welfare of independents does not indicate a course that turns away from anti-hysteria and punitive campaigns and a direction of their energies and thoughts into more constructive, more productive lines of endeavor.[72]

Finally, one last interrelationship between politics and economics remains to be examined — the economic effects of these political responses to economic problems. We have already noted changes in chains' policies toward agriculture and labor, but the effects of state chain taxes have not been discussed. The most comprehensive generalization is that these taxes were comparatively unimportant; they only accelerated some changes which were already under way. Most taxes were fairly mild, imposing levies of but two or three hundred dollars on units in top brackets, and could cause the closing only of marginal units.[73] Indiana's tax, with a top rate of $150, seemed to have no effect on chains in the period 1929–1935, most types of chains increasing their share of the Indiana market at a rate

---

[72] "The Lesson from California," editorial in *Progressive Grocer*, December 1936, in Bloomfield, pp. 165–166.

[73] The James Butler grocery chain did convert itself into a voluntary chain, but the primary reason lay in financial difficulties, and the effect of chain taxes was only a minor factor. Beckman and Nolen, p. 265.

much faster than they achieved elsewhere. In 1929, before the tax, grocery chains commanded 31.8 per cent of the Indiana market and 38.4 per cent of the national market. By 1935, after several years of the tax, they had increased their share of Indiana sales to 39.4 per cent, but made only 38.8 per cent of national sales. Drug chains showed a rate of increase almost as great in Indiana as nationally, increasing their share of the Indiana market from 25.7 per cent in 1929 to 34.5 per cent in 1935, and their share of national sales from 18.5 per cent to 25.7 per cent.[74] The number of chain stores in Indiana decreased somewhat, but this drop was not much greater than that experienced by chains throughout the nation. Maine, too, had imposed a moderate tax with a maximum rate of $150. It was the only state in New England to tax chains, yet from 1933 to 1935 its number of chain units increased more than it did in any other New England state, and it was one of four states in the nation in which chains increased their proportion of total sales in this period.[75]

Thus most state taxes had but little effect. The severe taxes which were enacted in a few states caused some chains to close marginal units but had an insignificant effect on national totals. In the decade 1929–1939, when chain taxes first took effect, chains slightly increased their share of total retail sales, going from 20.3 per cent in 1929 to 21.7 per cent in 1939.[76] If these taxes had any appreciable effect, it would be reflected in a reduction in the number of chain units. But, if we omit grocery and filling-station chains, the number of chain units actually

[74] *Ibid.*, p. 267.
[75] Thorp, *American Economic Review*, p. 81.
[76] *1939 Census of Business*, vol. I, part 1, p. 10. Chains made an even larger proportion of total sales in the middle of this decade, reaching 25.2 per cent in 1933 and 23.3 per cent in 1935. The decline in chain percentages after 1933 does not demonstrate the effectiveness of state taxes, for it reflects general increases in consumer income. Chains are most successful in groceries and other staples which account for a larger proportion of the consumer's budget in times of economic distress. In 1933 over 27 cents in the retail dollar was spent in food stores, in 1929 only 22 cents.

increased slightly during the decade.[77] It might also be expected that these taxes would increase average sales volume of chain units. Because taxes were based on length rather than volume, chains would tend to increase total volume through a policy of increasing average volume per store in preference to opening new units or maintaining marginal ones. But, again if we omit grocery and filling-station chains, average chain volume declined during this decade.[78]

Clearly, then, if the taxes had any effect, it was on grocery and filling-station chains. Since these are the two kinds of chain with lowest average volume and profits per store,[79] it would be easy to conclude that chain taxes had caused them to close marginal units and to concentrate their volume in fewer units. In fact, however, taxation was but a contributing factor in this process, and not the major one. Among grocery chains an emphasis on greater volume per store and abandonment of the policy of steadily increasing the number of outlets antedates discriminatory chain taxes by half a decade. A & P, for example, had increased average store sales from $31,000 in 1924 to $68,000 in 1929.[80] This emphasis on fewer and larger-volume units received a fresh impetus in the early 1930's when the supermarket appeared. After remaining aloof for a few years, virtually all major chains were erecting supermarkets by the later years of the decade. Chain taxes did no more than somewhat hasten the adoption of supermarkets and other large retail units. Thus these taxes had no lasting effects on grocery chains.

[77] From 70,477 to 72,554. *Ibid.*, vol. I, part 1, p. 11.

[78] From $92,589 to $82,489, or a decline of 8.3 per cent. However this was a small *relative* increase, for retail trade as a whole decreased 13 per cent. *Loc. cit.*

[79] It will be remembered that units of shoe chains had an average volume as low as, or lower than, those of grocery chains, but their average profits were more than two-and-one-half times as large.

[80] Thorp, *American Economic Review*, pp. 80–81. Some chains had pursued this policy much more vigorously than had A & P. Safeway, for example, in 1937 had average sales per unit of about $100,000, compared with $60,000 for A & P.

They did have a greater effect on filling stations, but, here too, their role was that of a contributing factor. The number of chain filling stations dropped by almost two-thirds from 1929 to 1939,[81] but, since most states exempted filling stations from chain taxes, this decline was due primarily to other causes. Chain taxes were only one of many factors influencing the decision of the major refiners to lease filling stations rather than to operate them directly. These other reasons included the desire to enable stations to adopt more flexible price policies, the discovery that men were willing to receive as proprietors a lower margin in dollars than they had previously received in wages as salaried managers — in part because they were able to supplement their margins through repair, service, and accessory sales — and the desire to avoid the consequences of wage, hour, and social security legislation. Indeed, although this policy of transferring refiner-owned stations to lessees was dubbed the "Iowa Plan" because a severe chain tax in that state in 1936 caused refiners to transfer most of their stations, in fact the policy had been begun well before that year. By 1935 almost one fourth of all company-owned stations had already been transferred to independent management.[82] Thus, as was also the case with grocery chains, the effect of chain taxation was primarily only the acceleration of already operative trends. Throughout distribution, then, these taxes had but minor effects.

[81] From 28,617 to 10,291. *1939 Census of Business*, vol. I, part 1, p. 11.
[82] TNEC Hearings, Part 15, p. 8699.

## The Robinson-Patman Act

The Robinson-Patman Act, one of the two federal acts resulting from intertype conflict in the 1930's, offers further illustration of the political repercussions of economic conflict. While we will not examine in any detail the legal and administrative background and consequences of this Act, a brief discussion of Section 2 of the Clayton Act is necessary for a full understanding of even the political aspects of the Robinson-Patman Act. Probably designed to prevent temporary local price cutting to eliminate small competitors by a large firm which could recoup its losses through higher prices in other, monopolized markets,[1] this section forbade price discrimination but allowed a number of important and broad exceptions.[2] To be illegal, the discrimination had to "substantially lessen competition," and discrim-

[1] Such predatory price-cutting tactics by Standard Oil, American Tobacco, and National Cash Register had contributed greatly to popular revulsion against the "Trusts" and were commonly regarded as one of the principal methods of creating a monopoly.

[2] ". . . it shall be unlawful for any person . . . to discriminate in price between different purchasers . . . where the effect of such discrimination may be to substantially lessen competition or tend to create a monopoly in any line of commerce: *Provided*, That nothing herein contained shall prevent discrimination in price between purchasers . . . on account of differences in the grade, quality, or quantity of the commodity sold, or that makes only due allowance for difference in the cost of selling or transportation, or discrimination in price . . . made in good faith to meet competition. . ."

inations were legal when they were "on account of differences in grade, quality, or quantity," when they made "only due allowances" for differences in selling or transportation costs, or when they were made "in good faith to meet competition."

Seldom applied to local price cutting,[3] this clause became the focus of the struggle between independent distributors and chains. Much of this struggle, as we have seen, centered on chain advantages in buying prices. Confronted with an established pattern of functional discounts and of limited quantity discounts, chains demanded functional discounts and increases in quantity discounts. Independent wholesalers and retailers tried to persuade manufacturers to classify chains as retailers, thereby denying them functional discounts, and to maintain or decrease their quantity discounts. To independents this was precisely the situation which should have been covered by the Clayton Act, whose aim was to preserve competition and to prevent monopoly. Identifying the preservation of competition with the preservation of independent competitors and regarding the growth of large chains as a trend toward monopoly, they believed that the Act's prohibition of price discrimination should have barred large chain discounts. They stressed the analogy between special chain allowances and discounts and the railroad rebates which had enabled Standard Oil to construct its monopoly. They contended that when chains received larger discounts than did wholesalers these discounts were price discriminations whose effect was "to substantially lessen competition" — i.e., enable the chains to achieve great size.

Statutory loopholes and judicial interpretation, however, prevented Section 2 from aiding independent distributors. Any

---

[3] Of the thirteen cease-and-desist orders issued by the FTC under this clause prior to its amendment by the Robinson-Patman Act in 1936, only one — *Pittsburgh Coal Co. of Wisconsin et al.,* 8 F.T.C. 480 (1925) — dealt with local price discrimination of the traditional sort. See John Perry Miller, *Unfair Competition; a Study in Criteria for the Control of Trade Practices* (Cambridge, Mass.: Harvard University Press; 1941), p. 132. In addition, four complaints had charged local discrimination but had been dismissed. M. W. Watkins, p. 63.

discount was legal if "made in good faith to meet competition," so a chain buyer could play off one manufacturer against another. Furthermore, chains usually received larger discounts because they purchased in larger lots. These discounts could make "only due allowance" for differences in selling and transportation costs but were legal if made "on account of" differences in quantities sold. There was no apparent statutory requirement that quantity discounts bear any close relationship to differences in cost of manufacture.

Finally, for the first fifteen years of the Act's life the courts held that the concern of Section 2 with competition "in any line of commerce" did not mean what it said. The FTC had recognized the section's obvious applicability to intertype competition and had seen that discriminatory discounts had as much effect on competition among distributors as they did on competition among manufacturers. But in two early cases circuit courts held that, despite the phrase "any line of commerce," the competition to be maintained through the prohibition of price discrimination was that between the firm granting the discrimination and his competitors.[4] Under this interpretation it was unlikely that any discount policy would run afoul of Section 2, since the more discriminatory a policy was the greater would be the opportunity for competing manufacturers to gain sales among those distributors who were being discriminated against. Not until 1929 did the Supreme Court reverse this interpretation.[5] Even with this barrier removed, other implications of the two earlier cases were confusing. In the Mennen case the FTC had charged that a manufacturer's refusal to grant wholesaler discounts to a coöperative organization of drug retailers which ordered in wholesale lots was discrimination. But the Circuit Court held that the manufacturer was legally justified in classifying his customers and that, as a

---

[4] *Mennen Co. v. F.T.C.*, 288 Fed. 774 (1923); and *National Biscuit Co. v. F.T.C.*, 299 Fed. 733 (1924). In both cases the Supreme Court denied certiorari. 262 U.S. 759 (1923); 266 U.S. 613 (1924).

[5] *George Van Camp & Sons v. American Can Co.*, 278 U.S. 245.

matter of law, the coöperative should be classified as a retail organization since the real parties in interest sold to consumers. In the National Biscuit case the court's argument was muddy, but it upheld the right of a manufacturer to grant a chain quantity discounts based on the system's total purchases, although he delivered to each chain unit, and there were no savings in delivery costs. These two opinions seem to conflict, but both contain one crucial implication — that a manufacturer is free to classify his customers as he sees fit, and that he may price his products as he wishes.[6] In other words, distributors could be given any concessions their power could extort, provided that this power was not based upon group action constituting a restraint of trade. Despite statements in the Mennen case, if a manufacturer was to be free to make his own discount policies, then no market structures are given special protection. Competing channels are free to enjoy whatever gains they can wrest from manufacturers. These two cases hindered the FTC in applying Section 2 to intertype problems. For eight years it issued no orders at all under this section. Then in 1933 it began proceedings against the Goodyear Tire and Rubber Company in an ambitious attempt to inject some meaning into the section,[7] but the Robinson-Patman Act had been passed long before this case had finished its round of the courts.

Judicial negation of Section 2 had thus left manufacturers free to find their own solution to the conflicting demands of

[6] Hence the significance of a sentence buried in the National Biscuit opinion: "Effective competition requires that merchants have freedom of action in conducting their own affairs." Watkins (pp. 73-74) notes the similarity of this view to that expressed in an earlier private suit brought under the Clayton Act. "Before the Sherman Act it was the law that a trader might reject the offer of a . . . buyer for any reason that appealed to him. . . That was purely his own affair. . . Neither the Sherman Act . . . nor the Clayton Act has changed the law in this particular. We have not yet reached the stage where the selection of a trader's customers is made for him by the government." *Great Atlantic and Pacific Tea Co. v. Cream of Wheat Co.*, 227 Fed. 46 (1915) at 49.

[7] 22 F.T.C. 236.

independents and chains. During the late 1920's, as the FTC's chain store investigation showed, chains won substantial quantity and special discounts. Independents' increasing concern with discounts was reflected in the fact that the NARG-instigated Senate resolution directing the FTC to investigate chain stores stressed the problem of quantity discounts.[8] With the onslaught of the Great Depression, more and more manufacturers increased quantity discounts, often disguised as advertising and promotional allowances or brokerage fees. Where many had formerly disposed of their output through the older channels, the depression had dried up many of their markets, leaving them burdened with overhead costs which had to be spread over a smaller volume. In this situation they were more willing to grant special discounts. Any price which enabled a manufacturer with idle capacity to cover more than his marginal costs on sales to chains would help him meet some of his overhead costs. Most chains were comparatively successful in maintaining their volume [9] — and hence their bargaining power — because they benefited from increased consumer price consciousness and because their sales were largely concentrated in necessities and staples. Consequently, the difference between the prices charged chains and those charged smaller distributors apparently widened, and the attention of independents was increasingly focused on discounts.

Under the NRA independent distributors were given a taste of a more protected life and an appreciation of the importance

---

[8] ". . . the Commission is directed to inquire into and report in full . . . (d) how far the rapid increase in the chain-store system of distribution is based upon actual savings in costs of management and operation and how far upon quantity prices available only to chain-store distributors . . . (e) whether or not such quantity prices constitute a violation of either the Federal Trade Commission Act, the Clayton Act, or any other statute and (f) what legislation, if any, should be enacted with reference to such quantity prices." S. Res. No. 224, 70th Cong., 1st Sess.

[9] While net sales by merchant wholesalers declined 55.8 per cent between 1929 and 1933, those billed by chain-store warehouses declined only 25.8 per cent. NRA, Research and Planning Division, *Report on Changes in Wholesaling and Retailing between 1929 and 1933*, p. 4.

of discounts in determining the conditions of intertype competition, although few of them received all that they desired in the way of code provisions.[10] In most trades, the manufacture, wholesaling, and retailing of products were covered by three different codes, and discounts were dealt with in manufacturers' codes. Although discounts had great effect on retail intertype competition and on the position of wholesalers, distributors had little to say in the writing of code provisions regarding discounts. Nevertheless, many manufacturing codes did shelter traditional distributors from some of the rigors of intertype competition. This was especially true of food manufacturing and processing, where discount structures had been quite stable until shattered by chain buyers, who had promoted price competition among manufacturers for their orders. If manufacturers wished to avoid price competition, they had to restore stability and uniformity to discount policies. Consequently, most food manufacturing or processing codes limited the discounts chain buyers could secure. Most codes forbade secret rebates and many prohibited all rebates. Most required that detailed terms and conditions be specified in the granting of advertising allowances — an attempt to ensure that such a payment be a *quid pro quo* and not a disguised price concession — and a few barred all such allowances. Almost half prohibited the payment of brokerage commissions to buyers, and a majority banned free deals. Most forbade discrimination of various types, some limited quantity discounts, and a few required functional discounts through a classification of customers, thereby denying wholesale discounts to a retailer.[11]

[10] For a general discussion of the effects of the NRA on intertype competition in distribution, see Zorn and Feldman, pp. 28–39.

[11] This summary of code provisions based upon data in NRA, Division of Review, Work Materials No. 35, "The Content of NIRA Administration Legislation; Part C; Trade Practice Provisions in the Codes," by Daniel S. Gerig, Jr., and Beatrice Strasburger, pp. 7–25. For a general discussion of efforts to control channels of distribution in all industries, see President's Committee on Industrial Analysis, *The National Recovery Administration*, H. Doc. 158, 75th Cong., 1st Sess. (Washington: GPO; 1937), ch. XVI. Some material on this

Thus, although many codes broke down after some months, independents were given some relief from their disadvantage in buying prices and an appetite for more. In addition, many distributors derived valuable political and organizational experience from preparing and administering codes. By the end of the NRA some distributors were highly group conscious, well organized, and had focused their attention on the problem of discounts. This was especially true of wholesalers. While they were seldom able to exercise direct control over manufacturers' discount policies, their wholesale codes show that this problem had become of major concern to them. The basic wholesale code permitted the code authority in each trade to prescribe a minimum functional discount. If a manufacturer refused to discriminate between wholesalers and retailers by at least the amount of this functional discount, all code members were prohibited from dealing with him — a legal and mandatory boycott.[12]

A better indication of wholesalers' goals is afforded by the codes which they proposed, rather than by those actually approved. The code which probably went the furthest was that proposed by the National Wholesale Druggists' Association (NWDA), largely composed of general-line, full-service wholesalers. It opened with a preamble which claimed sovereignty over the wholesale drug trade, describing the NWDA as being "fully qualified and equipped to fulfill *all* the needs and requirements of . . . retail druggists." Section 6 directed that no wholesaler "shall purchase or distribute a product of any manufacturer whose policy shall not conform" to certain principles.[13] These principles required a manufacturer to grant

---

same subject is also to be found in Leverett S. Lyon, *et al.*, *The National Recovery Administration; An Analysis and Appraisal* (Washington: Brookings Institution; 1935), pp. 568–577, 651–664, 700–704.

[12] Zorn and Feldman, pp. 32–33.

[13] (My italics.) For a partial text of this proposed code, see NRA Work Materials No. 57, pp. 349–353. This code was a tentative memorandum and never officially filed.

wholesalers at least a 15 per cent functional discount and not less than a 2 per cent cash discount. Retail chains were denied wholesale discounts. A boycott of manufacturers violating these principles was to be made effective through the official publication of what amounted to a "white list" — a list of at least ten thousand drug products on which manufacturers granted at least the minimum functional discounts demanded. The implication was that products not on this list would not be carried by wholesalers. In addition, a bid for retailer support was made by including similar provisions to guarantee a retail margin of at least 27 per cent.

Thus by the end of the NRA most wholesalers were seeking to protect their position by insisting upon a discount structure which would deny chain buyers any price advantages through direct purchases from manufacturers. While retailers usually focus their attention on chain selling prices and make control of them their primary political demand, for a number of reasons 1935 found them ready to ally themselves with the wholesalers in a campaign directed at chains' buying prices. As we have seen, because of a wholesaler's greater size, because of the frequency of wholesaler-retailer contacts, because the retailer is often dependent on his wholesaler, and because both share a common enemy in the chains, a retailer is apt to accept the political leadership of wholesalers. Probably for some years wholesaler representatives had been telling their retailer customers that low chain retail prices were due principally to (unfair) discounts and concessions chains received from manufacturers. This is such a simple and appealing argument that it is equally probable that it was fully accepted by retailers. Furthermore, schemes to control directly chain retail prices were beyond the power of the federal government and would antagonize consumers. In addition, the FTC had just concluded its six-year investigation of chain stores,[14] and its erroneous conclusion "that lower buying prices than are available

[14] Its final report had been submitted on December 14, 1934.

to independents are a most substantial, if not the chief, factor in these lower [chain] selling prices," [15] as well as much of its detailed evidence about special concessions received by chain buyers,[16] provided ammunition for those attacking chain buying practices and served further to focus attention on discounts. Of probably greater importance were the hearings of the Patman Committee. Although this committee had been established to investigate the lobbying activities of the American Retail Federation, Patman had seized upon the occasion to launch an investigation of chain buying tactics and had made public the special discounts and allowances received by large grocery and drug chains. The eight million dollars in special concessions received by A & P in one year was especially publicized and seemed to shock many sections of the general public, although it amounted to but 1 per cent of the concern's gross sales. The Patman Committee hearings, held in June and early July of 1935, were front-page news, and sales of the hearings reached a total never attained by any previous special committee.[17]

Finally, the need to appeal to the general public also caused retailers to center their attention on chain buying prices. It would have been difficult to muster general support for a direct attack on low chain retail prices, but the special concessions chains received because of their buying power coincided neatly with the quite common view that Big Business was expropriating huge profits at the expense of the farmer, worker, and small businessman. Special discounts appeared to be an example of the way in which monopoly — identified with size — eliminated competition — identified with the preservation of

[15] FTC, *Final Report*, p. 53. It will be remembered that in Chapter III, above, it is shown that the Commission's data on grocery chains do not support this conclusion.

[16] See FTC, *Special Discounts and Allowances — Grocery Trade; Special Discounts and Allowances — Drug Trade; and Special Discounts and Allowances to Chain and Independent Distributors — Tobacco Trade*, S. Doc. No. 86, 73d Cong., 2d Sess. (Washington: GPO; 1934).

[17] *Cong. Record*, vol. 79, part 12, p. 12655.

existing competitors — and produced monopolistic profits at the expense of the remainder of the economy.

The stage was set for a drama in which independent retailers would accept the leadership of wholesalers in a political campaign to limit the special concessions received by mass distributors. In brief, it was a process in which: (1) wholesalers secured the aid of independent retailers and took the offensive, seeking to promote their group interests through drastic limitations on the power of chain buyers to win discounts; (2) chains and other mass distributors tried to preserve the *status quo* or to hold to a minimum limitations on their bargaining power; and (3) manufacturers and agricultural producers supported the independents only to the extent that their own interests were served through limiting chain vertical power but then threw their weight in with the chains to block the remainder of the independents' program, which would have limited too greatly their own freedom of action and subordinated them to the vertical power of independents.

The Robinson-Patman bill began as an expression of wholesalers' goals. The original bill was written by the counsel for the United States Wholesale Grocers' Association (USWGA) [18] before the death of the NRA, but apparently in anticipation of it, in an attempt to utilize the FTC's request for corrective legislation as a springboard for the Association's own program. The bill was approved by a USWGA convention in the spring of 1935, and within forty-five hours of the Schechter decision the USWGA had issued a call to its members for their support. Casting about for a sponsor, they selected Representative Patman, who had recently been successful in pushing through a veterans' bonus bill, who was about to gain considerable publicity as chairman of the special committee investigating the

[18] Representative Patman, who first introduced the bill, testified that "Mr. Teegarden [attorney for the Association] wrote this bill." House Committee on the Judiciary, *Hearings on H. R. 8442, H. R. 4995, H. R. 5062 to Amend the Clayton Act,* 74th Cong., 1st Sess. (Washington: GPO; 1935), p. 9. (Hereafter cited as Sumners Committee Hearings.)

American Retail Federation, and who was in a position to use this investigation to probe and publicize chain buying practices. On June 11, 1935, fifteen days after the Blue Eagle had been pronounced dead, Patman introduced the USWGA's bill.[19] Despite the particularistic nature of its parentage and of its original provisions, the bill was so presented as to give the appearance of broader purposes. The bill's promoters claimed that it was simply a more effective way to deal with the evils uncovered by the FTC's chain store investigation than were the Commission's own recommendations.

> The Federal Trade Commission's report . . . showed . . . the competitive evils at which this bill is aimed and . . . the inadequacy of existing law to deal with them. This bill is entire harmony with its recommendations for legislation, but more definite and specific in its provisions and, therefore, more easily and effectively enforceable.[20]

This was not true. The original bill went far beyond the legislative recommendations issued by the FTC at the conclu-

---

[19] H. R. 8442. It is not clear whether the USWGA selected Patman to sponsor its bill *because* he was investigating chain buying practices, or whether it selected him because, as chairman of the special investigating committee, he would be in a position to investigate and publicize these buying practices. The timing, however, strongly suggests that the latter was the case and that the Association persuaded him to use the committee's investigatory powers as a means of whipping up popular support for the bill. Patman was given the bill at least several days before he introduced it on June 11 (Sumners Committee Hearings, p. 9); his committee investigating the American Retail Federation did not begin its hearings until June 5; and he did not introduce his resolution enabling the committee to broaden the scope of its investigation to include "the trade practices of individuals, partnerships, and corporations engaged in big-scale buying and selling of articles at wholesale or retail" until June 3 (H. Res. 203). On June 8 the USWGA informed its members that it had already completed arrangements to have its bill introduced. (Newell W. Ellison, "Robinson-Patman Act; Its Political and Commercial Background; Its Legislative History," in Trade Association Executives, *Conference Proceedings on Robinson-Patman Anti-Discrimination Act* [New York: 1936], p. 8.) Patman himself, however, denied that there was any such relationship, claiming that the USWGA did not approach him until after the American Retail Federation hearings had begun. (Sumners Committee Hearings, p. 42).

[20] From a prepared statement submitted by Mr. Teegarden, Sumners Committee Hearings, p. 39.

sion of its six-year, one-million-dollar investigation. The FTC had stressed the need to strengthen Section 7 of the Clayton Act to prevent further consolidation or merger of chains where the effect might be to lessen competition. On the question of discounts, its recommendations were indefinite. Even after its long investigation, it was still unable to determine whether chain concessions were in excess of actual cost savings and said that it was further investigating this crucial question.[21] Yet the assumption of the backers of the Robinson-Patman bill was that the FTC had demonstrated that many of these concessions had no basis in cost savings.

The Commission believed that, even if "only due allowance" was made for cost savings, "serious economic and social problems grow out of price concessions made to large chain-store organizations."[22] It declined, however, to recommend legislative answers to these problems, contenting itself with noting, on the one hand, the possibility that "ultimate injury to the public interest outweighs any temporary benefits," and, on the other hand, that to outlaw large chain discounts would produce "a consequent addition to the cost of living" and would "tend toward an arbitrary frustration of whatever saving in cost of production and distribution results from integration of the functions of producer, wholesaler, and retailer."[23] It elsewhere said that to amend Section 2 of the Clayton Act in order to

[21] "The Commission is giving further study to the question whether any of the special price concessions given by manufacturers to chain stores . . . make 'only due allowance' for the cost of selling and quantity." FTC, *Final Report*, p. 65.

[22] ". . . it may be that the effect of price discrimination which makes only such allowance will be to give to chain stores . . . powerful advantages which may produce quite similar results [monopoly or substantial lessening of competition]. . . . Serious economic and social problems grow out of price concessions made to large chain-store organizations with resources vastly in excess of most individual independents. Such concessions may be regarded as lawful because bearing a reasonable relationship to the far larger quantity of the chain's purchases. Whether the resulting competitive advantage should be curbed by new legislation may ultimately prove to be an important social and economic question." *Ibid.*, pp. 90–91.

[23] *Ibid.*, pp. 91–92.

eliminate the advantages chains received because of their scale of operation and because of their integration of distributive functions "would involve radical interference with the rights of private ownership and initiative, virtual abandonment of the competitive principle, and destruction of the public advantages represented by lower prices and lower cost of living." [24] Consequently, its only recommendation about price concessions was that Section 2 be amended to make it unlawful "to discriminate unfairly or unjustly in price between different purchasers of commodities," [25] in the hope that it could, case by case, build up concrete definitions of "unfair" and "unjust" price discriminations.

Thus at this stage we have a situation the contrary of that presented by the demands of automobile dealers for legislation. There the inability of dealers to agree on a legislative program gave the FTC a relatively free hand in the recommendation and partial effectuation of policy. Here the ability of well-organized distributors to agree on a program and to act together in pursuit of that program caused the FTC's policy recommendations to be discarded. Its recommendations were incorporated into two bills which were assigned to the same House Committee which considered the Robinson-Patman bill.[26] As far as the hearings disclose, these two bills were never seriously considered. Cohesive and well-organized groups prevented the FTC from having any real influence on policy. During the legislative course of the Robinson-Patman bill, all but a few Congressmen and witnesses before committees clearly regarded the FTC's thirty-four reports only as a source of ammunition to be used in pursuit of policy objectives already determined and on whose determination the Commission's findings had little effect.

Although the original bill was written by wholesalers and

[24] FTC, *Annual Report*, 1935, p. 32.
[25] FTC, *Final Report*, pp. 96–97.
[26] H. R. 4995 and H. R. 5062, both introduced by Representative Mapes.

designed primarily to improve their position, it was almost invariably presented as a bill to protect the small *retailer*. That the relatively large wholesalers presented their bill as one to protect small retailers again shows how group conflicts occur within, and must be related to, a framework of broader values and beliefs. At times elements of the broader framework may be manipulated quite successfully, but the very necessity of redefining group goals in terms of broader values may substantially alter them. Wholesalers were also able to disguise the bill's particularism by stating their goals in terms of some of the dominant political themes of the day. The relationship between widespread antipathy toward chains and general disenchantment with Big Business has already been mentioned. Furthermore, to an Administration and majority party which had just seen one of its major programs, the NRA, voided, the Robinson-Patman bill offered a new way to limit price chiseling — which many still thought responsible for the depression and causing exploitation of labor — and to drive a wedge between the small businessmen, who might continue to support the New Deal, and large businessmen, who had declared their permanent hostility. The wholesalers received some Administration support, especially the crucial aid of the Senate Majority Leader and Administration stalwart, Senator Robinson, who placed his potent name on the bill and introduced it in the Senate on June 26.[27]

Despite this success in disguising the bill's particularistic goals, the identity of its major supporters is clear. At least two other distributive trade associations shared credit with the USGWA as the bill's most influential sponsors. One of these,

[27] As S. 3154. However, the bill was not a party issue nor was the New Deal wing of the Democratic Party predominant among its supporters. Many Republican Congressmen, apparently especially sensitive to the small distributors in their constituency, supported the bill in its original form and opposed all attempts to weaken it. Others, more sensitive to the wishes of the farmers or manufacturers in their district, supported amendments to the bill, and some Democratic Congressmen, leaders in the New Deal wing of their party but representing urban districts, opposed the bill consistently.

the National Food Brokers' Association, shared a common interest with wholesalers in limiting or reversing grocery chain advances. The NARD, long the most cohesive and active of the distributive trade associations and having enjoyed the most protective of all NRA retail codes, also strongly backed this measure as one method of limiting retail price competition. Under their code minimum retail prices were manufacturers' wholesale list prices per dozen.[28] Since this was approximately the price paid by a small dealer, a floor was placed under retail price competition, and chain or pine board selling prices could not reflect their lower buying prices. It was the druggists' hope that this bill would similarly raise their intertype competitors' retail prices by stopping their large discounts. However, the astute NARD leaders must have known that lower buying prices of drug chains accounted for but a fairly small part of the difference between chain and independent selling prices.[29] They probably backed the Robinson-Patman bill with such vigor — Patman once declared that "no organization rendered greater service or more effective service in behalf of this cause than the National Association of Retail Druggists" [30] — because concessions on buying prices were often of greater importance to pine-boards. Moreover, the NARD, unlike the retail grocers, did not place the bulk of its eggs in the Robinson-Patman basket. At this very time it devoted equal energy to fair-trade legislation and substantial pressure to the support of such measures as chain taxes, state unfair-practices acts, and state laws confining the extremely profitable sale of prophylactics to drugstores.

In addition, while no record of their activities exists in Congressional hearings or debate, it appears that drug wholesalers were also active. In sponsoring a speaking tour by Patman to

[28] NRA Work Materials No. 57, pp. 65–66.
[29] See Notes 5 and 6 in Chapter IV, above, and those portions of the text to which they refer.
[30] *NARD Journal,* June 18, 1936, p. 791. Also see the NARD Washington representative's comments on the passage of the bill, *ibid.,* June 4, 1936, p. 697.

explain the Act, McKesson & Robbins took credit for having helped to secure its passage. Because the bill purported to further the interests of small business, however, it is probable that the large drug wholesalers, especially McKesson & Robbins, operated through the NARD, as they did in securing fair trade legislation. Finally, the NARG also participated in hearings, but it did not seem to have much direct influence. Many grocers apparently did communicate their support of the bill to their Congressmen, but this was as individuals and not as members of the national association. Once again, small grocers failed to exercise to the full their potential strength.

The provisions of the original bill give final evidence of its particularistic origins, for its purpose clearly was to straitjacket chain buyers. In brief, the bill would have altered Section 2 of the Clayton Act to make it

. . . unlawful for any person . . . to discriminate in price or terms of sale between different purchasers of commodities of like grade and quality. . . *Provided,* That nothing herein contained shall prevent differentials in prices as between purchasers depending solely upon whether they purchase for resale to wholesalers, to retailers, or to consumers . . . nor differentials which make only due allowance for differences in the cost of manufacture, sale, or delivery resulting from the differing methods or quantities in which such commodities are to such purchasers sold or delivered. . .

In addition, in three subsections the bill: (1) prohibited brokerage payments to any except completely independent brokers, (2) barred payments for a customer's services or facilities unless the payment "is offered on proportionally equal terms to all other customers competing in the distribution of such products or commodities," and (3) created a method for establishing presumptive damages for private suits by injured competitors under section 4 of the Clayton Act. While some problems are raised by these three subsections, for our purposes they can be dismissed as simple attempts to eliminate the use of brokerage commissions and advertising or promotional allowances as disguised discounts and to facilitate enforcement of the law through private suits.

It is the quoted portion of the bill which best reveals its purposes. It was designed to protect wholesalers' functional discounts but to endanger mass distributors' quantity discounts. It explicitly authorized functional discounts but required the classification of buyers according to the buyers' customers, thus preventing mass distributors from receiving a wholesaler's discount even though they performed the wholesaling function. Under the original terms of Section 2 of the Clayton Act no quantity discounts were to be questioned if they were "made in good faith to meet competition," or unless their effect was "to substantially lessen competition." These clauses were removed by the original Robinson-Patman bill, and quantity discounts were illegal unless they made "only due allowance" for differences in manufacturing, selling, and delivery costs. Thus, the bill seriously restricted competition. Manufacturers could compete for chain purchases only within the range of quantity discounts permitted under the bill's definition of cost savings resulting from quantity purchases — a definition which, as we shall see shortly, was intended to be most narrow. A manufacturer whose costs only slightly exceeded those of his competitors might find it impossible to compete for sales to chains. Furthermore, intertype competition was limited. Manufacturers were invited to use functional discounts, which would deny mass distributors the economies resulting from their performance of wholesaling functions. What was intended to be a narrow definition of a manufacturer's savings from quantity sales would also inflate a chain's costs. Thus, intertype price competition was to be restrained and retail prices were to be hindered in the performance of their function — to reflect costs accurately.

The bill's sponsors defined extremely narrowly the cost savings that might legally be reflected in quantity discounts. The bill permitted only those quantity discounts "which make only due allowance for differences in the cost of manufacture, sale or delivery resulting from the differing methods or quantities in which such commodities are . . . sold or delivered." To a business concern "cost" is an accounting term and varies with the accounting methods employed. The quoted portion of the bill does imply a method of computing costs, but its precise meaning is uncertain. The intent of its sponsors, however, was made clear in an illustration by Mr. Teegarden, the bill's author.

Suppose manufacturer A maintains a system of branch sales offices and a corps of traveling salesmen for the purpose of canvassing and selling to the wholesale trade, and that the costs of this sales organization, including its overhead, represents 25 per cent of his gross sales. Suppose then that chain X comes to A's headquarters office and offers him a large order for delivery direct to his chain retail outlets throughout the coming year and demands on that order a 25 per cent discount on the plea that it has not required the services of A's selling organization in any respect. If the same additional quantity of business had been sold to A's wholesaler customers it would have cost him, say, 3 per cent more for salesmen's traveling expenses and perhaps salaries of some additional salesmen, but otherwise would have been absorbed under his existing sales overhead.

In such case the chain might be given the 3 per cent discount but not a 25 per cent discount. The manufacturer is not able to abandon his whole selling organization merely by reason of the order of this chain, nor is he able to reduce his costs to an amount representing 25 per cent of this chain's order.[31]

While their reports were somewhat confusing and contradictory, the House and Senate Committees which reported out the Robinson-Patman bill apparently shared this narrow definition of cost savings. The Senate Committee report said that the bill

limits the differences in cost which may be honored in support of price differentials, to those marginal differences demonstrable as between the particular customers concerned in the discrimination. It is designed . . . to preclude the grant of a discrimination to a par-

---

[31] Prepared brief, submitted by Mr. Teegarden. Sumners Committee Hearings, p. 34.

ticular customer equal to the whole saving in cost resulting to the seller's entire volume of business as augmented by that customer's patronage; to preclude also differentials based on allocated or imputed . . . differences in cost, representing particular facilities or departments which the favored customer may not have immediately utilized, but with which the seller cannot dispense in the general conduct of his business. . . No particular customer should be permitted distinctively to bear the burden, of the immediate use or nonuse of facilities which the seller must maintain for his business generally.[32]

Under this construction few manufacturings savings could be passed on to mass buyers. Although a manufacturer with idle capacity might be willing to grant quantity discounts large enough to reduce his prices to a level which did little more than cover his marginal costs, the bill forbade the computation of costs upon such a basis. The lower unit costs resulting from an increase in production had to be reflected, if at all, in lower prices to all buyers. Put another way, all overhead costs had to be spread equally over all units produced. This also held for selling and delivery costs. Even though a chain buyer did not utilize the distributive services of a manufacturer, the prices of the goods he bought had to include their share of the manufacturer's general distributive expenses. Part of the cost of selling and delivering to independents had to be paid by the chain buyer as a part of the general fixed costs of the manufacturer. Obviously, this interpretation would have sharply reduced the advantage in buying prices enjoyed by chains.

This was the Robinson-Patman bill in its original form. Clearly particularistic in purpose, it sought to protect wholesalers and other functional middlemen, which it did by encouraging functional discounts and discouraging quantity discounts. It also aided independent retailers in their competition with chains, but this was only a secondary result. While the bill would have reduced drastically, and perhaps have eliminated,

---

[32] Senate Report No. 1502, 74th Cong., 2d Sess., pp. 5–6. Cf. H. Rept. No. 2287, 74th Cong., 2d Sess., especially at p. 10.

chain buying advantages, it would have had little effect on the retail operations of chains. Even if chains and wholesalers paid the same prices, chain warehouses distribute much more efficiently and could bill chain retail units at prices substantially lower than those paid by independent retailers. And if, because of functional discounts granted wholesalers but denied chains, a chain patronized wholesalers, it would still benefit in these purchases from whatever quantity discounts the wholesaler could legally give. More important, although the bill would have increased the prices paid by chains, it must be remembered that advantages in buying prices account for but a small proportion of the difference between the selling prices of chains and independents, the bulk of this difference resulting from more efficient performance of distributive functions. While the bill would have substantially improved the position of the wholesaler and might have caused chains to patronize him, it would have only partially shielded independent retailers.

Much of the bill's legislative history continues to be an account of group goals and of processes of group compromise and conflict in pursuit of those goals. In brief, what happened was that other groups sought to alter the bill in their own interests. Manufacturing and agricultural groups occupied a strategic position and usually commanded a balance of power. The initiative, however, lay with the independents. After some months there was little doubt that some bill would be passed, so that what manufacturing and agricultural groups did was to amend a bill already assured of passage.

The independents had marshaled their forces and their arguments effectively. Manufacturers apparently had not taken the bill seriously at first,[33] and the first hearings, held in the second

[33] Almost no manufacturers testified at the first Congressional hearings (by the Sumners Committee) in July, 1935. The president and the counsel of the American Grocery Manufacturers' Association (AGMA) filed written statements opposing the bill, but the president was not present to testify because he had what he considered to be more important engagements elsewhere. See Sumners Committee Hearings, pp. 128 ff., 236.

and third weeks of July, were largely devoted to testimony by independents and by a few representatives of chain stores and mail-order houses. These hearings soon showed that each participating member of the House Judiciary Committee had already decided that chains had concentrated enough power to endanger the continued existence of independent merchants, that this power had enabled them to extort shockingly large and economically unjustified special discounts, and that these concessions had enabled them to compete unfairly with independents. This attitude was shown in the way the Committee accepted the exaggerations and misconceptions of Representative Patman, whose factual ignorance of distribution was exceeded only by his unfamiliarity with the tools of economic analysis. The overly statistical and unemotional arguments of chain spokesmen, on the other hand, were universally shrugged off with comments to the effect that "anyone who has traveled through my district just *knows* the contrary." Even Representative Michener, the Committee member who was most critical of the bill, very early in the hearings conceded the "evil condition of things. We know this condition exists, we know the chains are doing irreparable damage . . . it is the process, or formula, or prescription that we want . . . we all want to go to Heaven. . . But we want to know the route. . ."[34]

The existence of this feeling among all members of a sizable committee shows that the groups behind this bill were taking advantage of an already existing belief. Such a widespread conviction was not one manufactured on short notice, although the bill's sponsors were highly successful in whipping up and harnessing this feeling. Throughout June and early July, in his investigation of the American Retail Federation, Patman had spotlighted the special and often secret discounts received by large grocery chains. Through speeches and newspaper releases Patman had further agitated the public and apparently had caused many usually inarticulate and still unorganized distribu-

[34] *Ibid.*, pp. 15–16.

tors to write their Congressmen demanding that remedial action be taken. Organized distributors had fanned popular concern and had mobilized their members to bombard Congressmen with demands for the Act's passage. Several Congressmen commented on the great volume of mail received: ". . . there has been considerable lobbying going on. . . I presume every Member has had terrible pressure from back home, just as I have had, to commit himself to this legislation." [35]

Representative Michener, who had criticized the bill in Committee hearings for its severity, later announced that he would support the bill and said, although denying that this was the cause for his support, that "no bill in this Congress has been subjected to so much propaganda as the Robinson-Patman bill." [36] While the bill was still in committee he had at one time received more than a hundred wires and letters a day as the result of a notice which had been sent to all of the retail druggists in his district and which read:

URGENT! URGENT! URGENT! We are informed . . . Michener opposing action on Robinson-Patman bill in present form. Also trying to amend bill to make it worthless. Suggest you write or wire him today demanding he support bill in present form. . . Get all merchants in other lines to write or wire him. . . Don't mince words. Let the gentleman know your attitude toward his present opposition. Act now! Passage of this bill is new hope for small businessman. Detroit Druggists' Association.[37]

Much of this success in eliciting widespread support of the bill resulted from the ability of the bill's spokesmen to appeal to many different groups and to different sections of the general public through an almost simultaneous use of arguments which, although somewhat interrelated, were diverse and even con-

[35] Representative Ramspeck, *Cong. Record,* vol. 80, part 8, p. 8226.

[36] *Ibid.,* vol. 80, part 7, p. 8136. This was also the boast of the *NARD Journal,* which claimed that "congressmen and senators have said that in their entire legislative experience they had never witnessed a piece of controversial legislation which brought so much correspondence to their desks. . ." July 2, 1936, p. 904.

[37] *Cong. Record,* vol. 80, part 7, p. 8137.

tradictory. Undoubtedly this was in part a calculated attempt to make the bill all things to all men. Yet the Congressional debates and hearings indicate that much of this conflict in arguments and in believed consequences of the bill also reflect a simple failure to recognize the conflicts. This is especially true of Patman, whose simple and naïve conception of distribution and whose ignorance of even the most rudimentary tools of economic analysis enabled him to pass blithely from inconsistency to inconsistency. But this was also somewhat true of many able and conscientious Congressmen who apparently never really grasped the essential features of the conflicts within distribution.

While any classification imposes an overly simple and rational form on arguments which were varied and often highly irrational,[38] there were three broad arguments made for the bill. The first frankly described the bill as antichain, designed to prevent chains from wiping out independents and to reverse the growth of corporate concentration together with the threat it offered to social institutions and to self-government. This argument tried to elicit the support of independent distributors, of those of the general public who identified competition with the continued existence of small business, and of those who feared or hated chains as a symbol of corporate concentration and Wall Street domination. A few examples will illustrate the general nature of this argument and some of its variations.

. . . there is a conspiracy existing between a few Wall Street bankers and some of the heads of the biggest business interests in this Nation to absolutely get control of retail distribution. They expect to do that through the chain-store system.[39]

---

[38] E.g., one Representative supported the bill because chains operated on Sundays. (*Ibid.*, vol. 80, part 7, p. 8129.) Another supported the bill because he grew nostalgic about the sport of spitting on the pot-bellied stove in an old general store. (*Ibid.*, p. 8135.) Yet another, whose concept of the bill must have been somewhat confused, attacked chains for not lowering their prices sufficiently. (*Ibid.*, p. 8136.)

[39] Patman in *ibid.*, vol. 79, part 11, p. 11572.

Monopoly is creeping up on us, and if we do not exercise just a little vision and forethought now I do not know what is going to happen to this country. Whenever you see all of these vacant store buildings, they were caused by monopoly; and people out of work, caused by consolidation and mergers. . .[40]

There are a great many people who feel that if we are to preserve democracy in government, in America, we have got to preserve a democracy in business operation . . . we must make some effort to maintain the yeomanry in business.[41]

This bill has the opposition of all cheaters, chiselers, bribe takers, bribe givers, and the greedy who seek monopolistic powers which would destroy opportunity . . . and which would eventually cause Government ownership, as the people . . . will not tolerate private monopoly.[42]

[The bill] will restrict the chain-store and mail-order octopuses which are gradually but surely destroying the small businessman in every section of the country.[43]

The American people are not going to stand for a few lords of industry destroying this country.[44]

I feel like there is an evil existing in this country in our economic system. . . I speak specifically of consolidation of food and grocery chain stores. . . The result is . . . that the day of the independent merchant is gone unless something is done and done quickly. He cannot possibly survive. . . So we have reached the crossroads; we must either turn the food and grocery business of this country . . . over to a few corporate chains, or we have got to pass laws that will give the people, who have built this country in time of peace and who saved it in time of war, an opportunity to exist. . .[45]

This argument assumed that mass distributors were socially, politically, and economically undesirable and that the bill's

[40] Patman in House Committee on the Judiciary, Subcommittee, *Hearings on H. R. 4995, H. R. 8442, and H. R. 10486 to Amend the Clayton Act*, 74th Cong., 2d Sess. (Washington: GPO; 1936), p. 395. (Hereafter cited as Utterback Committee Hearings.)

[41] Representative Sumners, chairman of the Judiciary Committee, in *ibid.*, p. 437.

[42] Patman in *Cong. Record*, vol. 80, part 3, p. 3446.

[43] Representative Sabath in *ibid.*, part 7, p. 8102.

[44] Representative Sumners in *ibid.*, p. 8110.

[45] Patman in Sumners Committee Hearings, pp. 5–6.

primary effect would be to safeguard independent retailers against competition, although, as we have seen, retail competition would have been affected only indirectly. Admitting that the bill's purpose was to cripple chains, in furtherance of this end it attacked chain discounts without regard to their basis in equity or economics. Yet this argument was inconsistent with the second major argument offered by the bill's backers, which held that this was not an antichain bill — this statement occurred repeatedly in the Congressional debate — but rather was intended to promote equality among all distributors, chain and independent, by ensuring that all receive the same discounts. This argument appealed, although not as strongly, to all those who sympathized with the first argument, for such equality would have hurt chains. It also appealed to those of the general public whose sense of equity was offended by unequal discounts, whatever their basis in quantity and service differences, and to those who, in a period of much cutthroat competition, of general economic strain, and of high economic mortality rates, wished to relax competitive rigors and to recapture the "live and let live" philosophy which had characterized much of the NRA.

. . . we must live and let live in this country and everybody is entitled to a living. We do not want to give anybody any undue advantage . . . we want to give them all equal rights. . .[46]

We recognize . . . the rights of chain-stores and mail-order houses to do business. . . This bill is not intended to destroy any right or benefit that they have . . . this bill proposes to give all of the independent merchants of this country the same rights, privileges, benefits, and other opportunities as the large concerns receive and no more. . .[47]

. . . if the Robinson-Patman bill is enacted . . . all merchants will receive the same prices from the manufacturers that the chain stores now receive. . . It is not a subsidy for a small group, but it will

[46] Patman in Utterback Committee Hearings, p. 395.
[47] Patman in Sumners Committee Hearings, p. 4.

be giving all independents the same prices, so that all their customers will be benefited along with the chain customers.[48]

The bill has the support of those who believe . . . that the policy of live and let live is a good one; that it is one of the first duties of Government to protect the weak against the strong and prevent men from injuring one another, that greed should be restrained and the Golden Rule practiced.[49]

This argument, then, described the bill as protecting small business by requiring equal discounts. Equality of opportunity was to be more highly valued than economic efficiency. Yet proponents of the bill also offered a third argument, which held that the purpose of the bill was not to hobble chains but rather to promote economic efficiency. It argued that many, or most, of the special discounts received by chains resulted from the ruthless use of buying power and held that the bill would confine chain discounts to those justified by cost savings and prevent abuse of vertical power by large retailers. When this third argument was made in the bill's later stages, it was a recognition that new objectives had been substituted for those of the original bill. It was a measure of the impact of manufacturing and agricultural groups, who opposed the original bill but who gladly agreed to provisions which protected them from exploitation by limiting the discounts that could be wrested from them. Senator Robinson, for example, who apparently never had a clear conception of the original bill and who seldom fought to prevent its amendment, believed its purpose to be "to correct the defects in the Clayton Antitrust Act which undertook to prevent by law unfair price discriminations which gave to those who had the power to do so the opportunity to destroy their competitors and to gain a monopoly. . ." [50]

When some of the more knowledgeable backers of the original bill made this third argument, they were probably trying to mask the purposes of the bill so as to appeal for support to

[48] Patman in *Cong. Record*, vol. 80, part 3, p. 3446.
[49] Patman in *ibid*. p. 3447.
[50] *Ibid*., part 6, p. 6277.

manufacturers and to the general public by seeming to desire only equity and efficiency. This is certainly true of the USWGA's clever attorney, Mr. Teegarden, who had written the original bill and who had so extremely narrowly defined cost savings. On the first day of the hearings he had blandly assured the Committee that the purpose of the bill was to prevent "the use of large buying power in concentrated hands to compel the granting of . . . concessions and discriminations . . . which are not warranted by corresponding economies . . . and which therefore result in unfair preference and advantage to those who exercise this power. . ." [51]

But Patman combined these conflicting second and third arguments so frequently that the conclusion is inescapable that he never saw the conflict. Blinded by his own prejudices, he attributed virtually all chain discounts to the unfair exercise of power and so failed to appreciate that there were economic bases for these discounts.

> . . . a few rich, powerful organizations by reason of their size and their ability to coerce and intimidate manufacturers have forced those manufacturers to give them their goods at a lower price than they give to the independent merchants under the same and similar circumstances and for the same quantities of goods. . . We are attempting to stop it, recognizing the right of the manufacturer to have a different price for a different quantity where there is a difference in the cost of manufacture.[52]

He apparently failed to see that few independents can purchase in large quantities. More important, he did not appreciate the great cost savings which result from quantity purchases and from chain performance of wholesaling functions. Consequently, he failed to see the conflict, believing that the elimination of abuses of power by chains would enable all retailers to buy at virtually the same prices.

> . . . if corporate chains can save the consumers three-quarters of a billion dollars a year when they are doing only 25 per cent of the

[51] From his prepared statement, Sumners Committee Hearing, p. 30.
[52] *Cong. Record*, vol. 80, part 7, p. 8111.

retail business, the consumers of the country will be saved billions of dollars a year when the independents who do the other 75 per cent . . . receive prices from manufacturers on the same basis as the corporate chains. . . It [the bill] will not cause manufacturers to charge the corporate chains more, but it will require them to give independents and smaller chains the same price for the same quantity.[53]

This frequently repeated statement admirably illustrates Patman's twofold error. He is unaware of the great differences in volume between chains and independents, and he believes that it was only unfair and unjustified special discounts which enabled chain stores to underprice their independent competitors. This belief is absurd. We have seen that differences in buying prices account for perhaps a quarter of the difference in retail prices, and that most special concessions to chains were economically justified. The fact that Patman apparently really entertained this view indicates that most independent retailers probably also shared this misconception. This would be natural enough. An independent would find it far easier to attribute his competitive woes to the evil machinations of his chain competitors than to the inefficiency and costliness of his own operations, especially when his store barely yielded him a living. Finding that his chain competitor was selling a product for less than it cost him at wholesale, his natural reaction would be to claim unfair competition and to ascribe the chain's lower price to collusion between the big fellows who owned the chain and the big fellows who made the product. This reaction explains the widespread retailer support for a bill designed to protect wholesalers and paved the way for a frustration of their purposes. To the extent that wholesalers shared this misconception, they, too, were destined for frustration.

The original bill, of course, was not in harmony with the third argument. It encouraged functional discounts without regard to their economic justification, and it defined extremely

[53] *Ibid.*, p. 7760.

narrowly the cost savings on which quantity discounts must rest. But the final act was much in accord with this argument. What happened was, as we have indicated, the subjection of this group program to criticism and amendment in terms of the goals of other groups, who, however, had been slow either to perceive what the bill really proposed to do, or to appreciate the strength of its support. The leading officials of the AGMA at first had not considered it worth their while to testify, although the bill had such obvious significance for grocery manufacturers. At the bill's first hearings, held in mid-July of 1935 by the full House Judiciary Committee, almost no manufacturers or agricultural producers appeared.[54] As a result, the hearings largely produced only fulsome praise for the bill. A few chain-store and mail-order house spokesmen appeared, but the Committee, already sold on the bill's merits, received their arguments coldly.

The Committee made no attempt to determine whether chains really were actual or potential monopolies, apparently accepting Patman's hazy figures and generalizations. Virtually the only effective criticism which the bill received was that made by a representative of voluntary group retailers, who opposed the bill because it would interfere with their buying activities.[55] The sponsors of the bill had won the first round by default.

Although the bill had been introduced in June, 1935, and although the House held hearings in July of that year, it was not until the next February that the middle groups — manufacturers and agricultural producers — appreciated the significance of the bill or the likelihood of its passage. Even the mass distributors had been lethargic, assuming that the bill would

[54] A few did appear to defend chain buying practices, but, to counter this, the NARD was able to command the support of a number of equally tame manufacturers who responded to Association secretary Dargavel's command to inform the Committee that almost no savings accrued from large orders. Sumners Committee Hearings, p. 50.

[55] Summers Committee Hearings, pp. 114 ff.

die.[56] Apparently the middle groups and the groups under attack were taken by surprise when on February 3, 1936, the Senate Committee reported the bill favorably,[57] although it had held no hearings. It also became evident at about this time that the House Judiciary Committee was about to report out its bill. Because of active distributor support and a general conviction that chains needed to be limited, Congress was about to pass a law which would have vital consequences for both the middle groups and the mass distributors. Yet the former had not expressed their views, and the latter had been able to win no Congressional support. It was almost too late. They had missed their opportunity to alter the bill in its committee stages, usually the best opportunity for expression of group purposes, for the Senate had already reported its bill, and the House Judiciary Committee held its final round of hearings between February 3 and 7,[58] before these groups were sufficiently aroused to participate, and reported out the bill on March 31.[59]

The Senate bill shows no evidence that any groups other than its original supporters had influenced the Senate Committee. The Committee did add an important amendment which made only those discriminations unlawful which have the effect of "substantially lessening competition or tending to create a monopoly," but this is simply a paraphrase of Section 2 of the Clayton Act, differing from it only in that it avoids the infinitive split by the earlier act. This amendment can be attributed to the force of the prevailing competitive myth on Senators who did not appreciate the anticompetitive implications of the bill, or who accepted the sponsors' definition of competition.

[56] At later hearings the representative of the Mail Order Association of America stated that after the completion of the Sumners Committee hearings "we proceeded on the assumption for quite a while that . . . you would see that you could not set up an ironclad strait jacket for business, without getting into such a terrific amount of complications that . . . the bill would die of its own weight." Utterback Committee Hearings, pp. 384–385.

[57] S. Rept. No. 1502, 74th Cong., 2d Sess.

[58] Utterback Committee Hearings.

[59] H. Rept. No. 2287, 74th Cong., 2d Sess.

To this clause, moreover, was added another designed to limit chain discounts by taking into account intertype competition. It declared illegal those discounts whose effect was "to injure, destroy, or prevent competition with any person who either grants or receives the benefit of such discrimination, or with the customers of either of them. . ." Since functional discounts had been expressly declared legal, this clause could affect only quantity discounts. The Committee also amended the bill to authorize the FTC to set absolute limits on quantity discounts regardless of their justification in cost savings.

The House Committee's amendments show that only the sponsoring groups and voluntary group retailers had had any influence on its deliberations. The original bill had forbidden the payment of brokerage commissions to a party to a sale, burdening voluntary chains as much as corporate chains. As a concession to voluntary group retailers the somewhat ambiguous phrase "except for services rendered" was inserted, but they were unable to secure any further changes. Since they had adopted many chain buying practices, it would have been impossible to free them of restraints without also freeing the corporate chains. The Committee also added an amendment permitting price discriminations which resulted from price changes made in response to changes in market conditions. This amendment was in the interests of the middle groups, but the necessity of it is so obvious that its acceptance did not reflect their influence. In Committee hearings it was not opposed by the bill's sponsors, whose only concern was to prevent its use to evade the Act.

While other groups thus failed to influence the Committee, the groups backing the original bill maintained their dominance and even tightened up the bill. Where the original bill had specifically authorized functional discounts — "differentials in price as between purchasers depending solely upon whether they purchase for resale to wholesalers, to retailers or to consumers" — the Committee, to ensure the denial of these discounts to mass distributors, added that "for the purpose of such classification of customers as wholesalers or jobbers, or retailers, the character of the selling of the purchaser and not the buying shall determine the classification." This grant of preferential treatment to wholesalers shows how much this was still a wholesaler's bill.

In an attempt to make the bill more workable, however, the House Committee further amended it in an important way. It eliminated the section dealing with presumptive damages under private suits but added Subsection 2 (e),

Upon proof being made . . . that there has been discrimination in price, the burden of rebutting the prima-facie case thus made by showing justification shall be upon the person charged with a violation of this section, and unless justification shall be affirmatively shown, the Commission is authorized to issue an order terminating the discrimination.

Thus far, the subsection makes it even more difficult for manufacturers to grant quantity discounts. But to this the Committee added the proviso

That nothing herein contained shall prevent a seller rebutting the prima-facie case thus made by showing that his lower price . . . was made in good faith to meet an equally low price of a competitor.

Why had the Committee, so sympathetic to the aims of the original bill, added this clause, making discrimination easier? The answer lay not in a change of heart but in a recognition that the absence of such a clause would have produced impossible competitive situations — further evidence of how incompatible with competition were the goals of the original bill. Its absence, for example, might have made it impossible for a national manufacturer, faced with local price competition, to lower his prices to meet that competition unless he lowered his whole price structure. To omit the clause would have worked great hardships, completely disrupted many marketing channels, and might have made the Act unconstitutional. Yet, as

Congressional debate shows, the bill's backers feared that a reiteration of the good-faith competition clause of the Clayton Act [60] would have opened wide the door to price discrimination, enabling a manufacturer to justify all discriminations by alleging that he was only meeting competition. Accordingly, this proviso was so drafted as to try to make the justification it provided for quantity discounts far less sweeping than that provided by the Clayton Act. Congressional debate never made clear the extent of protection believed to be afforded a discriminating manufacturer by this proviso, but it did show that the Committee thought that this proviso was merely procedural and did not weaken the bill's prohibitions against discrimination.[61] Consequently, the addition of this clause was not a defeat for the forces promoting the bill.

It was not until after the bill had picked up momentum and after the chance to influence regular committee deliberations had passed, that manufacturing and agricultural groups finally reacted in strength to safeguard their interests and that mass distributors exerted their full force. Their pressure became fairly intense during March, several Congressmen commenting on the receipt of great volumes of mail reflecting varying views on the proposed legislation. Some of these communications protested the failure of the Senate Judiciary Committee to hold

[60] "That nothing herein contained shall prevent discriminations in prices in the same or different commodities, made in good faith to meet competition."

[61] Representative Utterback, who managed the bill in the House, declared that the proviso "does not set up the meeting of competition as an absolute bar to a charge of discrimination in the bill. It merely permits it to be shown in evidence. This provision is entirely procedural. It does not determine substantive rights, liabilities and duties. They are fixed in the other provisions of the bill. It leaves it a question of fact to be determined in each case, whether the competition to be met was such as to justify the discrimination given, as one lying within the limitations laid down by the bill, and whether the way in which the competition was met lies within the latitude allowed by those limitations. This procedural provision cannot be construed as a carte blanche exemption to violate the bill so long as a competitor can be shown to have violated it first, nor so long as that competition cannot be met without the use of oppressive discrimination in violation of the obvious intent of the bill." *Cong. Record*, vol. 80, part 9, p. 9560. As we shall see below, the Supreme Court did not share this interpretation.

hearings, and on short notice that Committee announced hearings on the Borah-Van Nuys bill,[62] which dealt with the same subject.

These hearings,[63] held on March 24 and 25, were given over almost entirely to manufacturers, who had not presented their views at earlier hearings, and to mass distributors, who had failed to win converts earlier. Technically devoted to the Borah-Van Nuys bill, the hearings actually concerned the Robinson-Patman bill and afforded an opportunity to rebut the arguments presented at the earlier House hearings. Of the 27 witnesses who testified, not one supported the Robinson-Patman bill, and 21 found the Borah-Van Nuys bill less objectionable, the lesser of two evils. While this bill was not an amendment of the Clayton Act but a criminal statute, it, too, dealt with price discrimination. Modeled on a Canadian act, it provided criminal penalties for the granting or receiving of any discriminatory "discount, rebate, allowance, or advertising service charge . . . [on] a sale of goods of like grade, equality, and quantity," and provided the same penalties for geographical price discrimination or the sale of goods at "unreasonably low prices" where the purpose was that "of destroying competition or eliminating a competitor." Despite the seeming ferocity of this bill, it was much milder than the Robinson-Patman bill. Its provisions regarding geographical discrimination and predatory price-cutting would not have much effect on mass distributors,[64] and even the first provision had little real application, for it did not apply unless the goods were of "like grade, quality and *quantity*." As long as a chain buyer bought in quantities different from his competitors, no question of illegal

[62] S. 4171, introduced on March 4. The timing suggests that this bill may have been introduced in order to enable the Committee to reopen hearings on the subject of price discrimination, although this bill was a consolidation of two earlier ones, S. 3670, introduced by Senator Borah on January 16, and S. 3835, introduced by Senator Van Nuys on January 30.

[63] Senate Committee on the Judiciary, Subcommittee, *Hearings on S. 4171; Price Discrimination*, 74th Cong., 2d Sess. (Washington: GPO; 1936).

[64] See the discussion of these provisions in Zorn and Feldman, pp. 254–265.

discrimination was raised. Indeed, the bill did not even require equal *prices*; it only required that discounts, allowances, and rebates be equal.

Mass distributors made more of this opportunity to attack the Robinson-Patman bill than did the middle groups, who did not turn out in as great numbers or express their views as forcefully as might be expected. No major farm groups testified, although they became interested in the bill in the next few months. The chains presented their case more effectively than they had at previous hearings, offering only a minimum of their arguments directly. Instead, in an anticipation of the technique they were to develop more fully in the next few years,[65] they induced other groups and individuals to present arguments against the bill. Marketing experts, a few small consumer organizations, department stores, a few tame manufacturers and agricultural producers all defended the chains. This technique strongly suggests that some of the criticism of the bill by manufacturers, such as that made by the AGMA, while in pursuit of their own interests, was invited and elicited by mass distributors. It is probable that chains spurred on the producing groups, realizing that the programs of these middle groups would limit somewhat their buying power but that such limitations would be less stringent than those of the original Robinson-Patman bill.

While the subcommittee never issued a report and allowed the Borah-Van Nuys bill to die in committee — although it was shortly to be resurrected in a new form — these hearings and other expressions of opinion appear to have influenced a majority of Senators. Only a few weeks before, passage of the Robinson-Patman bill in approximately its original form had appeared assured. In early February the full Judiciary Committee had unanimously reported the bill favorably, adding only one weakening amendment. Now a majority of Senators

[65] See discussion of California referendum and the Congressional hearings on the Patman chain store tax in Chapter VI.

were uncertain about the bill. It would, they discovered, have important consequences for a host of established trade practices and policies. Expressions of support and opposition were confusing. Since chains had adopted a strategy of weakening of the bill through amendment rather than one of outright opposition, the Senators were confronted with a situation in which all groups seemed to support the regulation of price discriminations, but few agreed on how to do it. Most independents supported the bill in its original form, but associations of voluntary chains asked for modification of its brokerage and quantity discount provisions. Manufacturers and agricultural producers approved of the brokerage provisions, but thought the provisions regarding advertising allowances and quantity discounts unduly restrictive. Both agricultural and consumer coöperatives opposed the mandatory classification of distributors, while chains and other mass distributors sought substantial revision of the whole bill.

Most Senators were evidently confused by a flood of expressions of varying points of view [66] and by the inherent difficulties of framing a clear standard for the complex problem of price discriminations which could be applied to a countless number of different market situations. Many Senators, under the leadership of Senator Logan, held firmly to their earlier beliefs and tried to fight off all amendments. But Senate debate on the bill, from April 28 to April 30, showed that more Senators, including Robinson, were somewhat baffled by these confusions and complexities.[67] While the minority of Senators who strongly supported the original bill defeated some weakening amendments,

[66] "Judging by my mail . . . outside of Congress there is a wide difference of opinion about this bill." Senator Walsh, *Cong. Record*, vol. 80, part 3, p. 3115. ". . . I want to explain the bill the best I can because I wish to relieve myself of the tremendous amount of correspondence, briefs, telegrams, and all kinds of pamphlets that come to my desk. . ." Senator Logan, *ibid.*, p. 3116.

[67] Senator Robinson, in referring to the House hearings on the Robinson-Patman bill, declared that "there are hearings already available . . . that no one in this body has read completely unless it be the Senator from Kentucky [Logan]." *Ibid.*, vol. 80, part 6, p. 6277.

it was unable to block others. The passage of some amendments indicated that the groups sponsoring the initial bill had lost their sure Senate majority, but the amendments accepted on the Senate floor vary so in effect that they do not indicate that this majority had shifted to a more moderate but consistent position. Instead, they had simply become confused. They were unable to compromise the varying aims of the groups concerned. Some successful amendments were intended to tighten up the bill. One amendment made a buyer who received a price discrimination equally guilty with the seller who granted it, if the buyer was aware of the concession.[68] Another amendment was copied from the House Committee's amendment making the proof of a price discrimination a prima-facie violation but allowing a rebuttal showing that the concession was made in good faith to meet competition.[69] And the Senate rejected an amendment which applied the broader justification of discrimination afforded by the terms of the Clayton Act's good-faith competition clause.[70]

But it also accepted some which substantially weakened the bill. Three important amendments were passed in rapid succession, exempting from coverage under the Act the sales of commodities purchased for further manufacture or for use in the production of a new product,[71] the sale of mineral products or metals,[72] and the sale of imported commodities.[73] They had been introduced in response to strong pressure from the producing and importing groups concerned. They were accepted, not because of a general agreement that the original bill was too restrictive, but because the Senate, faced with conflicting group interests, had abandoned hopes of compromising them behind a coherent policy. The Senate had given up. "I do not approve

[68] *Ibid.*, p. 6666.
[69] *Ibid.*, p. 6674.
[70] *Ibid.*, p. 6665.
[71] *Ibid.*, p. 6674.
[72] *Ibid.*, p. 6670.
[73] *Ibid.*, p. 6674.

of this amendment," Senator Robinson said at one point, but
"I am not going to make further objection. . ." [74]

That the Senate had reneged in the performance of its legislative function is more clearly manifested in its acceptance of
the entire Borah-Van Nuys bill as an amendment to the Robinson-Patman bill. Now this was an absurd mating of two quite
dissimilar pieces of legislation. One was an amendment to the
Clayton Act, a measure establishing standards for the FTC to
enforce and for the courts to apply in civil proceedings; the
other was a separate criminal statute. And while they dealt
with the same general subject, they were different in substance
and consequences. Why, then, did the Senate unite them? It
did so simply because it was unable to formulate a policy regarding quantity discounts and so was passing the buck to the
Conference Committee which it knew would have to be created.

. . . it was my desire to secure . . . the adoption of the Borah-
Van Nuys bill as an amendment to the Robinson bill so that we may
have the entire subject matter in conference, because there is where
it ultimately will go. In my judgment, the measure which will really
pass will be the measure which the conference works out.[75]

. . . all I ask is that the bill be taken up; that the Senate give it
fair consideration and send it to the other House which . . . is likely
to substitute its bill. . . That will throw the whole subject matter
into conference and give the conferees the opportunity of reconciling
the differences. . . I see no objection to incorporating as an amendment the provisions of the Borah-Van Nuys bill, so that if the conferees finally prefer the plan of that bill to either the House bill or
the Senate bill . . . they will have the opportunity of doing so.[76]

The House ignored the Senate bill and passed its own bill
on May 28.[77] While in the Senate the groups promoting the

[74] *Ibid.*, p. 6671.
[75] Senator Borah, *ibid.*, p. 6276.
[76] Senator Robinson, *ibid.*, p. 6277.
[77] *Ibid.*, part 8, p. 8242. Because the House did not consider the Senate bill,
S. 3154, but passed its own bill, H. R. 8442, in order to establish a conference
on the same numbered bill, it was technically necessary for the Senate to
consider H. R. 8442. It passed this bill on June 1, but substituted the provisions
of its own bill. *Ibid.*, part 9, pp. 8689–8690.

original bill had lost their control, in the House the bill remained under the firm control of Congressional leaders — Representatives Patman, Utterback, and Miller — who were able to defeat every amendment of which they disapproved. This is not to say, however, that the desires of the recently roused middle groups had no influence, for in explicit recognition of their interests the bill's managers themselves proposed and secured the passage of two major amendments. One was no setback for the independents, but it did reflect the influence of manufacturing groups. It struck from the bill a definition of price, added by the Judiciary Committee, which would have explicitly made basing point price systems illegal. The bill's managers had been forced to agree to this amendment in order to get the bill released from the Rules Committee, some of whose members, it seems, had been subjected to pressure from manufacturing groups who opposed this feature of the bill.[78]

The other amendment was a major defeat for the independents and an explicit moderation of their program in order to avoid opposition. This example of programmatic compromise struck from the bill its classification clause, which prevented the granting of functional discounts to retailers who bypassed wholesalers. This clause had been vigorously, if belatedly, opposed by agricultural organizations, including the powerful Farm Bureau Federation and the National Grange, because it would have required manufacturers to discriminate against farmer coöperatives as well as against chains.[79]

These farm groups also feared that the bill might prevent coöperatives from adjusting their prices to conditions prevail-

[78] See Patman's explanation of the amendment, ibid., pp. 8113, 8223.

[79] See ibid., pp. 8117–8118, for copy of letter opposing this and other provisions of the bill and signed by representatives of the American Farm Bureau Federation, the National Grange, the Northwest Farmers' Union Legislative Committee, National Cooperative Milk Producers' Federation, and the Farmers' National Grain Corporation. The tardiness of agricultural groups in awakening to the significance of some of the provisions of this bill is indicated by the fact that this letter — the first fully stated opposition to the bill by them — was not written until May 25.

ing in different markets and that the requirement that advertising allowances be offered "on proportionately equal terms to all other customers" might prevent producers' coöperatives from concentrating limited advertising budgets on strategically chosen markets. The bill's managers did not amend the bill to meet these objections, but they did change their interpretation of some of its provisions.[80] In regard to advertising allowances, for example, it was explained that the bill only required that allowances be offered to all " 'customers competing in the distribution of such products or commodities' — that means the same city or community." [81]

Although the bill's managers made some concessions to middle groups, they retained an unquestioned command of the House, caused the bill to be passed by a resounding margin — 290 to 16 — and sent the bill to conference. There were to meet again these two legislative twins, the Senate bill and the House bill, both born of the USWGA and given to trusted Congressional guardians but one of which had been carefully guided through its limited contact with other groups and had retained most of its pristine particularistic purity, while the other had escaped its guardians and had been corrupted through contact with other groups. It was the task of the Conference Committee to make one bill out of this now dissimilar pair and to choose between the moderated particularism of the House bill and the utter confusion of the Senate bill.

The Committee reported agreement after but a short conference.[82] It appears, however, that this was an agreement to disagree. There is no record of what actually occurred at this conference — even the astute and informed NARD professed ignorance on this score [83] — but the Committee's composition

[80] E.g., see Representative Boileau's interpretations offered in response to these objections, *ibid.*, pp. 8122–8123.

[81] *Ibid.*, p. 8123.

[82] The Committee was not appointed until June 1, yet on June 6 it reported a rewritten bill to both houses of Congress.

[83] *NARD Journal*, October 1, 1936, p. 1408.

suggests that there was head-on conflict. Of the seven members appointed by the House, four were among the strongest proponents of the original bill, while all five of the Senate's representatives had sat on the Committee which had conducted the Borah-Van Nuys hearings and so had heard the arguments against the original bill. Only one of the five Senators had strongly supported the original bill and three had advocated weakening it. The bill which the Committee wrote, and which became the Robinson-Patman Act, suggests that the Committee never succeeded in compromising this conflict and instead amalgamated into one bill the opposing views of the conferees. It was similar to the bill passed by the House but also included the text of the Borah-Van Nuys bill. Now this was an irrational wedding. The House bill was the wholesalers' program, somewhat modified to placate agricultural groups, but the Borah-Van Nuys amendment resulted from the inability of the Senate to agree on policy when confronted with the conflicting demands of independents, manufacturers, and mass distributors. In short, the Committee reported the bill in response to the demand of independents that their bill be passed, but struck out the classification clause in deference to agricultural groups, and added the Borah-Van Nuys bill to show that they also recognized the validity of the arguments of manufacturers and chains.

Thus the Act reflects group conflicts but not the art of political compromise. It may enable compromise, but Congress did not negotiate this compromise; it passed that task on to the FTC, whose perplexing duty it was to administer this melange of partially incongruous and often vague provisions.

The original bill was a wholesaler's measure, sharply differentiating between quantity discounts, which it limited to extremely narrowly defined cost savings, and functional discounts, which were unlimited in amount but which were denied to mass distributors. The final Act differed in many important respects. Its provisions regarding brokerage payments and advertising or promotional allowances were substantially the same, but all mention of functional discounts had disappeared, leaving a manufacturer free to grant them to mass distributors. Quantity discounts could still make "only due allowance" for savings in cost, but the Congressional definition of these cost savings was no longer the narrow one, offered by the USWGA's Mr. Teegarden and seconded by the House and Senate Committees, which required mass distributors to pay a proportionate share of a manufacturer's total manufacturing and distribution costs, regardless of whether they used the services and facilities reflected in these costs. The Conference Committee radically altered Congressional interpretation of this clause. In explaining the conference report to his colleagues, Representative Utterback, formerly one of the more vigorous supporters of the original bill, said:

> So also when a manufacturer or merchant sells to some customers through traveling-salesman solicitation, to others across the counter, and to others by mail order from catalogue *price differentials may be made to reflect the differing costs of such varying methods of sale* . . . the bill permits the translation of differences in cost into price differentials as between the customers concerned, no matter where these differences arise.[84]

This interpretation permits a manufacturer to differentiate materially in price between large and small buyers in cases where, for example, the former do not require sales effort and do not use his storage and distributive facilities, or where they enable him to purchase his raw materials more advantageously or in larger lots, to lower the ratio of preparation costs to actual costs of production, and to produce in off seasons. Now the FTC and the courts might have adopted this broad definition of cost savings anyway, but this Congressional change made it almost impossible for them to adopt the earlier definition and was a major setback for the independents.

The final Act had also been broadened by the good-faith

[84] *Cong. Record*, vol. 80, part 9, p. 9559. (My italics.)

competition clause, which the bill's Congressional guardians had reluctantly added in the House committee and on the Senate floor. Mindful of the broad sanction given discounts by the good-faith competition clause of the Clayton Act, they had tried to so phrase the Robinson-Patman clause that competition would not be a full defense of discrimination.[85] But the Supreme Court did not accept this interpretation and held that a showing that a price discrimination was made in good faith to meet competition is a complete defense under the Act.[86] It is not our purpose to deal with the Act's interpretation and administration, but it is significant that a majority of the Justices, perhaps deliberately closing their eyes to its legislative history and background, held that the Act must be interpreted as a means of protecting competition.

The heart of our national economic policy long has been faith in the value of competition. In the Sherman and the Clayton Acts, as well as in the Robinson-Patman Act, "Congress was dealing with competition, which it sought to protect, and monopoly, which it sought to prevent." [87]

Actually, the original bill promoted competition only if that term be equated with the continued existence of independent distributors. In any other sense of the word it was anticompetitive, designed to cripple the intertype competition offered by mass distributors. But the difficulty of applying the bill in competitive markets, where manufacturers would strongly object to being prevented from meeting discounts offered by competitors, and the need to make the bill seem harmonious with prevailing beliefs in the value of competition, had compelled the bill's managers to make at least a token obeisance to competition. This token, in turn, enabled an interpretation of the Act which was truly in harmony with competition. Thus a particularistic group program had been broadened through the neces-

[85] See Note 61, above.
[86] *Standard Oil Co. v. F. T. C.*, 71 S. Ct. 240 (1951). Three Justices dissented.
[87] *Ibid.*, at 249.

sity of adjustment to the dynamism of a vigorously competitive economy, to the goals of other groups, and to broad national values.

Finally, the Act may have been broadened by retention of the Borah-Van Nuys amendment. This section did not alter directly any of the remainder of the Act, and it was unlikely that it would lead to many criminal actions. If it has any meaning — and it may not — it shows that the Conference Committee, like the Senate, was clumsily reflecting the demands of the middle and chain groups for more moderate legislation. It may, then, have crudely symbolized the way in which the committee wanted the Act to be interpreted — as a measure to aid independents, but not to aid them to an extent which would seriously hurt manufacturers, agricultural groups, nor even mass distributors.

Thus the legislative process did purge the bill of most of its particularism. What had begun as an attempt to hobble chains by making it difficult for them to receive anything more than normal retailers' discounts ended as a law which was relatively sound in terms of equity and economic efficiency. In general, mass distributors are prohibited only from excessive use of vertical power. Functional discounts are not denied them, nor are quantity discounts which reflect demonstrable cost savings. Evasion of this moderate limitation on quantity discounts is made difficult by a fairly explicit injunction against the payment of brokerage commissions to a party to the transaction and by a less definite requirement that advertising and promotional allowances be offered to all competing buyers on proportionately equal terms. Independents are protected only from that intertype competition which involves excessive use of power and so may be called unfair competition. Manufacturers probably benefit more, receiving some protection in their dealings with powerful retailers but being free to match the discounts offered by other sellers. Despite the Act's complexity, its consequences do not differ greatly from those which might have accrued from such legislation as that recommended by the FTC. Nor are they greatly at variance with the results the Commission might have produced under the original terms of Section 2 of the Clayton Act, had it continued actions such as that brought against Goodyear.

But the record does not demonstrate that these relatively reasonable results are necesssary consequences of group conflict and compromise. While it shows that participation of other groups will significantly broaden a particularistic program, in this case that participation was almost fortuitous. Had the middle groups dozed a little longer, or had the mass distributors not adopted the tactic of awakening them and encouraging them to pursue their own interests, then a much different measure would have been enacted.

The record also illustrates some of the many factors which hinder the translation of economic grievances into political policies and which hamper the transfer of the potential strength of economic groups into effective political influence. Obviously this whole episode is meaningless except in terms of groups. What occurred was a process of conflict and compromise among groups which were economically defined and based. The resultant policy tended to be fixed by the relative strengths and goals of the groups concerned. Yet the political balance among groups is often a most imperfect reflection of the underlying economic balance. A group's political strength is not an automatic consequence of its potential size, resources, and interest as defined by economic circumstances. Certainly in the passage of this Act groups were not represented in proportion to their potential strength. The most sizable group concerned, the consumers, were, as usual, hardly represented at all. Even powerful manufacturing and agricultural groups never exerted an influence proportionate to their strength. While independent grocers did muster some political strength, more appeals were made in their name than by them. The pressure they did exert was elicited and manipulated to a considerable degree. It is only a slight exaggeration to say that they were tricked into supporting a wholesalers' bill.

Furthermore, these groups did not operate in a vacuum. Independents achieved even their limited victory only because they could harness a broad antipathy toward chains, which, as we have seen, can only partially be attributed to group clashes within distribution. This antipathy, however, was not an unmixed blessing. To the extent that independents, too, shared its irrational elements, they were hindered in formulating a sound program. This was especially true of the retailers. Believing that most of the competitive gains made by chains resulted from abuse of vertical power, they were deluded into a belief that an elimination of unfair or uneconomic price concessions would substantially ease their competitive situation. In fact, however, the independents may have promoted an Act which at times actually worsens their lot, for the Act is a two-edged sword. By forcing manufacturers and wholesalers to reëxamine their traditional discount structures with the tools of cost accounting, the Act has led many of them to a realization that the prices charged for small orders were insufficient to cover costs.

Yet another factor to which the independents had to adjust their program was the prevailing competitive myth. Despite the fact that their program was anticompetitive in its effects, they had to give their bill the appearance of promoting competition. But the good-faith competition clause, included to give this appearance, permitted an interpretation of the Act which truly did promote competition. They had sought to utilize the garb of the competitive myth to cloak their particularistic purposes; instead, their purposes were subordinated to those valued by the myth.

A final factor inhibiting the independents was the dynamically competitive nature of the economy, to which the inclusion of the good-faith competition clause was, in part, a tribute. Even had the original bill passed unamended, it is doubtful whether mass distribution could really have been crippled by such a shallow and patchworklike attempt to hobble the competitive vigor of mass distributors through an attack on some of the surface reflections of the revolution which had already taken place in the channels of trade. It was an attempt to strike at the symptoms of the change, not at its causes. So great a premium does the economic system pay for changes producing efficiencies and so relatively easy does it make these changes, that mass distributors probably could have evaded or avoided most of the supposed consequences of the original bill. Some of the steps taken by grocery chains to avoid the effects of even the moderate act passed — such as a shift to the purchase, or even direct production, of goods made to a retailer's specifications, and to the purchase of the entire output of small manufacturers — suggest some of the steps mass distributors could have taken to avoid the effects of more stringent legislation. In short, in this sector the economy was too dynamic to be channeled to an important degree by the amount of governmental regulation which could be evoked by the political strength mustered by independents.

# VIII

## The Fair-Trade Laws

The NARD's broad and forceful campaign for "fair-trade," or resale price maintenance, legislation — permitting the fixing of minimum wholesale and retail prices on trademarked goods — in the 1930's was extraordinarily successful, leading to the designation of that Association as "the Nation's most powerful trade association today." [1] Congressman Patman told its national convention that "no organization . . . has more power, prestige, or influence. . ." [2] Although I use this episode only to test my generalizations about the interrelations of politics and economics within distribution, this campaign was so successful that a fuller description would be a valuable case study in pressure politics.[3] Within an eight-year period, 1933–1940, the NARD secured the passage of resale price maintenance acts in 44 states — half again as many as passed chain taxes. In one year alone, 1937, 28 states passed such laws.[4] That this was a centrally directed and carefully organized campaign is indicated by the fact that the acts of 16 states are closely modeled on the California statute, which had been passed at the insistence of the organized retail druggists of that state,

[1] *Business Week*, August 28, 1937, p. 42.

[2] *NARD Journal*, October 1, 1936, p. 1937.

[3] For a description of some of this campaign, see FTC, *Report on Resale Price Maintenance* (Washington: GPO; 1945), especially chapters III, IV, V. (Hereafter referred to as FTC, *RPM*.)

[4] *Ibid.*, pp. 69–70.

and those of 20 states are direct or close copies of the NARD's "Model Act." [5] These acts were such close copies and were pushed through so hastily that 16 states repeated California's wrongful use of the word "content" where "container" was intended,[6] and 11 states actually copied a stenographic error in the California act which made an important section of the law unintelligible, substituting "in delivery" for "any dealer." [7]

The NARD's success on the federal level was equally striking. It won passage of the Miller-Tydings Amendment to the almost sacred Sherman Act in 1937, despite the fact that every session of Congress since 1914 had seen that body reject resale price maintenance legislation [8] and despite the opposition of a President who had just received overwhelming support in the 1936 elections.

Economic factors explain much of this legislative success. In Chapters II, III, and IV we saw that there are many economic and other factors which make retail druggists more cohesive than perhaps any other retail merchants, enabling them to form a militant, well organized, highly disciplined trade association, capable of conducting effective political campaigns. Of probably equal importance is the trade's power structure. It will be remembered that the power structure within automobile distribution had hindered dealers in mobilizing political power and had narrowly confined the gains which could be won. The drug trade's power structure offers a sharp contrast. Because the retailer often performs the crucial function of selection — determining which brand a consumer will buy — manufacturers are dependent on his good will and hesitate to antagonize him. In addition, because of inelastic consumer demand for drugs and cosmetics, resale price maintenance, and its consequent raising of retail margins, does not lose manufac-

---

[5] For a comparison and analysis of these laws, see *ibid.*, pp. 71–87.

[6] Stanley A. Weigel, *The Fair Trade Acts* (Chicago: Foundation Press; 1938), pp. 66, 89–100.

[7] FTC, *RPM*, p. 68.

[8] E. T. Grether, p. 7.

turers much volume. And, since the consumer had never made much use of his potential economic power and could be expected to be politically quiescent, druggists were relatively free to promote a program designed to increase retail margins.

Finally, it was unlikely that intertype competitors would muster strong political opposition to the druggists. The logical opponents, the chains, had come to accept nonprice competition and to mute their price appeal. The deepest price competition confronting druggists was that offered by pine-board stores and department stores. But the former's economic base was so marginal and personal — resting on their ability to secure distress merchandise, to get by with minimum product ranges, and to find low-rental quarters — that they could not generate or organize effective political power. Accordingly, the burden of mustering and expressing intertype political opposition to the NARD's program had to be borne by department stores, whose political strength was confined to cities.

Thus, the economic bases for a political victory of the independent retail druggists are readily apparent. Even a quick summary of the political campaign shows how much of its success is due to these economic bases. While other retailers — notably liquor dealers and booksellers — aided the druggists, this was the NARD's program, and it was the NARD which directed and organized the campaign and which exerted the preponderance of force in support of it.

. . . it is to be borne in mind that the pharmacists . . . have been the ones who have carried the brunt of the fight to secure fair-trade legislation. While grocers, jewelers, confectioners, etc., gave their moral support . . . they had little or no part in actually bringing it to pass.[9]

At work here was the same militant cohesion which had made the NARD one of the major forces behind the Robinson-

[9] From speech of R. L. Swain, chairman of the NARD's fair trade committee, in FTC, *RPM*, p. 157. And the *NARD Journal* boasted that "It is essentially an N.A.R.D. victory. Many others helped . . . but . . . the N.A.R.D. led the way and shouldered the brunt of the burden." August 26, 1937, p. 1239.

Patman bill and which had enabled it, through an unusual amount of pressure, to obtain the most protective of all NRA retail codes.[10] And retail druggists were considerably aided by their vertical allies. The wholesalers naturally allied themselves with the retailers. Maintenance of retail prices and margins would tend to protect wholesale margins. Indeed, there are some suggestions that drug wholesalers, especially McKesson & Robbins, played a major role in promoting and financing the campaign,[11] but little concrete evidence is available.[12] Manufacturers, too, were inclined to support resale price maintenance. A manufacturer whose product had been made a loss leader often found that, as a consequence, independents were reluctant to stock it and some consumers balked at paying its normal retail price. Retailers often were not content with purely voluntary support from manufacturers; they blacklisted or boycotted manufacturers who did not support their program, and maintained white lists of coöperating manufacturers.[13] The experience of the Pepsodent Company is the best example of how a manufacturer could be "persuaded" to support the druggists.[14] In 1935 Pepsodent withdrew from its California fair-trade contracts for fear of violating the Sherman Act. Druggists' associations quickly reacted by urging their members to boycott Pepsodent. Almost to a man the retailers responded. The executive secretary of the Northern California Retail Druggists' Association reported that

. . . to my great delight and the great delight of our executive com-

[10] For an account of this pressure and a description of the Retail Drug Code, see NRA Work Materials No. 57.

[11] E.g., see testimony of Dr. Ruth Ayres, TNEC Hearings, part 8, p. 3375.

[12] A Connecticut grand jury, however, found that the NARD and McKesson & Robbins had shared the expenses involved in securing, through bribery, the passage of a fair-trade act in that state. Kenneth G. Crawford, *The Pressure Boys; The Inside Story of Lobbying in America* (New York: Julian Messner; 1939), p. 23.

[13] For examples, see TNEC Hearings, Part 8, pp. 3465–3467; FTC, *RPM*, pp. 153–154.

[14] For accounts of this episode, see Grether, pp. 99–100; FTC, *RPM*, pp. 143, 166–167, 169, 195–196.

mittee all the druggists in California refused to sell Pepsodent tooth-paste or Pepsodent products. They put them in the basement. Some were enthusiastic enough to throw them into the ash can.[15]

The boycott was almost completely successful. For a while it was possible to buy Pepsodent products only in a few pine-boards. News of the boycott was passed on to druggists in other states, and the Company's national sales fell appreciably. Here was a clear demonstration of the vertical power of drug-gists and of their surprising group solidarity. Pepsodent was a relatively powerful firm. Through extensive advertising it had won about as much consumer preference and hence had gener-ated about as much vertical power as any manufacturer could. Yet it had been decisively defeated by the organized druggists. After a few months of drastically declining sales, Pepsodent capitulated, again signed price maintenance contracts, *and* donated a check of $25,000 to the NARD to be used in support of the campaign for fair-trade acts. Following this good-will offering, other manufacturers voluntarily contributed to the fund, and still others were requested to donate.

Their vertical power permitted druggists to present what appeared to be industry-wide support for price maintenance at Congressional hearings and probably at hearings before state legislative committees. At all Congressional hearings on the Miller-Tydings Amendment [16] manufacturers as well as whole-salers joined retailers in supporting the legislation. Much of this support clearly was by command of the NARD.[17] This

[15] FTC, *RPM*, p. 143.

[16] Senate Committee on the Judiciary, Subcommittee, *Hearings on S. 3822, Resale Price Maintenance*, 74th Cong., 2d Sess. (Washington: GPO; 1936); House Committee on the Judiciary, Subcommittee, *Hearings on H. R. 1611, Resale Price Maintenance*, 75th Cong., 1st Sess. (Washington: GPO; 1937); Senate Committee on the Judiciary, Subcommittee, *Hearings on S. 100, Resale Price Maintenance*, 75th Cong., 1st Sess. (Washington: GPO; 1937). Hereafter referred to, respectively, as Hatch Committee Hearings, 1936; Miller Committee Hearings; and Hatch Committee Hearings, 1937.

[17] One group of telegrams from manufacturers supporting the Miller-Tydings Amendment and submitted to Congressional committee were addressed, not to that committee, but to the NARD. One of these wires was prefaced with

political solidarity was possible because of the same factor which gave the retailers their economic power: the silence of the consumer — unorganized, inarticulate, and probably unaware. At these three hearings only one witness testified for the consumer, and she was a self-appointed representative.[18] Spokesmen for the Farm Bureau Federation and the National Grange also opposed the bill in the interests of farmers as consumers, but their opposition was so perfunctory and ill-informed that the Congressional committees could have safely assumed that farmer-consumers were not much concerned.

That consumers are congenitally difficult to organize and arouse is a political truism. Yet the task is not hopeless. As we have seen, grocery chains finally mustered considerable consumer support in opposition to the Patman tax bill. This political support, however, had been based upon a prior economic support. Having successfully appealed to consumers with lower prices, the grocery chains were then able to generate some political support for a continuation of those prices. But drug chains had given up the effort to elicit consumer support for lower prices, accepting fatter margins in preference to promoting intertype competition. Where once they had vigorously opposed resale price maintenance legislation, they now supported it, seeking protection from pine-boards and department stores.[19] "Today chains are working shoulder to shoulder with the independents in behalf of fair trade legislation," said the NARD.[20] Consequently, if there were to be any consumers' tribunes to mobilize consumer support for a continuation of deep price cuts, they had to arise from the pine-boards or the

---

the statement that it was in response to "Your telegram forwarded to me here." Miller Committee Hearings, pp. 84–86. One also wonders how spontaneous was a wire from Pepsodent. *Ibid.*, pp. 81–82.

[18] Dr. Jessie V. Coles of the American Home Economics Association. *Ibid.*, pp. 87 ff.; Hatch Committee Hearings, 1937, pp. 14 ff.

[19] E.g., see testimony of F. J. Griffiths, Secretary of the National Association of Chain Drug Stores. Hatch Committee Hearings, 1936, p. 18; Miller Committee Hearings, pp. 22 ff.

[20] *NARD Journal*, October 3, 1935, p. 1251.

department stores. But the former were too marginal and small to play an effective role, and sent not a single representative to the Congressional hearings. From among the ranks of the department stores, R. H. Macy, long a leading price-cutter, did try to assume this role. It fought federal and New York legislation vigorously and forcefully. But even in New York, where it elicited some consumer opposition, it could not prevent passage of a fair-trade act. In Washington it was almost alone in its opposition, commanding the support of only the department stores' trade association, the National Retail Dry Goods Association, and the Mail Order Association.

Thus the drug trade presented a united front, facing the opposition of only a few department stores. The economic bases, then, do explain much of the NARD's political success. Yet this is not a full explanation. Economic circumstances explain why virtually the whole drug trade supported fair trade; they do not explain how it was possible for the nation's 50,000 druggists, together with other drug interests, to gain such a sweeping political victory with so little support from other retailers. The absence of effective opposition from other groups is only a partial answer, for the Miller-Tydings Amendment was opposed by a strong President. And every previous session of Congress since 1914 had seen similar legislation fail, although many earlier bills were backed by broad group coalitions.[21]

The political process was more than a simple reflection of underlying economic forces. The NARD's great success — the passage of 28 state acts and one federal statute in a single year — suggests extraordinary political skill and organization. The NARD was immodest, perhaps, but accurate in attributing victory to "a combination of brilliant leadership and direction, plus loyal and active support by the members."[22] It has frequently taken pride in its "constant militance and vigilance"[23]

---

[21] For an account of these earlier attempts to secure a federal resale price maintenance law, see FTC, *RPM*, pp. 39–50.

[22] *NARD Journal*, August 26, 1937, p. 1239.

[23] E.g., *ibid.*, June 16, 1938, p. 860.

and has said that "legislative activity has been one of the major divisions of the Association's work since its beginning." [24] Little wonder that its secretary should boast that "the N.A.R.D. can do anything in reason that the retail druggists want it to do. . ." [25] And the political skill of its leadership was matched by the cohesion and effectiveness of its organization. Its *Journal* was justified in exulting, after the passage of the Miller-Tydings Amendment, that "once again . . . ORGANIZATION WINS!" [26] Its political skill and organizational cohesion were amply demonstrated throughout this decade. In addition to its sweeping fair-trade victory, the Association had been a major force behind the Robinson-Patman Act, had assisted in the passage of state chain taxes and unfair trade practices acts, and had induced at least 11 states and over 200 cities to confine the profitable sale of prophylactics to drug stores.[27] This mastery of the political arts cannot be dismissed as a mere reflection of economic circumstances.

Not much material is readily available on the state campaigns conducted by the NARD,[28] but apparently it took advantage of a relative lack of opposition to push through its legislation speedily and easily. This speed and ease are indicated by the number of bills passed in one year, by the fact that hasty legislatures enacted bills with stenographic errors, and by the fact that few legislatures even conducted hearings.[29] The campaign was, however, centrally directed. "The outstanding work of the N.A.R.D. has been of extreme importance in the enactment of these laws. The Association furnished state

[24] *Loc. cit.*
[25] *Ibid.*, June 4, 1936, p. 697.
[26] *Ibid.*, July 15, 1937, p. 1125.
[27] *Ibid.*, January 7, 1937, p. 80; May 6, 1937, p. 679.
[28] Apparently frequent use was made of the technique of deluging a state capital with busloads of pharmacists during crucial stages in the legislative course of the desired measures. In addition, in Connecticut direct, and pecuniary, contacts were established with legislators. Crawford, p. 23.
[29] Even in the four populous states of New York, New Jersey, Pennsylvania, and Illinois no legislative hearings were held. Hatch Committee Hearings, 1937, p. 12.

legislative committees with facts, figures, and a wealth of ammunition with which to fight these bills through legislatures."[30] And druggists' pressure on state legislators paralleled the NARD's method of influencing Congress.

Under a "Captain Plan," first developed in California and then applied nationally, the NARD organized a contact committee in every Congressional district, headed by a "Captain," who was intimately acquainted with the district's Representative.[31] By 1937 there were two thousand "Congressional contact men" in operation, and the number later rose to three thousand. Each of these men, in turn, was expected to form in his own local community a committee of ten other retailers "who will work and move as a unit when called upon by the N.A.R.D. Washington Office."[32] These committees exploited the especial malleability of candidates for office by approaching the nominees for House and Senate in the 1936 elections and asking for their pledges of support.[33] With such a disciplined army in the field, the NARD's GHQ could conduct a most effective political campaign, attacking on broad fronts or concentrating fire on one point of resistance after another.[34] They could bombard all Congressmen with demands for passage of the Miller-Tydings Amendment, producing "a flood of letters and telegrams coming from practically every community in the nation,"[35] or they could inundate members of a crucial committee. The *NARD Journal* for 1936 and 1937 reads like a file of battle orders. At one time one thousand communications were ordered sent to each member of a committee considering the

[30] *NARD Journal*, June 18, 1936, p. 830.
[31] For descriptions of this plan, see FTC, *RPM*, pp. 64–66, 144; TNEC Hearings, part 8, pp. 3460–3463.
[32] *NARD Journal*, January 7, 1937, p. 36.
[33] *Ibid.*, June 17, 1937, p. 932.
[34] "Members of these congressional contact committees are the shock troops of the National Association of Retail Druggists which are used in legislative emergencies in the Nation's Capital. They have rendered wonderfully effective work in the past. . ." *Ibid.*, October 5, 1939.
[35] *Ibid.*, June 17, 1937, p. 932.

bill; at another time each druggist was commanded to write a letter a week to his Representative and Senator; in the later stages of the bill's consideration "a constant barrage of letters and telegrams and letters" was ordered.[36] Direct pressure was applied on the President and the FTC, and state governors were strongly urged to communicate their support of the bill to the President and the Commission. Determined and organized attempts were made to gain allies. Instructions were given on methods of securing consumer support and of lining up support from other retailers.[37] Manufacturers were "persuaded" to support the bill and unsympathetic newspapers were attacked.[38] In short, while the economic environment had minimized opposition and made victory possible, the achievement of that victory required positive political action and a mastery of the weapons of political warfare.

Equally responsible for its victory was the way in which the NARD had framed and presented the issues. Seeking to lessen criticism of its program as "price-fixing" — criticism which had defeated all earlier federal price maintenance bills — it combined an appeal to general antichain, antibigness sentiment with an appeal to equity. It argued that chains had grown primarily because of an unfair trade practice — loss leaders — and that only the prohibition of this practice would enable independents to survive.

These unfair trade practices have . . . been peculiarly helpful to . . . large distributors. . . . Thus large concerns have become larger. . . . Monopoly now casts its insidious shadow over the land that was meant to symbolize free and open opportunity for all.[39]

We are up against the question of whether we want to protect small business enterprises against powerful aggregations of capital. . . . I am not out to destroy big business, but . . . it must be properly

[36] *NARD Journal*, February 18, 1937, p. 273.
[37] For examples, see TNEC Hearings, part 8, pp. 3463–3465.
[38] *Ibid.*, p. 3466.
[39] R. L. Swain, chairman of the NARD fair-trade committee, Miller Committee Hearings, p. 4.

regulated . . . for not to regulate it so the small businessman can survive is to tend toward monopoly and no competition at all.[40]

. . . the small retail distributors are rapidly approaching the time when they will be forced completely out of an independent business existence. . . Even if this situation were the outcome of fair methods of competition . . . it would be deplorable. . . These small businesses have been and are the backbone of the communities of this country. . . If we ask ourselves, honestly, whether we want this country to become a nation of clerks or to remain a nation of opportunity for individual enterprise, there can be only one answer consistent with American ideals.[41]

The bill's supporters devoted most of their arguments to attacks on loss leaders, which they assailed for injuring: a manufacturer, by cutting off some of his marketing channels or by damaging the reputation of his products; a wholesaler, by disrupting "normal" trade channels; an independent retailer, by cutting his sales; and a consumer, by deceiving him into the belief that all products in a cut-rate store were priced on an equally low level and by bankrupting the fully-stocked druggist and so depriving the consumer of ready access to a full stock of drugs.[42] This was a persuasive argument. Loss leaders can be defended as a method of advertising, but there are also sound and, to the members of the Congressional committees, convincing reasons for terming their use a deceptive, perhaps even predatory, trade practice. But the argument against loss leaders was only a smokescreen. Had it really been the NARD's goal to outlaw them, then the most direct method would have been state acts prohibiting sales below cost. Indeed, 25 states had passed such legislation by 1940.[43] While these laws may

[40] Senator Tydings, Hatch Committee Hearings, 1936, p. 40.
[41] E. G. Kelley, secretary of the American Pharmaceutical Association, *ibid.*, p. 43.
[42] For a full statement of this argument, see memorandum filed by Edward S. Rogers, counsel for the fair-trade committee of the NARD, Hatch Committee Hearings, 1936, pp. 7–12.
[43] See FTC, *RPM*, pp. 87–92; Fainsod and Gordon, p. 603; Zorn and Feldman, pp. 317–326.

be held unconstitutional unless cost is defined narrowly, they do effectively bar loss leaders.

The major purpose of fair-trade acts was, rather, to give druggists what they had always considered to be their just recompense and what had long been a shibboleth of organized druggists — a margin of 33⅓ per cent (a markup of 50 per cent on cost) — and to prevent their competitors from cutting prices reflecting this margin. At the NARD's 1935 convention its president said:

> The principle that 33⅓-per cent margin from the suggested minimum price is necessary is as old as the National Association of Retail Druggists, and the cornerstone upon which the Association was founded. . . With the passage of so many State fair trade laws it soon became apparent that . . . the retailer would be able to demand compliance with this principle from participating manufacturers.[44]

Fair-trade acts permit the manufacturer of a trademarked, branded, or otherwise identified product, or his authorized agent or distributor, to prescribe by contract the minimum prices at which the product may be resold at wholesale and at retail. The nonsigner clause of these laws makes the observance of the prices set by a contract signed with any one distributor mandatory on all other distributors within the state upon the serving of notice.[45] Thus a manufacturer or his distributor can set minimum resale prices for his goods at all stages in their distribution. Although such contracts conflict with common-law doctrines of contract, in 1936 the Supreme Court sustained them as a valid method of protecting a manufacturer's good will, and upheld the constitutionality of the Illinois and California statutes.[46]

[44] FTC, *RPM*, p. 212.

[45] For more detailed analysis and description of these state laws, see *ibid.*, pp. 67–87; Weigel, pp. 36–65.

[46] *Old Dearborn Distributing Co. v. Seagram-Distillers Corporation*, 299 U. S. 183. This opinion also covered several similar cases: *Triner v. McNeil*; and, from California, *The Pep Boys, Manny, Moe & Jack of California v. Pyroil Sales Co.* For an account of earlier cases dealing with resale price maintenance when not authorized by state legislation, see FTC, *RPM*, pp. 17–36.

This grant of legal authority to set minimum resale prices enables a manufacturer to do much more than stop loss leaders; it empowers him to set all distributive margins and to restrain or end retail price competition. Consequently, the argument against loss leaders is irrelevant, and an evaluation of fair trade requires examination of its effects on horizontal competition among manufacturers and retailers, vertical relations within marketing channels, and intertype competition among different channels of distribution. Although its purpose was to protect independent retailers, the Congressional backers of the Miller-Tydings Amendment, perhaps not entirely ingenuously,[47] evaluated it only in terms of competition among manufacturers, holding, in effect, that this was the only form of competition which it was necessary to preserve and that its preservation was sufficient to protect consumers.

. . . this bill cannot be unfair to the public because if prices are set too high by any manufacturer, competition will take his trade away from him. . . Manufacturers still compete with each other. . . Competition remains — and it is fair competition. . .[48]

This argument is unsound because it fails to consider retail competition and vertical relations. The vertical power of organized independent retailers enables them to exercise some of the legal authority to set resale prices conferred on manufacturers. In efforts to achieve margins of $33\frac{1}{3}$ per cent or more, druggists can force manufacturers to set minimum resale prices so high that they tend to become the going retail prices, and price competition disappears.[49] Different products may still compete — although resale price maintenance makes easier horizontal

[47] Senator Tydings' law partner was in the pay of the NARD during the campaign for federal legislation. Crawford, pp. 20–21.

[48] Senator Tydings, Hatch Committee Hearings, 1936, p. 23. Although this was his principal argument, he also held that retail price competition would also continue to exist, assuming, as he apparently did, that the minimum resale prices really would be minimum prices and only place a floor under a range of retail prices.

[49] For a study of the effects of resale price maintenance on retail drug prices, see FTC, *RPM*, pp. 639–710.

agreements, tacit or explicit, among manufacturers [50] — but the prices of intertype competitors cannot reflect the differences in their costs of distribution.

The most effective argument of fair-trade supporters at the national level, however, was a procedural one. The Miller-Tydings Amendment did not directly authorize price maintenance; instead, it amended the Sherman Act so as to prevent that Act, or Section 5 of the Federal Trade Commission Act, from being applied against price maintenance contracts covering goods moving in interstate commerce but resold in a state legalizing these contracts. Accordingly, the Amendment's backers argued that it declared no policy; it simply left the states free to determine policy as they saw fit.

. . . the States should be free to deal with their own problems in their own way. . . Someone has referred to the States as so many legislative, social, and economic laboratories. . . It is through these legislative laboratories that we . . . test, in the acid of experience, new principles of liberty, and new principles of restraint.[51]

. . . if the people of Arkansas want to pass a law that will permit their citizens to deal in this way, that is the Arkansas people's privilege, and we should not pass any law to prevent that. . .[52]

These arguments and this technique paid off. At the last moment the bill was for a while blocked by President Roosevelt's vigorous opposition, expressed just as the bill was about to pass. Quoting the FTC's opinion that the bill would probably enable retailers and manufacturers to "abuse the power to arbitrarily fix resale prices by unduly increasing prices," he wrote to the Vice President on April 24 that "this bill should not, in my judgment, receive the consideration of the Congress until the whole matter can be more fully exlored." [53]

The clearly implied threat of a veto stymied the fair-trade supporters only a few weeks. As pressure from the militant

[50] *Ibid.*, pp. 540–547.
[51] R. L. Swain, quoting Senator Tydings, in Miller Committee Hearings, p. 6.
[52] Representative Patman, in *ibid.*, p. 21.
[53] *Cong. Record*, vol. 81, part 7, p. 749.

NARD reached a crescendo — the NARD high command ordered its troops to write to the President, and to their Senators and Representatives, to ask ten other retailers to do the same, to ask state legislators to write the President, to hold mass meetings, to ask state legislatures to memorialize the President and Congress, and to circulate petitions to the President and to Senators and Representatives [54] — on July 2 Senator Tydings attached the bill as a rider to a District of Columbia appropriations bill which had to be signed so that the District could meet some pressing obligations.[55] With the passage of the Amendment on August 17, state legislators were permitted to define a part of national economic policy. Any assumption that state legislatures would consider fair-trade legislation more thoroughly than had Congress in its brief and inadequate study was, as we have seen, ill-founded. Evidently few state legislators knew, or cared, that price maintenance laws invited price fixing, for only Wisconsin expressed concern over the prices set by fair-trade contracts.[56] And the NARD avoided debate wherever possible. Having directed that each drugstore be transformed into "an outpost of political influence and education" so that the druggist could make the most of his "unparalleled opportunity to put in his best licks for the fair candidates for office, and to take care of those who are unfair," [57] the NARD counseled its members to

. . . avoid all reference to Fair Trade laws . . . unless the customer himself brings them up. The principles which are fundamental to the Fair Trade movement are deep, and for an uninformed customer to understand them would require a lengthy explanation which might lead to an argument — and no one ever won an argument.[58]

[54] *NARD Journal*, May 20, 1937, p. 759.

[55] The President signed with considerable reluctance and criticized the practice of attaching irrelevant measures to urgent legislation.

[56] This state provided that upon complaint an administrative agency would determine whether a price was "unfair and unreasonable." If the agency so found, the contract was to be nullified. FTC, *RPM*, pp. 76–77.

[57] *NARD Journal*, January 2, 1936, p. 36.

[58] *NARD Journal*, June 16, 1938, p. 42.

Even this brief description of the NARD's vigorous and artful campaign shows that the economic circumstances which enabled the NARD to mobilize the whole drug trade are not a full explanation of the political events. The economic bases of the conflict made the NARD's political victory possible, but they did not produce that victory. They created political potentials which took positive and vigorous political actions to be realized.

This episode also sheds light on other interrelations of politics and economics. While the effectiveness of trade regulation is often questioned, the vigor with which druggists sought political redress of their economic woes under the existing rules of the game suggests that this regulation had been quite effective. In view of the frequency with which druggists have tried to avoid price competition through both horizontal and vertical agreements, only to be frustrated by actions under the Sherman or Federal Trade Commission Acts,[59] it is likely that, had it not been for these rules, the American drug trade would have resembled the British. In Britain the Proprietary Articles Trade Association controls all prices and margins under a scheme in which industry-wide boycotts of price cutters enforce prices and margins.[60] A high degree of security is enjoyed by most distributors, but this security has been purchased at considerable economic cost. Efficient firms and marketing media have been hobbled to protect the less efficient. The latter have been assured of high margins, but the very height of margins has attracted so many firms to the trade and allowed so many others to continue in existence that firm incomes remain low.

The previous impact of antitrust regulation is also indicated by the changes which fair trade has brought about. The most obvious change has been an increase in the concessions which druggists can exact from manufacturers. An FTC investigation

[59] Above, Chapter IV.
[60] E. T. Grether, *Resale Price Maintenance in Great Britain*.

showed that their vertical power has been repeatedly used to force manufacturers to sign price maintenance contracts which guarantee retail margins of at least 33⅓ per cent.[61] Outright boycotts have seldom been necessary after the spectacular and well publicized humbling of Pepsodent in California. But where persuasion fails, indirect boycotts are used. Uncoöperative manufacturers are listed by the NARD, state fair-trade committees, and state and local druggists' associations. This listing is often the signal for "off-the-shelf" programs in which low-margin products are not stocked, are hidden under counters, or their sale otherwise discouraged. Coöperative manufacturers may be rewarded by having their products energetically promoted. A state association, for example, may designate a "Dr. West Appreciation Week" or "Statewide Gem Razor Appreciation Days" in which all druggists display prominently and push the sales of high-margin, price-maintained products.

The effects of this power are not confined to the vertical plane. Thanks to the nonsigner clause, organized druggists can limit or end price competition. If they can control the resale price a manufacturer sets, they of course thereby control the prices their competitors charge. Fair trade has substantially narrowed the gap between independents' prices and those of their intertype competitors. Chain and department stores have had to raise their prices to the level specified by fair-trade contracts and independents have tended to charge minimum resale prices.

Thus many of the interrelations between the political and the economic are apparent. Faced with governmental limitations on their economic power, organized druggists mustered their political power — and used their economic power to generate yet more political power — so to control governmental power as to permit the freer exercise of their economic power. This somewhat circular process, however, does not allow perpetual and self-generating increases in power. Nor was this

[61] FTC, *RPM*, pp. 166–249.

political victory a final defeat for competition. Retail druggists are too inextricably enmeshed in a vigorously competitive economy always subject to dynamic change to insulate themselves from competition and change.

They have been able to translate their political victory into only limited economic gains. Vertically, their power is dominant but far from absolute. Shortly after the passage of the Miller-Tydings Amendment wholesalers induced manufacturers to sign manufacturer–wholesaler fair-trade contracts which forbade wholesalers to grant retailers a special 10 per cent discount on fast-moving products — a discount that wholesalers had previously granted out of their own margin to assist retailers in meeting intertype competition.[62] And fear of his competitors limits the increases in resale prices that a manufacturer can safely grant. Even when competing manufacturers act together, as appears to be the case at times, private brand competition limits price increases. Private brands also offer a check at the retail level. The greater the success of independent druggists in increasing margins and prices on nationally advertised products, the greater is the price appeal of private brands carried by chain and department stores. Fair trade improved somewhat the terms of trade for retailers but did not free them from competitive restraints.

And dynamic change has intensified these restraints. Attracted by high margins, supermarkets have recently been selling increasing ranges and amounts of drugs and toiletries. The very success of druggists in raising margins has made intertype competition more likely by making it more profitable. Surveys indicate that by 1950 food stores were making half or more of the total sales of many products usually regarded as "drugstore items." [63] Thus the luring of drug chains from

[62] For a brief account of this controversy, see *ibid.*, pp. 150–153, 206–212.

[63] E.g., a Nielsen survey indicates both the extent to which food stores have captured this market and the speed with which these gains continue to mount. In the period of April and May of 1946, the survey estimates, food stores made 58 per cent of total sales of dentifrices and had increased this share to 75 per

the path of vigorous price competition by the comfortable margins of nonprice competition has not for long protected independents from intertype competition. Supermarkets may do more than provide another source of supply for consumers. Since they stress prices and tend to make their customers more price conscious, they may cause consumers to extend their area of price consciousness to include drugs and toiletries, and so provide a firm basis for intertype competition. They may cause drug chains to adopt more vigorous price policies, just as earlier they spurred on the grocery chains at a moment when their zeal for price competition had begun to slacken. Strong intertype competition would have important effects on power relations within the older avenues of distribution. It would lessen, for example, the dependency of a manufacturer on the good will of retailers and might limit the retail margins he can grant by confronting him with vigorous private-brand competition.

Thus even a hasty glance at contemporary conditions in the trade indicates how limited were the economic fruits gained by the organized druggists. The consumer lost a political battle, but the druggists did not gain as much as they expected. They were unable to shackle to any important degree the basic competitive dynamism of the economy.

---

cent by the period of June and July of 1950. Other comparable figures were: shampoos, 50 per cent and 70 per cent; shave creams, 48 per cent and 61 per cent; hand lotions, 41 per cent and 48 per cent; face powders, 25 per cent and 23 per cent; toothbrushes, 35 per cent and 42 per cent; baby oils, 14 per cent and 38 per cent; blades and razors, 79 per cent and 83 per cent. (Survey reported in Boston Globe *Retail Memo*, vol. 5, no. 9, March 28, 1951, p. 3.) Also see "Grocer Horns in on Druggist," *Business Week*, February 16, 1952, p. 158 ff.

I X

## Conclusions

If the trades I have examined are well chosen, this study shows that distribution's basic conflict in this period was one between large-scale organization and small, between new methods of organizing marketing and old. This was obviously the case in groceries and drugs, where mass distributors threatened independents. It was also the issue in the struggle between automobile dealers, who wanted to function as independent merchants, controlling their own purchases and expenses, and manufacturers, who regarded retailing as but one phase of an integrated process of production and marketing.

The course and outcome of this battle have revealed much of the intricate interweaving of politics and economics which characterizes our political economy. To the extent that distributive markets are imperfect, participants possess power. Organization, which is usually the basis of dynamic and creative marketing changes, breeds more power. And organization tends to induce counterorganization and yet more power. Although classical economic analysis defines it away, this economic power is often important in market operations, may become of concern to government, and may be translated into political power. Similarly, political policy-making processes are importantly affected by economic factors.

Probably the two most basic causative factors at work here, themselves somewhat interrelated, are the general legal and political framework and the elemental dynamism of the economy. Distribution's conflicts arose from marketing innovations which emerged from the bowels of the economy and which were conceived, initiated, and brought to fruition by business firms. But these innovations were permitted, encouraged, and protected by general governmental policies which were only moderately altered by the political battles of the 1930's. While government has not produced these changes in marketing techniques and in methods of organizing distributive functions, and while governmental policy cannot guarantee that innovations will take place, it has broken the ground and prepared the soil, enabling the innovator to plant his seed, and then has protected the seedling from joint attacks by more mature growths.

By reducing fraud, deception, and collusive restraints of trade, antitrust and trade practice regulation has lessened the extent to which prices reflect factors other than costs of production and marketing, has enhanced the concern of distributors with efficiency, and has enabled the consumer to be a better and more rational judge of the products he buys. Regulation has restrained many anticompetitive actions of distributors, has sufficed to make some horizontal competition, such as that in automobiles, usually vigorous and effective, and has encouraged innovations leading to intertype competition. And it has further encouraged intertype competition by narrowly limiting the ability of older distributors to cut innovators' supply lines by boycotts and other joint actions. Where consumers have been competent to judge, governmental policy has enabled the economy to produce vigorous and effective competition which allows the consumer meaningful choice in selecting his preferred combination of price, quality, and service. In the field of drugs, where consumers have been incompetent judges, druggists have usurped consumers' vertical power, and competition has usually been relaxed and uncreative.

Although the economy's dynamism and the relatively free play given it by general governmental policy promote innovations and, hence, group struggles between newer and older distributive media, they weaken the Bentley group hypothesis by hampering political settlement of these disputes and at the same time promote economic settlement of them and the achievement of new economic equilibria. Grocery chains revolutionized trade channels and endangered hundreds of thousands of independent grocers. Yet none of the legislative aids gained by independents were sufficient to help them appreciably, and free consumer choice was allowed to strike a new equilibrium. Chains have not increased their share of grocery sales in twenty years,[1] and, although small independents have steadily lost ground, larger independents have fairly easily met chain competition [2] by matching their prices or bettering their services. Changes in market conditions did more for car dealers in their relations with manufacturers than all the governmental aid they were able to invoke, and even the powerful and successful druggists have not succeeded in insulating themselves from basic competitive market forces.

Independents' political attacks on mass distribution and large-scale organization, full of sound and fury, accomplished little. Competition had become so much a way of life in the

[1] In 1929 grocery chains made 38.5 per cent of total grocery sales; in 1948, 37.6 per cent.
[2] In 1939 there were 424,558 independent food stores with annual sales of less than $20,000, and they accounted for 40.8 per cent of total independent food sales. In 1949 there were 194,550, making 11.1 per cent of total sales. In 1939 there were 4,518 independent "superettes," with volumes between $100,000 and $300,000, accounting for 9.8 per cent of total independent sales. In 1949 there were 32,250, making 34.0 per cent of total sales. And in 1939 there were 544 independent supermarkets, with volumes of over $300,000, accounting for 4.7 per cent of total independent sales. In 1949 there were 4,700, making 15.3 per cent of total sales. *1939 Census of Business*, vol. I, part 2, pp. 671–2; *Progressive Grocer: Facts in Food and Grocery Distribution* (1950), pp. 4, 5, 8, 14. These statistics of course reflect inflation as well as physical growth.

grocery and automobile trades, and had come to be so valued by consumers, that neither manufacturers nor legislators would allow distributors to choke off the competition which had so disadvantaged them. While the sweeping political victory of the druggists has narrowly confined some areas of price competition, it did not long shackle the economy's dynamism, for supermarkets are making spectacular inroads on drugstore sales. Neither chain taxes nor the Robinson-Patman Act significantly affected mass distribution, and the automobile investigation had no lasting results. And, with the exception of resale price maintenance, all of these attacks were seriously weakened by the need to reconcile them to the values underlying general competitive policies. The confused but generally anticompetitive goals of automobile dealers were frustrated by the FTC's reliance on competitive values. Its good-faith competition clause greatly lessened the intended impact of the Robinson-Patman Act, and, because of the necessity of justifying them in terms of other goals, few chain taxes seriously hurt their targets.

Thus these conflicts can be settled politically, and a group can shield itself from competition and innovation, only by strong measures. But, at the risk of unnecessary reiteration, we have seen that many factors operate to blur the translation of group programs into public policies and make it unlikely that strong measures will emerge. Some of these factors, such as the necessity of adjusting policies to the interests or values of other groups, as was the case in the Robinson-Patman Act, are consistent with the Bentley group hypothesis. Others are serious limitations on the validity of this approach and show us that the identification of the potential groups concerned in an issue merely begins the task of analyzing the policy-making process. Group analysis of the economic environment only tells us what potential groups may become agitated over an issue. Whether these groups become operative depends on environmental circumstances and on political processes. An understanding of the policy-making process requires far more than a simple measurement of group pressures and goals.

Some of the barriers to an easy transfer of the pursuit of economic goals to the political sphere, such as extreme geographical dispersion and separation and, in some trades, high turnover, incompetence, and lack of strong interest or motivation, are somewhat peculiar to distribution, making most of it politically a low pressure area. Other barriers are perhaps less peculiar to distribution. Imperfect mobilization of groups is a more general, and extremely important, phenomenon, for the picture of a militant group which really organizes its potential membership and causes them to act as one is usually only the invention, and the unrealized hope, of trade association executives. Independent grocers never functioned as a group and were only a potential source of support which could be appealed to and manipulated by other groups or by legislators. In the case of chain taxes, the Bentley group hypothesis would have been more valuable to a politician looking for ways in which to woo voters than it is to a student of the policy-making process.

Nor are groups free to wander at will in the political sphere. They carry with them a network of economic power relationships which condition their political behavior. Some are hampered by their dependence on other groups; others are strengthened by their ability to command the support of other groups. Car dealers who are economically at the mercy of manufacturers have their political efforts weakened by that dependence, and small grocers tend to walk politically hand-in-hand with their paternal wholesalers. The political influence of the NARD, on the other hand, was greatly enhanced by its ability to use vertical power to summon up allies.

Finally, group programs must be fought for within a general environment which affects their chances for success. The legislative success of the chain tax movement in the early and middle 1930's, and its rapid decline thereafter, were due to factors beyond the control of the independents.

The drug trade is a high-pressure area because, as we have seen, a number of factors, economic and professional, operate to make druggists exceptionally cohesive and capable of effective and relatively complete mobilization. Accordingly, the Bentley hypothesis is a largely valid explanation of events. The fair-trade acts were an unadulterated group program and their passage entirely due to the efforts of organized groups. Yet even here druggists were unable thereby to insulate themselves from the effects of dynamic innovation, and, while resale price maintenance protects them from strong price competition on standard brands, this protection is weaker than that afforded by the Tri-partite Agreement, which was voided by general governmental policy. Private brand competition limits the retail margins they can safely receive under fair trade, and supermarkets apply new and potentially dynamic competitive restraints on them. It is also significant that much of the political power of druggists results from the failure of consumers to exercise their economic power. The usurpation of most of this power by druggists through their exercise of the crucial function of selection explains their vertical predominance and their ability to mobilize virtually the whole trade behind their political programs. Consumer apathy also explains the limited success of chains and of drug sections of department stores and the general toning down of intertype competition and of price appeals. And it is this lack of apathy in the consumer's automobile and grocery purchases which underlies and generates vigorous competition among automobile manufacturers and dealers and among and between chain and independent grocers.

If, then, policy does more than simply register group drives and strengths, and if the policy-making process is partially autonomous, then there is some point to a summary of competitive criteria in the light of experience in this field. Although these legislative battles arose from reactions against prevailing general regulatory policies, except for fair trade, they produced no major modifications in those policies. And even though fair trade obviously conflicts with general competitive principles, it imposes only moderate quantitative limitations on the competitiveness of the economy's distributive markets. The general principles still stand.

Experiences within distribution show that the market structure test of competition, which makes the goal of competitive policy the absence or minimization of economic power, is not, and should not be, the ultimate criterion. Instead, as I argued in Chapter V, few structural situations or exercises of power can be condemned *per se*; generally, power has been, and should be, evaluated in terms of its consequences, actual or intended. The existence of power is accepted as a necessary concomitant of increasing economic interdependence and large-scale organization, and only that power is condemned which "restrains trade" by lessening the competitiveness of behavior. This explains the seemingly inequitable distinction between exercises of power by loose associations and by large corporations. The former is attacked because it is used to limit the competitiveness of members of the association or of outsiders; the latter is usually upheld because it is often in itself competitive behavior or is used to make more competitive the behavior of others.

Thus, although the existence of power is incompatible with the concept of perfect competition, in practice the exercise of power is often competitive behavior and produces competitive results. The power of an innovator, usually deriving from large-scale organization, may, as Schumpeter saw, enable him to introduce almost explosively creative improvements in product or service, as was the case with grocery chains and automobile manufacturers. Or power at one distributive level may, as Galbraith says, balance and restrain power at another level. Chains, for example, used their power to smash traditional discount structures and caused prices to reflect costs more accurately. Chain power countered the power of large manufacturers and prevented them from insulating themselves from competition. Yet, as we have seen, Galbraith's apparent belief in the almost automatically beneficent consequences of "countervailing power" is not justified. The clash of power between druggists and manufacturers is of little benefit to the consumer. Druggists use their power to inflate retail margins, and manufacturers usually can only strengthen their vertical position by extensive advertising notorious for its lack of objective content and sometimes further increasing retail prices. And, while the organization of countervailing power by automobile dealers did remove some inequities from manufacturer–dealer relations and, by easing pressure on dealers, may have lessened deceptive and fraudulent retail trade practices, it also substantially restrained retail competition in some areas and aimed at general limitations on competition. Clearly, although the existence of substantial power is inevitable, and although power is usually at least partially balanced by other power, it may be abused.

The question of whether to identify competition with specific market structures or with behavior and consequences was the issue usually presented by distributors' political battles in the depression decade, especially in the struggles over the Robinson-Patman and Patman bills. The outcome of these struggles constituted a refusal to accept the former definition and an acceptance of the economy's dynamism. This decision has obvious material advantages in efficiency and productivity. Undoubtedly we will continue to face problems in defining and attacking abuses of power, and acceptance of power will raise new problems of policy. Even now it is possible that General Motors has achieved such size that its power can hardly be used without endangering competition and that social and political values are endangered, although this danger is not readily apparent in its marketing activities. A & P's buying subsidiary, Acco, similarly may have had so much power in a few commodity markets as to make competition difficult.

For the most part, however, mass distributors have not developed sufficient unrestrained power to endanger our economic, social, or political values. And these values are certainly served by an acceptance of consumer freedom to choose among distributive channels.

Furthermore, the alternative is unreal. The choice is not between a Brandeisian world of sturdy, efficient, small businessmen-yeomen and one of top-heavy, corporate concentration of resources and irresponsible power. Under free intertype competition many consumers still prefer traditional channels, and new equilibria have been reached. Mass distributors possess much power, but in most markets this power is effectively limited in proportion to the effectiveness of competition — generally more effectively limited than is the power of the independent druggists. To adopt the alternative policy, that of protecting existing market structures, would not eradicate power. Power would still exist, but it might be more irresponsible and might produce cartelized trades. And to adopt this policy would certainly be to subsidize inefficiency and to reduce the vigor and creativity of this section of the economy.

# INDEX

A & P: discounts and special allowances, 65n, 66n, 67–68, 196; buying practices, 69, 73–74; political activities, 173–174, 180–181; mentioned, 61, 168, 175–176, 183, 186, 261
Adelman, M. S., 39n, 40n, 66n, 70n, 73n
AGMA, 216–222
Agricultural groups: oppose chain taxes, 173–174, 180; role in legislative history of Robinson-Patman Act, 197, 207–208, 216–223, 225–228, 231–232; oppose fair trade, 240
Allowances. See Discounts
American Retail Federation: investigation of, 175, 196–198, 208
Antichain movement: description, 160–165; lack of organization, 166–168, 177–182; decline of, 168–181; and Robinson-Patman Act, 201, 210–212, 233; and fair trade, 244–245
Antitrust Division. See Sherman Act
Automobile manufacturers. See Manufacturers
Automobile Manufacturers' Association, 129
Automobile trade: description and analysis, 107–158; mentioned, 255, 257

Bargaining power. See Discounts; Power
Beckman, T. N., 5n, 6n, 7n, 14n, 18n, 41n, 61n, 62n, 79n, 82n, 160n, 184n, 185n
Bentham, Jeremy, 49
Bentley, Arthur, 2
Bentley hypothesis. See Group analysis
Berle, A. A., Jr., 40n, 132n
Blacklists. See Boycotts
Boer, A. E., 13n, 93n
Borah, William, 225
Borah-Van Nuys bill, 221–222, 225, 228, 231

Boulding, Kenneth E., 30n
Boycotts: use of by organized distributors, 34; as reaction to intertype competition, 44–48; by grocery wholesalers, 85–87; by druggists, 95–96, 238–239, 251; mentioned, 52
Brands. See Private brands
Brokerage provisions: of Robinson-Patman Act, 203–204, 218, 223, 228–229, 231
Burns, Arthur R., 59n
Business performance test, 146–153, 261
Byoir, Carl, 180

California referendum, 173–174, 184
Captain Plan, 243–244
Car dealers: size, 10, 107, 127, 156; manufacturers' power over, 107–121, 125–129, 141–144, 156–157; own vertical power, 115–116; controls over trade practices and trade-in allowances, 122–126; profits, 122, 144–145; organizational weaknesses, 127–128, 155–157; political activities, 128–135, 138–140; FTC report on automobile industry, 135–138; mortality, 144; trade practices evaluated, 143–153; interrelation of competition and power, 152–153; mentioned, 159, 164, 200, 254, 256–258, 261
Chains: growth, 7–8, 159–160; impact on independents, 7, 17, 39–40; antichain movement, 159–165, 168–181; political campaigns of, 172–174, 180–181, 183–184, 222–223; Patman chain tax bill, 175–181; effects of chain taxes, 184–187; role in legislative history of Robinson-Patman Act, 197, 207–208, 216–223, 225–228, 231–232; attacks on vertical power of, 189–208, 210–215; effects of Robinson-Patman Act, 222, 230–234; effects of fair trade, 251–253; mentioned, 53. See also Discounts